Air Fryer Cookbook
for Beginners

600 5 Ingredients Simple, Easy and Delicious Air Fryer
Recipes for Beginners and Advanced Users

By Stephanie Newman

Table of Content

Introduction

With so many cooking appliances and techniques in the market, you can quickly get confused about your choice and approach towards healthy and delicious cooking. The choice of the perfect cooking appliance is the first step towards healthy and delicious food; this furthermore guarantees your health. This book is going to cover the vast world of Air Fryers for you, enabling you to understand what it is, and of course why you should opt for it in the first place.

Air Fryers were introduced initially to Australian and European consumers in the year 2010. After having an overwhelming response air fryer were launched in the markets of North America and Japan. And they have received such a wild reaction from the users that you can almost spot them in every second household now. And amazingly every region is using the best of it in its way. The Japs are using them for frying their prawns while the Dutch and British are making their all-time favorite chips with them. Even Indians are using them to prepare their finger-licking spicy samosas with the Air Fryer. And here in the United States, chicken wings are the favorite recipes when it comes to using Air Fryers in your kitchens.

Various experts in culinary and dietary domains have drafted this introduction for users who are wholly new to the world of Air Frying. The book is aiming to break down every essential aspect associated with cooking with an Air Fryer. It also tells you how you can utilize it to the maximum possible level. The book explains the entire working of the Air Fryer that involves the Rapid Air Frying Technology. It also aims to explain how various kind of fats are concerned with air frying and to what extent they are good or bad depending upon their nature. Moreover, we have drafted the perfect steps to clean your Air Fryer after you use it. This is a vital portion because appliances involving electronic equipment are tricky with cleaning and washing.

This book ensures not only that you master the art of cooking but also provide you with the healthiest possible recipes. And this comes with without taking into account the cooking or air frying skills you already have. These recipes are your guarantee towards perfect health and delicious taste. All the recipes are well scripted, with every step involved, portion sizes, and cooking time. Moreover, the recipes are using only a minimal amount of 5 ingredients only. This makes it unique and yet ensure the best possible taste for you and your loved ones. In short, this book is going to make you an expert on cooking with an Air Fryer. That too by not only making you understanding the mechanisms on which the Air Fryer works. But it also breaks down the techniques to cook with it more efficiently and without altering the taste at all.

Chapter-1: Getting Familiar with an Air Fryer

How Does the Air Fryer Works?

The underlying mechanisms behind the effective working of an Air Fryer are that it uses the circulation of hot air inside and cooking the food over the heat produced by the warm air. The Air Fryer uses Rapid Air Technology to cook your food with very little oil; instead of immersing them in a bulk of fatty oils. The Rapid Air Technology works on the principle of circulation of hot air having approximately 200 degrees Celsius for frying foods like chips, chicken, pastries, and fish, etc. Rapid Air Technology has become the most state of the art innovation in the modern-day cooking world. It has changed the entire concept of frying foods by providing adequate and smarter cooking appliances. The Air Fryer fries your meal to a perfect brown and crispy level and uses 80 percent lower oil; than any other conventional frying approach.

Labeled Air Fryer Controls

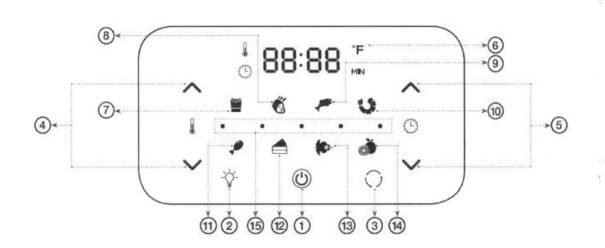

1. **Power/Start-Stop Button-** Once unit is plugged in, the Power Button will light up.

Selecting the Power Button once 'will cause the full-panel to be illuminated. Selecting the Power Button a second time will activate the cooking process at the default temperature of 370° F (190° C) and time of 15minutes. Selecting the Power Button at any time during the cooking process will shut down the unit causing display to go dark within 20 seconds the fan will continue running for 20 seconds to cool down the unit

2.**Internal Light** . Selecting this button will help you check cooking progress while Unit is in operation.

NOTE: Opening the door during the cooking process will pause the Unit. Internal light will illuminate if doors open.

3.**Rotation Button** - Select this button when cooking anything using the Rotisserie Mode.Function can be used with any preset. The icon will blink while in use.

4. Temperature Control Buttons - These buttons enable you to raise or lower cooking

temperature by 50 F (2.7° C) intervals starting from150 F (65° c) to 400 F (200 C). Dehydration is fromn90F (30° C)to 170°F (75C).

5. Time Control Buttons . These buttons enable you to select exact cooking time to the minute,from 1 to 60 minutes in all modes except when dehydrating, which uses 30 minute intervals and an operating time from 2 to 24 hours.

6. LED Digital Display- The Digital Numeric Display will switch between Temperature and Time Remaining during the cooking process.

7 - 14. Cooking Presets - Selecting any of these will set Time an Temperature to a default setting for that particular food. You may over-ride these presets with Time and Temperature Buttons.View presets on the next page.

15. Running Lights- These lights will blink in sequence while cooking is in progress and continue blinking up to 20 seconds once you shut Unit down.

Mastering Air Frying

There are various steps in mastering the art of Air Frying, which includes adjusting your Air Fryer to Cooking with it. This portion is going to explain them to you in a convenient manner.

Adjusting your Air Fryer

* **Lowering the Cooking Temperature by 15°C (25°F)**

Almost all the recipes come with their specific cooking temperatures for perfect cooking. You should lower down the required temperature of the particular recipe you want to cook/fry in the Air Fryer by 25°F. This is to preheat the Air Fryer to the specific cooking temperature before adding your food into it. You can also have various online charts which are available online to understand and know the right cooking temperatures for different meals for perfectly cooking them.

* **Adjusting the Cooking Time by 20 percent**

You also have to customize your cooking time just like the cooking temperature while using an Air Fryer. In the starting, it might be a bit tricky. But generally, while using an Air Fryer, you can go for an optimal 20 percent reduced cooking time than the usual cooking time your meal requires. It means that if a recipe is needing 20 minutes for cooking, you should cook it for 16 minutes in the Air Fryer.

* **Use 2 Tbsp. Of Oil Approximately**

As explained earlier, Air Fryers uses much lesser amount of oils than any conventional cooking method. You will solely require 1 to 2 tbsp. of oil; per basket for fresh foods with an Air Fryer. You have to toss your food in it before putting it in the Air Fryer. Use a cooking spray or oil mist for spraying over the basket if your ingredients are battered or frozen. Once you are done placing the food inside the Air Fryer, use the same oil for a light spritz over the top. Moreover, you can use any oil for your Air Fryer.

Cooking with the Air Fryer

* **Don't Overload the Air Fryer**

Overloading of the Air Fryer affects the smooth and adequate circulation of the hot air and thus reduces the efficiency of the Air Fryer. For having a perfect and evenly fried or cooked crispy food, fill up your Fryer till the tray is covered. Leave out some space on the top for the smooth circulation of air, and preferably go for cooking in small batches to avoid any unwanted results.

- **Shake up the Food After Every 5 Minutes**

While cooking, open the Air Fryer and rotate or shake your food thoroughly every 5 to ten minutes. Smaller snacks like mozzarella sticks and fries require proper shaking. While more abundant foods like chicken breasts and meat cuts should be entirely rotated for exposing out their other sides.

- **Looks out If the Food is Cooked**

Cooking with an Air Fryer is usually much faster than any conventional cooking technique. So it is highly preferred to check on your food while cooking it with the Air Fryer. Observe your ingredients thoroughly while rotating or shaking it to see whether it is perfectly prepared or not. It helps you avoid the burning of your food.

- **Take Out Your Food When it's Golden**

You have to take out your food from the Air Fryer when it is crispy or golden brown. You should adequately check meats like chicken etc. to see if they are properly cooked or not before taking them out. In case they are not cooked properly, you have to use an oven for properly cooking them over. When you are done with preparing your food, you should dry it by dabbing with a paper towel and later on serve it crispy and hot.

Cleaning an Air Fryer

Considering how modern the Air Fryer is, cleaning it is simple, like any conventional cleaning approaches. The requirements for cleaning the Air Fryer includes cleaning brush, soap, hot water, sponge, and a damp clothing piece. Moreover, you can clean your Air Fryer in the following easy steps in less than 5 minutes. These steps include:

1. Cut off the power supply to the Air Fryer and let it get cooled down.
2. Use the damp clothing to clean the outer surface of the Air Fryer and remember not to use the damp cloth on the power outlets to avoid any mishap.
3. Use dishwashing soap and a non-abrasive sponge to clean up the inner surface of the Air Fryer.
4. Use a brush to brush off any leftover or sticky particles from the inner basket.
5. Dry or wipe down all the components of the Air Fryer.

The following tips can make your Air Fryer clean more effectively and conveniently. These include:

- For more effective cleansing of your Air fryer, always prefer a non-abrasive sponge to clean off any residing food particles leftover in the drip pan or the basket. Never go for using utensils to remove off these particles as there is a lining with a non-stick coating of air fryer components which are easily cleaned with scratching them off.
- In case the food particles are hardened over the surface of the basket or the pan, put them into soap and hot water for soaking. This technique is going to soften own these leftover particles and will become very easy to clean off.
- If you are making large quantities of food, you can wait unless you are done with your final batch of cooking and then cleanse your Air Fryer afterward.

There are various types of fats involved with Air Frying, and this portion is going to explain to them, their sources, and the harms associated with them.

1. Saturated Fats

They are solid at room temperature, and excessive intake can be harmful over a longer time. If consumed in excess, they are known to raise cholesterol levels which increases the risks of heart strokes and other cardiovascular diseases.

They are found in abundance in meat products, dairy products, poultry skin, meat (mammals), and even in processed foods like pastries, cakes, chips, and biscuits. They are also present in cocoa butter, coconut oil, and palm oil. A healthy diet usually has 10 percent saturated fats, and it is not recommended to replace saturated fats with refined carbs or even sugar.

2. Unsaturated Fats

These include both monounsaturated and polyunsaturated fats. They are derived from plant oils, explaining why are they called good fats.

- **Monounsaturated Fats**

They are known for lowering LDL and incrementing HDL levels if you reduce the saturated fat intake along with them. They are known to reduce the risks of cardiovascular diseases.

You can find them in olive oil, avocados, olives, peanut butter, and nuts.

- **Polyunsaturated Fats**

They are perfect for our health, especially Omega-e3 polyunsaturated fatty acids from fish. They are known to lower inflammation and the risk of heart complications. Omega-3 fatty acids are also useful for arthritis, skin issues, and joint problems.

Omega-6 fatty acids are present in vegetable oils and processed foods, and their excessive intake (common in the standard American Diet) might increase inflammation.

You can find them in safflower, sunflower oil, grapeseed, pastured eggs, nuts, oily fish (mackerel, sardines, trout, etc.) and seeds.

3. Trans Fats

They are produced synthetically and does not occur naturally. They are also called partially hydrogenated oils. They are not essential for human life; instead, they are considered harmful to our health. They increment LDL levels and lowers HDL levels causing an increased risk of heart diseases three times more than other fats. They are known to cause 50,000 deaths per year and are also known to increase the risk of type-2 diabetes. Many states and cities like Philadelphia, California, and New York City have banned or are about to ban their usage.

You can find them in fried foods like pies, biscuits, cookies, stick margarine, fast foods, shortenings, doughnuts, French fries, pizza dough, packaged foods, pastries, and many other baked foods. Any food labeled with partially hydrogenated oils is known to have Trans-fat. Your diet should not be having more than 5-6 percent Trans-fat at all, and this level is also harmful.

Air Fryer Cooking Time Table

It is essential to read your manufacturer's time and temperature instructions and then, you can adjust both to fit the recipe in question to ensure that you have well-cooked meals. Also, work with a food thermometer to aid you in reaching the accurate internal temperature of meats and seafood for safe consumption.

Vegetables

	Temp (°F)	Time (mins)		Temp (°F)	Time (mins)
Asparagus (1-inch slices)	400 °F	5	**Onions (quartered)**	400 °F	11
Beets (whole)	400 °F	40	**Parsnips (½-inch chunks)**	380 °F	15
Bell Peppers (1-inch chunks)	400 °F	15	**Pearl Onions**	400 °F	10
Broccoli (florets)	400 °F	6	**Potatoes (whole baby pieces)**	400 °F	15
Broccoli Rabe (chopped)	400 °F	6	**Potatoes (1-inch chunks)**	400 °F	12
Brussel Sprouts (halved)	380 °F	15	**Potatoes (baked whole)**	400 °F	40
Cabbage (diced)	380 °F	15	**Pumpkin (½-inch chunks)**	380 °F	13
Carrots (halved)	380 °F	15	**Radishes**	380 °F	15
Cauliflower (florets)	400 °F	12	**Squash (½-inch chunks)**	400 °F	12
Collard Greens	250 °F	12	**Sweet Potato (baked)**	380 °F	30 to 35
Corn on the cob	390 °F	6	**Tomatoes (halves)**	350 °F	10
Cucumber (½-inch slices)	370 °F	4	**Tomatoes (cherry)**	400 °F	4
Eggplant (2-inch cubes)	400 °F	15	**Turnips (½-inch chunks)**	380 °F	15
Fennel (quartered)	370 °F	15	**Zucchini (½-inch sticks)**	400 °F	12
Green Beans	400 °F	5	**Mushrooms (¼-inch slices)**	400 °F	5
Kale (halved)	250 °F	12			

Chicken

	Temp (°F)	Time (mins)		Temp (°F)	Time (mins)
Breasts, bone in (1 ¼ lb.)	370 °F	25	Legs, bone-in (1 ¾ lb.)	380 °F	30
Breasts, boneless (4 oz)	380 °F	12	Thighs, boneless (1 ½ lb.)	380 °F	18 to 20
Drumsticks (2 ½ lb.)	370 °F	20	Wings (2 lb.)	400 °F	12
Game Hen (halved 2 lb.)	390 °F	20	Whole Chicken	360 °F	75
Thighs, bone-in (2 lb.)	380 °F	22	Tenders	360 °F	8 to 10

Beef

	Temp (°F)	Time (mins)		Temp (°F)	Time (mins)
Beef Eye Round Roast (4 lb.s.)	400 °F	45 to 55	Meatballs (1-inch)	370 °F	7
Burger Patty (4 oz.)	370 °F	16 to 20	Meatballs (3-inch)	380 °F	10
Filet Mignon (8 oz.)	400 °F	18	Ribeye, bone-in (1-inch, 8 oz)	400 °F	10 to 15
Flank Steak (1.5 lb.s)	400 °F	12	Sirloin steaks (1-inch, 12 oz)	400 °F	9 to 14
Flank Steak (2 lb.s)	400 °F	20 to 28			

Pork & Lamb

	Temp (°F)	Time (mins)		Temp (°F)	Time (mins)
Bacon (regular)	400 °F	5 to 7	Pork Tenderloin	370 °F	15
Bacon (thick cut)	400 °F	6 to 10	Sausages	380 °F	15
Pork Loin (2 lb.)	360 °F	55	Lamb Loin Chops (1-inch thick)	400 °F	8 to 12
Pork Chops, bone in (1-inch, 6.5 oz)	400 °F	12	Rack of Lamb (1.5 – 2 lb.)	380 °F	22

Fish & Seafood

	Temp (°F)	Time (mins)		Temp (°F)	Time (mins)
Calamari (8 oz)	400 °F	4	**Tuna Steak**	400 °F	7 to 10
Fish Fillet (1-inch, 8 oz)	400 °F	10	**Scallops**	400 °F	5 to 7
Salmon, fillet (6 oz)	380 °F	12	**Shrimp**	400 °F	5
Swordfish steak	400 °F	10			

Frozen Foods

	Temp (°F)	Time (mins)		Temp (°F)	Time (mins)
Breaded Shrimp	400 °F	9	**French Fries (thick - 17 oz)**	400 °F	18
Chicken Nuggets (12 oz)	400 °F	10	**Mozzarella Sticks (11 oz)**	400 °F	8
Fish Sticks (10 oz.)	400 °F	10	**Onion Rings (12 oz)**	400 °F	8
Fish Fillets (½-inch, 10 oz)	400 °F	14	**Pot Stickers (10 oz)**	400 °F	8
French Fries (thin - 20 oz)	400 °F	14			

Volume Equivalents(Liquid)

US STANDARD	US STANDARD(OUNCES)	METRIC(APPROXIMATE)
2 TABLESPOONS	1 fl.oz.	30 mL
1/4 CUP	2 fl.oz.	60 mL
1/2 CUP	4 fl.oz.	120 mL
1 CUP	8 fl.oz.	240 mL
1 1/2 CUP	12 fl.oz.	355 mL
2 CUPS OR 1 PINT	16 fl.oz.	475 mL
4 CUPS OR 1 QUART	32 fl.oz.	1 L
1 GALLON	128 fl.oz.	4 L

Volume Equivalents (DRY)

US STANDARD	METRIC (APPROXIMATE)
1/8 TEASPOON	0.5 mL
1/4 TEASPOON	1 mL
1/2 TEASPOON	2 mL
3/4 TEASPOON	4 mL
1 TEASPOON	5 mL
1 TABLESPOON	15 mL
1/4 CUP	59 mL
1/2 CUP	118 mL
3/4 CUP	177 mL
1 CUP	235 mL
2 CUPS	475 mL
3 CUPS	700 mL
4 CUPS	1 L

Weight Equivalents

US STANDARD	METRIC (APPROXIMATE)
1/2 OUNCE	15g
1 OUNCE	30g
2 OUNCE	60g
4 OUNCE	115g
8 OUNCE	225g
12 OUNCE	340g
16 OUNCES OR 1 POUND	455g

Temperatures Equivalents

FAHRENHEIT (F)	CELSIUS(C) (APPROXIMATE)
250	121
300	149
325	163
350	177
375	190
400	205
425	218
450	232

Chapter 2 Breakfast and Brunch Recipes

Ham, Spinach and Egg in a Cup

Prep time: 10 minutes, cook time: 20 minutes; Serves 4

5 Ingredients:
- 1 pound fresh baby spinach
- 4 eggs
- 4 teaspoons milk
- 7-ounce ham, sliced
- 1 tablespoon unsalted butter, melted

What you'll need from the store cupboard:
- 1 tablespoon olive oil
- Salt and black pepper, to taste

Instructions:
1. Preheat the Air fryer to 350 °F and grease 4 ramekins with butter.
2. Heat olive oil in a skillet on medium heat and add baby spinach.
3. Cook for about 4 minutes and drain the liquid from the spinach completely.
4. Divide the spinach into the prepared ramekins and top with ham slices.
5. Crack 1 egg into each ramekin over ham slices and sprinkle evenly with milk.
6. Season with salt and black pepper and transfer into the Air fryer.
7. Cook for about 15 minutes and dish out to serve hot.

Nutrition Facts Per Serving:
Calories: 228, Fats: 15.6g, Carbs: 6.6g, Sugar: 1.1g, Proteins: 17.2g, Sodium: 821mg

Yummy Breakfast Frittata

Prep time: 15 minutes, cook time: 14 minutes; Serves 2

5 Ingredients:
- 6 cherry tomatoes, halved
- ½ cup Parmesan cheese, grated and divided
- 1 bacon slice, chopped
- 6 fresh mushrooms, sliced
- 3 eggs

What you'll need from the store cupboard:
- 1 tablespoon olive oil
- Salt and black pepper, to taste

Instructions:
1. Preheat the Air fryer to 390 °F and grease a baking dish with olive oil.
2. Mix together tomatoes, bacon, mushrooms, salt and black pepper in a bowl.
3. Transfer into the baking dish and place in the Air fryer.
4. Cook for about 6 minutes and remove from the Air fryer.
5. Whisk together eggs and cheese in a bowl.
6. Pour the egg mixture evenly over bacon mixture and cook in the Air fryer for about 8 minutes.

Nutrition Facts Per Serving:
Calories: 397, Fat: 26.2g, Carbs: 17.9g, Sugar: 11.2g, Protein: 27.3g, Sodium: 693mg

Toasties and Sausage in Egg Pond

Prep time: 10 minutes, cook time: 22 minutes; Serves 2

5 Ingredients:
- 3 eggs
- 2 cooked sausages, sliced
- 1 bread slice, cut into sticks
- 1/8 cup mozzarella cheese, grated
- 1/8 cup Parmesan cheese, grated

What you'll need from the store cupboard:
- ¼ cup cream

Instructions:
1. Preheat the Air fryer to 365 °F and grease 2 ramekins lightly.
2. Whisk together eggs with cream in a bowl and place in the ramekins.
3. Stir in the bread and sausage slices in the egg mixture and top with cheese.
4. Transfer the ramekins in the Air fryer basket and cook for about 22 minutes.
5. Dish out and serve warm.

Nutrition Facts Per Serving:
Calories: 261, Fat: 18.8g, Carbohydrates: 4.2g, Sugar: 1.3g, Protein: 18.3g, Sodium: 428mg

Sausage Bacon Beans Cancan

Prep time: 10 minutes, cook time: 20 minutes; Serves 6

5 Ingredients:
- 6 medium sausages
- 6 bacon slices
- 4 eggs
- 6 bread slices, toasted
- 1 can baked beans

What you'll need from the store cupboard:
- Salt and black pepper, to taste

Instructions:
1. Preheat the Air fryer at 320 º F and place the bacon and sausages in a fryer basket.
2. Cook for about 10 minutes and dish out.
3. Place the baked beans in first ramekin.
4. Place the eggs whisked with salt and black pepper in another ramekin.
5. Set the Air fryer to 390 degrees F and transfer the ramekins in it.
6. Cook for about 10 more minutes and divide the bread slices, sausage mixture, beans and eggs in 6 serving plates to serve.

Nutrition Facts Per Serving:
Calories: 518, Fat: 34.9g, Carbs: 20g, Sugar: 0.6g, Protein: 29.9g, Sodium: 1475mg

Bacon and Eggs Cup

Prep time: 10 minutes, cook time: 26 minutes; Serves 2

5 Ingredients:
- 1 bacon slice
- 2 eggs
- 2 tablespoons milk
- 1 tablespoon Parmesan cheese, grated
- 2 bread slices, toasted and buttered

What you'll need from the store cupboard:
- ½ teaspoon red pepper
- 1 teaspoon marinara sauce
- Freshly ground black pepper, to taste

Instructions:
1. Preheat the Air fryer at 355 º F and place the bacon in it.
2. Cook for about 18 minutes and remove from the Air fryer.
3. Cut the bacon into small pieces and divide into 2 ramekins.
4. Crack 1 egg over bacon in each ramekin and pour milk evenly over eggs.
5. Sprinkle with black pepper and top with marinara sauce.
6. Layer with the Parmesan cheese and transfer the ramekins in the Air fryer.
7. Cook for about 8 minutes and serve alongside the bread slices.

Nutrition Facts Per Serving:
Calories: 186, Fat: 11.7g, Carbs: 6.8g, Sugar: 1.7g, Protein: 13.2g, Sodium: 498mg

Luscious Scrambled Eggs

Prep time: 10 minutes, cook time: 10 minutes; Serves 2

5 Ingredients:
- 2 tablespoons unsalted butter
- 4 eggs
- ¼ cup fresh mushrooms, chopped finely
- 2 tablespoons Parmesan cheese, shredded
- ¼ cup tomato, chopped finely

What you'll need from the store cupboard:
- Salt and black pepper, to taste

Instructions:
1. Preheat the Air fryer at 285 º F and grease a baking pan.
2. Whisk together eggs with salt and black pepper in a bowl.
3. Melt butter in the baking pan and add whisked eggs, mushrooms, tomatoes and cheese.
4. Transfer in the Air fryer and cook for about 10 minutes.
5. Remove from the oven and serve warm.

Nutrition Facts Per Serving:
Calories: 254, Fat: 21.7g, Carbs: 2.1g, Sugar: 1.4g, Protein: 13.7g, Sodium: 267mg

Spanish Style Frittata

Prep time: 10 minutes, cook time: 11 minutes; Serves 2

5 Ingredients:
- ½ cup frozen corn
- ½ of chorizo sausage, sliced
- 1 potato, boiled, peeled and cubed
- 2 tablespoons feta cheese, crumbled
- 3 jumbo eggs

What you'll need from the store cupboard:
- 1 tablespoon olive oil
- Salt and black pepper, to taste

Instructions:
1. Preheat the Air fryer at 355 º F and grease the baking pan with olive oil.
2. Add chorizo sausage, corn and potato and cook for about 6 minutes.
3. Whisk together eggs, salt and black pepper in a small bowl.
4. Pour eggs over the sausage mixture and top with feta cheese.
5. Place in the Air fryer and cook for about 5 minutes till desired doneness.

Nutrition Facts Per Serving:
Calories: 327, Fat: 20.2g, Carbs: 23.3g, Sugar: 2.8g, Protein: 15.3g, Sodium: 316mg

Colorful Hash Brown

Prep time: 20 minutes, cook time: 25 minutes; Serves 4

5 Ingredients:
- 5 russet potatoes, peeled, cubed and soaked in water for 30 minutes
- ½ onion, chopped
- ½ jalapeño, chopped
- ½ red bell pepper, seeded and chopped
- ½ green bell pepper, seeded and chopped

What you'll need from the store cupboard:
- ½ tablespoon extra-virgin olive oil
- ¼ tablespoon dried oregano, crushed
- ¼ tablespoon garlic powder
- ¼ tablespoon ground cumin
- ¼ tablespoon red chili powder
- Salt and black pepper, to taste

Instructions:
1. Preheat the Air fryer at 330 º F.
2. Mix together potatoes and olive oil in a bowl and toss to coat well.
3. Place the potatoes into the Air fryer basket and cook for about 5 minutes.
4. Dish out the potatoes onto a wire rack and allow them to cool.
5. Add remaining ingredients in the bowl and toss to coat well.
6. Stir in the potatoes and mash well.
7. Set the Air fryer to 390 º F and transfer the potato mixture in the Air fryer basket.
8. Cook for about 20 minutes until desired doneness and serve warm.

Nutrition Facts Per Serving:
Calories: 220, Fat: 2.3g, Carbs: 46g, Sugar: 5.1g, Protein: 5.2g, Sodium: 27mg

Sweet Mustard Meatballs

Prep time: 15 minutes, cook time: 15 minutes; Serves 4

5 Ingredients:
- ½ pound ground pork
- 1 onion, chopped
- 2 tablespoons fresh basil, chopped
- ½ tablespoon cheddar cheese, grated
- ½ tablespoon Parmesan cheese, grated

What you'll need from the store cupboard:
- 1 teaspoon garlic paste
- 1 teaspoon mustard
- 1 teaspoon honey
- Salt and black pepper, to taste

Instructions:
1. Preheat the Air fryer to 395 º F.
2. Mix together all the ingredients in a bowl until well combined.
3. Make small equal-sized balls from the mixture and arrange in an Air fryer basket.
4. Cook for about 15 minutes until golden brown and serve hot.

Nutrition Facts Per Serving:
Calories: 110, Fat: 2.9g, Carbohydrates: 4.6g, Sugar: 2.7g, Protein: 15.9g, Sodium: 45mg

Delish Mushroom Frittata

Prep time: 15 minutes, cook time: 17 minutes; Serves 2

5 Ingredients:
- ½ red onion, sliced thinly
- 2 cups button mushrooms, sliced thinly
- 3 eggs
- Cooking spray, as required
- 3 tablespoons feta cheese, crumbled

What you'll need from the store cupboard:
- 1 tablespoon olive oil
- Salt, to taste

Instructions:
1. Preheat the Air fryer at 330 º F and grease a 6-inch ramekin with cooking spray.
2. Heat olive oil on medium heat in a skillet and add onion and mushrooms.
3. Sauté for about 5 minutes and dish out the mushroom mixture in a bowl.
4. Whisk together eggs and salt in a small bowl and transfer into prepared ramekin.
5. Place the mushroom mixture over the eggs and top with feta cheese.
6. Arrange the ramekin in Air fryer basket and cook for about 12 minutes.
7. Dish out and serve hot.

Nutrition Facts Per Serving:
Calories: 220, Fat: 17.1g, Carbohydrates: 6g, Sugar: 3.5g, Protein: 12.8g, Sodium: 332mg

Supreme Breakfast Burrito

Prep time: 15 minutes, cook time: 8 minutes; Serves 2

5 Ingredients:
- 2 eggs
- 2 whole-wheat tortillas
- 4-ounces chicken breast slices, cooked
- ¼ of avocado, peeled, pitted and sliced
- 2 tablespoons mozzarella cheese, grated

What you'll need from the store cupboard:
- 2 tablespoons salsa
- Salt and black pepper, to taste

Instructions:
1. Preheat the Air fryer at 390 º F.
2. Whisk together eggs with salt and black pepper in a bowl and transfer into a small shallow nonstick pan.
3. Arrange the pan into an Air fryer basket and cook for about 5 minutes.
4. Remove eggs from the pan and arrange the tortillas onto a smooth surface.
5. Divide the eggs in each tortilla, followed by chicken slice, avocado, salsa and mozzarella cheese.
6. Roll up each tortilla tightly and set the Air fryer at 355 º F.
7. Line an Air fryer tray with a foil paper and arrange the burrito in the prepared tray.
8. Place in the Air fryer and cook for about 3 minutes until the tortillas become golden brown.

Nutrition Facts Per Serving:
Calories: 281, Fat: 13g, Carbohydrates: 15.4g, Sugar: 1.8g, Protein: 26.2g, Sodium: 249mg

Crust-Less Quiche

Prep time: 5 minutes, cook time: 30 minutes; Serves 2

5 Ingredients:
- 4 eggs
- ¼ cup onion, chopped
- ½ cup tomatoes, chopped
- ½ cup milk
- 1 cup Gouda cheese, shredded

What you'll need from the store cupboard:
- Salt, to taste

Instructions:
1. Preheat the Air fryer to 340 º F and grease 2 ramekins lightly.
2. Mix together all the ingredients in a ramekin until well combined.
3. Place in the Air fryer and cook for about 30 minutes.
4. Dish out and serve.

Nutrition Facts Per Serving:
Calories: 348, Fat: 23.8g, Carbohydrates: 7.9g, Sugar: 6.3g, Protein: 26.1g, Sodium: 642mg

Crispy Bread Rolls

Prep time: 20 minutes, cook time: 20 minutes; Serves 4

5 Ingredients:

- 5 large potatoes, boiled and mashed
- 2 small onions, chopped finely
- 2 green chilies, seeded and chopped finely
- 2 tablespoons fresh cilantro, chopped finely
- 8 bread slices, trimmed

What you' ll need from the store cupboard:

- 2 tablespoons olive oil, divided
- ½ teaspoon ground turmeric
- ½ teaspoon mustard seeds
- 1 teaspoon curry powder
- Salt, to taste

Instructions:

1. Heat 1 tablespoon of olive oil on medium heat in a large skillet and add mustard seeds.
2. Sauté for about 30 seconds and add onions.
3. Sauté for about 5 minutes and add curry leaves and turmeric.
4. Sauté for about 30 seconds and add the mashed potatoes and salt.
5. Mix until well combined and remove from the heat.
6. Transfer into a bowl and keep aside to cool.
7. Stir in the chilies and cilantro and divide the mixture into 8 equal-sized portions
8. Shape each portion into an oval patty.
9. Wet the bread slices with water and squeeze the moisture with your palms.
10. Place one patty in the center of each bread slice and roll the bread around the patty.
11. Seal the edges to secure the filling and coat the rolls evenly with the remaining olive oil.
12. Preheat the Air fryer at 390 º F and grease the Air fryer basket with some oil.
13. Transfer the rolls into the prepared basket and cook for about 13 minutes until golden.

Nutrition Facts Per Serving:
Calories: 445, Fat: 8.1g, Carbohydrates: 85.5g, Sugar: 7.8g, Protein: 9.7g, Sodium: 191mg

Breakfast Creamy Donuts

Prep time: 10 minutes, cook time: 18 minutes; Serves 8

5 Ingredients:

- 4 tablespoons butter, softened and divided
- 2 large egg yolks
- 2¼ cups plain flour
- 1½ teaspoons baking powder
- 1 pinch baking soda

What you' ll need from the store cupboard:

- 1/3 cup caster sugar
- 1 teaspoon cinnamon
- ½ cup sugar
- 1 teaspoon salt
- ½ cup sour cream

Instructions:

1. Preheat the Air fryer to 355 º F.
2. Mix together sugar and butter in a bowl and beat until crumbly mixture is formed.
3. Whisk in the egg yolks and beat until well combined.
4. Sift together flour, baking powder, baking soda and salt in another bowl.
5. Add the flour mixture and sour cream to the sugar mixture.
6. Mix well to form a dough and refrigerate it.
7. Roll the dough into 2-inch thickness and cut the dough in half.
8. Coat both sides of the dough with the melted butter and transfer into the Air fryer.
9. Cook for about 8 minutes until golden brown and remove from the Air fryer.
10. Sprinkle the donuts with the cinnamon and caster sugar to serve.

Nutrition Facts Per Serving:
Calories: 303, Fat: 10.2g, Carbohydrates: 49.1g, Sugar: 21g, Protein: 4.8g, Sodium: 343mg

Egg in a Bread Basket

Prep time: 10 minutes, cook time: 10 minutes; Serves 2

5 Ingredients:
- 2 bread slices
- 1 bacon slice, chopped
- 4 tomato slices
- 1 tablespoon Mozzarella cheese, shredded
- 2 eggs

What you' ll need from the store cupboard:
- ½ tablespoon olive oil
- 1/8 teaspoon maple syrup
- 1/8 teaspoon balsamic vinegar
- ¼ teaspoon fresh parsley, chopped
- Salt and black pepper, to taste
- 2 tablespoons mayonnaise

Instructions:

1. Preheat the Air fryer to 320 º F and grease 2 ramekins lightly.
2. Place 1 bread slice in each prepared ramekin and add bacon and tomato slices.
3. Top evenly with the Mozzarella cheese and crack 1 egg in each ramekin.
4. Drizzle with balsamic vinegar and maple syrup and season with parsley, salt and black pepper.
5. Arrange the ramekins in an Air fryer basket and cook for about 10 minutes.
6. Top with mayonnaise and serve immediately.

Nutrition Facts Per Serving:
Calories: 245, Fat: 17.1g, Carbohydrates: 10.2g, Sugar: 2.7g, Protein: 12.8g, Sodium: 580mg

Tasty Egg Yolks with Squid

Prep time: 15 minutes, cook time: 20 minutes; Serves 4

5 Ingredients:
- ½ cup self-rising flour
- 14-ounce flower squid, cleaned and dried
- 2 green chilies, seeded and chopped
- 4 raw salted egg yolks
- 2 tablespoons evaporated milk

What you' ll need from the store cupboard:
- ½ cup chicken broth
- 1 tablespoon sugar
- 3 tablespoons olive oil
- 1 tablespoon curry powder
- Salt and black pepper, to taste

Instructions:

1. Preheat the Air fryer to 355 º F and grease an Air fryer pan.
2. Place the flour in a shallow dish and keep aside.
3. Sprinkle the flower squid with salt and black pepper and coat with flour.
4. Transfer the flower squid into the Air fryer pan and cook for about 9 minutes.
5. Remove from Air fryer and keep aside
6. Heat olive oil on medium heat in a skillet and add chilies and curry leaves.
7. Cook for about 3 minutes and add egg yolks
8. Cook, stirring for about1 minute and add the chicken broth.
9. Cook for about 5 minutes, stirring continuously and add evaporated milk and sugar.
10. Mix till well combined and toss in the fried flower squid until evenly coated.
11. 1Serve immediately.

Nutrition Facts Per Serving:
Calories: 311, Fat: 16.1, Carbohydrates: 19.8g, Sugar: 4.2g, Protein: 21g, Sodium: 197mg

Cherry Tomato Frittata

Prep time: 10 minutes, cook time: 10 minutes; Serves 2

5 Ingredients:

- ½ of Italian sausage
- 4 cherry tomatoes, halved
- 3 eggs
- 1 tablespoon Parmesan cheese, shredded
- 1 teaspoon fresh parsley, chopped

What you'll need from the store cupboard:

- 1 tablespoon olive oil
- Salt and black pepper, to taste

Instructions:

1. Preheat the Air fryer to 360 º F.
2. Place the sausage and tomatoes in a baking pan and transfer in the Air fryer.
3. Cook for about 5 minutes until done and remove the baking dish from oven.
4. Whisk together eggs with Parmesan cheese, oil, parsley, salt and black pepper and beat until combined.
5. Drizzle this mixture over sausage and tomatoes and place in the Air fryer.
6. Cook for about 5 minutes and serve warm.

Nutrition Facts Per Serving:
Calories: 293, Fat: 21.5g, Carbohydrates: 10.4g, Sugar: 7g, Protein: 16.8g, Sodium: 328mg

Jacket Potatoes

Prep time: 5 minutes, cook time: 15 minutes; Serves 2

5 Ingredients:

- 2 potatoes
- 1 tablespoon mozzarella cheese, shredded
- 1 tablespoon butter, softened
- 1 teaspoon chives, minced
- 1 tablespoon fresh parsley, chopped

What you'll need from the store cupboard:

- 3 tablespoons sour cream
- Salt and black pepper, to taste

Instructions:

1. Preheat the Air fryer to 355 º F.
2. Prick the potatoes with a fork and transfer the potatoes in the Air fryer.
3. Place and cook for about for about 15 minutes.
4. Mix together remaining ingredients in a bowl until well combined.
5. Cut the potatoes from the center and stuff in the cheese mixture.
6. Serve immediately.

Nutrition Facts Per Serving:
Calories: 247, Fat: 10.4g, Carbohydrates: 34.4g, Sugar: 2.5g, Protein: 5.2g, Sodium: 84mg

Tasty Toasts

Prep time: 10 minutes, cook time: 5 minutes; Serves 4

5 Ingredients:

- 4 bread slices
- 8 ounces ricotta cheese
- 4 ounces smoked salmon
- 1 shallot, sliced
- 1 cup arugula

What you'll need from the store cupboard:

- 1 garlic clove, minced
- 1 teaspoon lemon zest
- ¼ teaspoon freshly ground black pepper

Instructions:

1. Preheat the Air fryer to 355 º F and arrange the bread slices in an Air fryer basket.
2. Cook for about 5 minutes and remove from the Air fryer.
3. Put garlic, ricotta cheese and lemon zest in a food processor and pulse until smooth.
4. Spread this mixture over each bread slice and top with salmon, arugula and shallot.
5. Sprinkle with black pepper and serve warm.

Nutrition Facts Per Serving:
Calories: 143, Fat: 6g, Carbohydrates: 9.2g, Sugar: 0.7g, Protein: 12.2g, Sodium: 702mg

Cream Bread

Prep time: 20 minutes, cook time: 55 minutes; Serves 12

5 Ingredients:
- 1 cup milk
- 1 large egg
- 4½ cups bread flour
- ½ cup all-purpose flour
- 2 tablespoons milk powder

What you'll need from the store cupboard:
- ¾ cup whipping cream
- 1 teaspoon salt
- ¼ cup fine sugar
- 3 teaspoons dry yeast

Instructions:
1. Preheat the Air fryer to 375 º F and grease 2 loaf pans.
2. Mix together all the dry ingredients with the wet ingredients to form a dough.
3. Divide the dough into 4 equal-sized balls and roll each ball into a rectangle.
4. Roll each rectangle like a Swiss roll tightly and place 2 rolls into each prepared loaf pan.
5. Keep aside for about 1 hour and place the loaf pans into an air fryer basket.
6. Cook for about 55 minutes and remove the bread rolls from pans.
7. Cut each roll into desired size slices and serve warm.

Nutrition Facts Per Serving:
Calories: 215, Fats: 3.1g, Carbohydrates: 36.9g, Sugar: 5.2g, Proteins: 6.5g, Sodium: 189mg

Protein-Rich Breakfast

Prep time: 10 minutes, cook time: 23 minutes; Serves 4

5 Ingredients:
- 1 tablespoon unsalted butter, melted
- 1 pound fresh baby spinach
- 4 eggs
- 7-ounces ham, sliced
- 4 teaspoons milk

What you'll need from the store cupboard:
- 1 tablespoon olive oil
- Salt and black pepper, to taste

Instructions:
1. Preheat the Air fryer to 355 º F and grease 4 ramekins with butter.
2. Heat olive oil on medium heat in a skillet and add spinach.
3. Cook for about 3 minutes until wilted and drain the liquid completely from the spinach.
4. Divide the spinach into prepared ramekins and top with ham slices.
5. Crack 1 egg over ham slices into each ramekin and drizzle with milk evenly.
6. Season with salt and black pepper and transfer into the Air fryer.
7. Bake for about 20 minutes and serve hot.

Nutrition Facts Per Serving:
Calories: 228, Fat: 15.8g, Carbohydrates: 6.6g, Sugar: 1.1g, Protein: 17.2g, Sodium: 821mg

Air Fryer Sausage

Prep time: 5 minutes, cook time: 20 minutes; Serves 5

5 Ingredients:
- 5 raw and uncooked sausage links

What you'll need from the store cupboard:
- 1 tablespoon olive oil

Instructions:
1. Preheat the Air fryer to 360 º F and grease an Air fryer basket with olive oil.
2. Cook for about 15 minutes and flip the sausages.
3. Cook for 5 more minutes and serve warm.

Nutrition Facts Per Serving:
Calories: 131, Fat: 11.8g, Carbohydrates: 0g, Sugar: 0g, Protein: 6g, Sodium: 160mg

Nutty Zucchini Bread

Prep time: 15 minutes, cook time: 20 minutes; Serves 16

5 Ingredients:
- 3 cups all-purpose flour
- 2 teaspoons baking powder
- 3 eggs
- 2 cups zucchini, grated
- 1 cup walnuts, chopped

What you' ll need from the store cupboard:
- 1 tablespoon ground cinnamon
- 1 teaspoon salt
- 2¼ cups white sugar
- 1 cup vegetable oil
- 3 teaspoons vanilla extract

Instructions:
1. Preheat the Air fryer to 320 º F and grease two (8x4-inch) loaf pans.
2. Mix together the flour, baking powder, cinnamon and salt in a bowl.
3. Whisk together eggs with sugar, vanilla extract and vegetable oil in a bowl until combined.
4. Stir in the flour mixture and fold in the zucchini and walnuts.
5. Mix until combined and transfer the mixture into the prepared loaf pans.
6. Arrange the loaf pans in an Air fryer basket and cook for about 20 minutes.
7. Remove from the Air fryer and place onto a wire rack to cool.
8. Cut the bread into desired size slices and serve.

Nutrition Facts Per Serving:
Calories: 377, Fat: 19.3g, Carbohydrates: 47.9g, Sugar: 28.7g, Protein: 5.5g, Sodium: 241mg

Perfect Cheesy Eggs

Prep time: 10 minutes, cook time: 12 minutes; Serves 2

5 Ingredients:
- 2 teaspoons unsalted butter, softened
- 2-ounce ham, sliced thinly
- 4 large eggs, divided
- 3 tablespoons Parmesan cheese, grated finely
- 2 teaspoons fresh chives, minced

What you' ll need from the store cupboard:
- 2 tablespoons heavy cream
- 1/8 teaspoon smoked paprika
- Salt and black pepper, to taste

Instructions:
1. Preheat the Air fryer to 320 º F and grease a pie pan with butter.
2. Whisk together 1 egg with cream, salt and black pepper in a bowl.
3. Place ham slices in the bottom of the pie pan and top with the egg mixture.
4. Crack the remaining eggs on top and season with smoked paprika, salt and black pepper.
5. Top evenly with Parmesan cheese and chives and transfer the pie pan in the Air fryer.
6. Cook for about 12 minutes and serve with toasted bread slices.

Nutrition Facts Per Serving:
Calories: 356, Fat: 26.5g, Carbohydrates: 5.4g, Sugar: 1g, Protein: 24.9g, Sodium: 771mg

Milky Scrambled Eggs

Prep time: 10 minutes, cook time: 9 minutes; Serves 2

5 Ingredients:
- ¾ cup milk
- 4 eggs
- 8 grape tomatoes, halved
- ½ cup Parmesan cheese, grated
- 1 tablespoon butter

What you' ll need from the store cupboard:
- Salt and black pepper, to taste

Instructions:
1. Preheat the Air fryer to 360 º F and grease an Air fryer pan with butter.
2. Whisk together eggs with milk, salt and black pepper in a bowl.
3. Transfer the egg mixture into the prepared pan and place in the Air fryer.
4. Cook for about 6 minutes and stir in the grape tomatoes and cheese.
5. Cook for about 3 minutes and serve warm.

Nutrition Facts Per Serving:
Calories: 351, Fat: 22g, Carbohydrates: 25.2g, Sugar: 17.7g, Protein: 26.4g, Sodium: 422mg

Gourmet Cheesy Bread

Prep time: 10 minutes, cook time: 15 minutes; Serves 2

5 Ingredients:
- 3 bread slices
- 2 tablespoons cheddar cheese
- 2 eggs, whites and yolks, separated
- 1 tablespoon chives
- 1 tablespoon olives

What you'll need from the store cupboard:
- 1 tablespoon mustard
- 1 tablespoon paprika

Instructions:
1. Preheat the Air fryer to 355 º F and place the bread slices in a fryer basket.
2. Cook for about 5 minutes until toasted and dish out.
3. Whisk together egg whites in a bowl until soft peaks form.
4. Mix together cheese, egg yolks, mustard and paprika in another bowl until well combined.
5. Fold in egg whites gently and spread the mustard mixture over toasted bread slices.
6. Place in the Air fryer and cook for about 10 minutes.
7. Remove from the Air fryer and serve warm.

Nutrition Facts Per Serving:
Calories: 164, Fat: 9.2g, Carbohydrates: 11.1g, Sugar: 1.7g, Protein: 10.2g, Sodium: 199mg

Fluffy Cheesy Omelet

Prep time: 10 minutes, cook time: 15 minutes; Serves 2

5 Ingredients:
- 4 eggs
- 1 large onion, sliced
- 1/8 cup cheddar cheese, grated
- 1/8 cup mozzarella cheese, grated
- Cooking spray

What you'll need from the store cupboard:
- ¼ teaspoon soy sauce
- Freshly ground black pepper, to taste

Instructions:
1. Preheat the Air fryer to 360 º F and grease a pan with cooking spray.
2. Whisk together eggs, soy sauce and black pepper in a bowl.
3. Place onions in the pan and cook for about 10 minutes.
4. Pour the egg mixture over onion slices and top evenly with cheese.
5. Cook for about 5 more minutes and serve.

Nutrition Facts Per Serving:
Calories: 216, Fat: 13.8g, Carbohydrates: 7.9g, Sugar: 3.9g, Protein: 15.5g, Sodium: 251mg

Banana Bread

Prep time: 10 minutes, cook time: 20 minutes; Serves 8

5 Ingredients:
- 1 1/3 cups flour
- 1 teaspoon baking soda
- 1 teaspoon baking powder
- ½ cup milk
- 3 bananas, peeled and sliced

What you'll need from the store cupboard:
- 2/3 cup sugar
- 1 teaspoon ground cinnamon
- 1 teaspoon salt
- ½ cup olive oil

Instructions:
1. Preheat the Air fryer to 330 º F and grease a loaf pan.
2. Mix together all the dry ingredients with the wet ingredients to form a dough.
3. Place the dough into the prepared loaf pan and transfer into an air fryer basket.
4. Cook for about 20 minutes and remove from air fryer.
5. Cut the bread into desired size slices and serve warm.

Nutrition Facts Per Serving:
Calories: 295, Fat: 13.3g, Carbohydrates: 44g, Sugar: 22.8g, Protein: 3.1g, Sodium: 458mg

Flavorful Bacon Cups

Prep time: 10 minutes, cook time: 15 minutes; Serves 6

5 Ingredients:
- 6 bacon slices
- 6 bread slices
- 1 scallion, chopped
- 3 tablespoons green bell pepper, seeded and chopped
- 6 eggs

What you' ll need from the store cupboard:
- 2 tablespoons low-fat mayonnaise

Instructions:
1. Preheat the Air fryer to 375 º F and grease 6 cups muffin tin with cooking spray.
2. Place each bacon slice in a prepared muffin cup.
3. Cut the bread slices with round cookie cutter and place over the bacon slices.
4. Top with bell pepper, scallion and mayonnaise evenly and crack 1 egg in each muffin cup.
5. Place in the Air fryer and cook for about 15 minutes.
6. Dish out and serve warm.

Nutrition Facts Per Serving:
Calories: 260, Fat: 18g, Carbohydrates: 6.9g, Sugar: 1.03g, Protein: 16.7g, Sodium: 805mg

Crispy Potato Rosti

Prep time: 10 minutes, cook time: 15 minutes; Serves 2

5 Ingredients:
- ½ pound russet potatoes, peeled and grated roughly
- 1 tablespoon chives, chopped finely
- 2 tablespoons shallots, minced
- 1/8 cup cheddar cheese
- 3.5 ounces smoked salmon, cut into slices

What you' ll need from the store cupboard:
- 2 tablespoons sour cream
- 1 tablespoon olive oil
- Salt and black pepper, to taste

Instructions:
1. Preheat the Air fryer to 365 º F and grease a pizza pan with the olive oil.
2. Mix together potatoes, shallots, chives, cheese, salt and black pepper in a large bowl until well combined.
3. Transfer the potato mixture into the prepared pizza pan and place in the Air fryer basket.
4. Cook for about 15 minutes and dish out in a platter.
5. Cut the potato rosti into wedges and top with smoked salmon slices and sour cream to serve.

Nutrition Facts Per Serving:
Calories: 327, Fat: 20.2g, Carbohydrates: 23.3g, Sugar: 2.8g, Protein: 15.3g, Sodium: 316mg

Healthy Tofu Omelet

Prep time: 10 minutes, cook time: 29 minutes; Serves 2

5 Ingredients:
- ¼ of onion, chopped
- 12-ounce silken tofu, pressed and sliced
- 3 eggs, beaten
- 1 tablespoon chives, chopped

What you' ll need from the store cupboard:
- 1 garlic clove, minced
- 2 teaspoons olive oil
- Salt and black pepper, to taste

Instructions:
1. Preheat the Air fryer to 355 º F and grease an Air fryer pan with olive oil.
2. Add onion and garlic to the greased pan and cook for about 4 minutes.
3. Add tofu, mushrooms and chives and season with salt and black pepper.
4. Beat the eggs and pour over the tofu mixture.
5. Cook for about 25 minutes, poking the eggs twice in between.
6. Dish out and serve warm.

Nutrition Facts Per Serving:
Calories: 248, Fat: 15.9g, Carbohydrates: 6.5g, Sugar: 3.3g, Protein: 20.4g, Sodium: 155mg

Stylish Ham Omelet

Prep time: 10 minutes, cook time: 30 minutes; Serves 2

5 Ingredients:
- 4 small tomatoes, chopped
- 4 eggs
- 2 ham slices
- 1 onion, chopped
- 2 tablespoons cheddar cheese

What you' ll need from the store cupboard:
- Salt and black pepper, to taste

Instructions:
1. Preheat the Air fryer to 390 º F and grease an Air fryer pan.
2. Place the tomatoes in the Air fryer pan and cook for about 10 minutes.
3. Heat a nonstick skillet on medium heat and add onion and ham.
4. Stir fry for about 5 minutes and transfer into the Air fryer pan.
5. Whisk together eggs, salt and black pepper in a bowl and pour in the Air fryer pan.
6. Set the Air fryer to 335 º F and cook for about 15 minutes.
7. Dish out and serve warm.

Nutrition Facts Per Serving:
Calories: 255, Fat: 13.9g, Carbohydrates: 14.1g, Sugar: 7.8g, Protein: 19.7g, Sodium: 543mg

Peanut Butter Banana Bread

Prep time: 15 minutes, cook time: 40 minutes; Serves 6

5 Ingredients:
- 1 cup plus 1 tablespoon all-purpose flour
- 1¼ teaspoons baking powder
- 1 large egg
- 2 medium ripe bananas, peeled and mashed
- ¾ cup walnuts, roughly chopped

What you' ll need from the store cupboard:
- ¼ teaspoon salt
- 1/3 cup granulated sugar
- ¼ cup canola oil
- 2 tablespoons creamy peanut butter
- 2 tablespoons sour cream
- 1 teaspoon vanilla extract

Instructions:
1. Preheat the Air fryer to 330 º F and grease a non-stick baking dish.
2. Mix together the flour, baking powder and salt in a bowl.
3. Whisk together egg with sugar, canola oil, sour cream, peanut butter and vanilla extract in a bowl.
4. Stir in the bananas and beat until well combined.
5. Now, add the flour mixture and fold in the walnuts gently.
6. Mix until combined and transfer the mixture evenly into the prepared baking dish.
7. Arrange the baking dish in an Air fryer basket and cook for about 40 minutes.
8. Remove from the Air fryer and place onto a wire rack to cool.
9. Cut the bread into desired size slices and serve.

Nutrition Facts Per Serving:
Calories: 384, Fat: 2.6g, Carbohydrates: 39.3g, Sugar: 16.6g, Protein: 8.9g, Sodium: 189mg

Yummy Savory French Toasts

Prep time: 10 minutes, cook time: 4 minutes; Serves 2

5 Ingredients:
- ¼ cup chickpea flour
- 3 tablespoons onion, chopped finely
- 2 teaspoons green chili, seeded and chopped finely
- Water, as required
- 4 bread slices

What you' ll need from the store cupboard:
- ½ teaspoon red chili powder
- ¼ teaspoon ground turmeric
- ¼ teaspoon ground cumin
- Salt, to taste

Instructions:
1. Preheat the Air fryer to 375 º F and line an Air fryer pan with a foil paper.

2. Mix together all the ingredients in a large bowl except the bread slices.
3. Spread the mixture over both sides of the bread slices and transfer into the Air fryer pan.

4. Cook for about 4 minutes and remove from the Air fryer to serve.

Nutrition Facts Per Serving:
Calories: 151, Fat: 2.3g, Carbohydrates: 26.7g, Sugar: 4.3g, Protein: 6.5g, Sodium: 234mg

Aromatic Potato Hash

Prep time: 10 minutes, cook time: 42 minutes; Serves 4

5 Ingredients:
- 2 teaspoons butter, melted
- 1 medium onion, chopped
- ½ of green bell pepper, seeded and chopped
- 1½ pound russet potatoes, peeled and cubed
- 5 eggs, beaten

What you' ll need from the store cupboard:
- ½ teaspoon dried thyme, crushed
- ½ teaspoon dried savory, crushed
- Salt and black pepper, to taste

Instructions:
1. Preheat the Air fryer to 390 º F and grease an Air fryer pan with melted butter.
2. Put onion and bell pepper in the Air fryer pan and cook for about 5 minutes.
3. Add the potatoes, thyme, savory, salt and black pepper and cook for about 30 minutes.
4. Meanwhile, heat a greased skillet on medium heat and stir in the beaten eggs.
5. Cook for about 1 minute on each side and remove from the skillet.
6. Cut it into small pieces and transfer the egg pieces into the Air fryer pan.
7. Cook for about 5 more minutes and serve warm.

Nutrition Facts Per Serving:
Calories: 229, Fat: 7.6g, Carbohydrates: 30.8g, Sugar: 4.2g, Protein: 10.3g, Sodium: 103mg

Pumpkin and Yogurt Bread

Prep time: 10 minutes, cook time: 15 minutes; Serves 4

5 Ingredients:
- 2 large eggs
- 8 tablespoons pumpkin puree
- 6 tablespoons banana flour
- 4 tablespoons plain Greek yogurt
- 6 tablespoons oats

What you' ll need from the store cupboard:
- 4 tablespoons honey
- 2 tablespoons vanilla essence
- Pinch of ground nutmeg

Instructions:
1. Preheat the Air fryer to 360 º F and grease a loaf pan.
2. Mix together all the ingredients except oats in a bowl and beat with the hand mixer until smooth.
3. Add oats and mix until well combined.
4. Transfer the mixture into the prepared loaf pan and place in the Air fryer.
5. Cook for about 15 minutes and remove from the Air fryer.
6. Place onto a wire rack to cool and cut the bread into desired size slices to serve.

Nutrition Facts Per Serving:
Calories: 212, Fat: 3.4g, Carbohydrates: 36g, Sugar: 20.5g, Protein: 6.6g, Sodium: 49mg

Zucchini Fritters

Prep time: 15 minutes, cook time: 7 minutes; Serves 4

5 Ingredients:

- 10½ ounces zucchini, grated and squeezed
- 7 ounces Halloumi cheese
- ¼ cup all-purpose flour
- 2 eggs
- 1 teaspoon fresh dill, minced

What you'll need from the store cupboard:

- Salt and black pepper, to taste

Instructions:

1. Preheat the Air fryer to 360 ° F and grease a baking dish.
2. Mix together all the ingredients in a large bowl.
3. Make small fritters from this mixture and place them on the prepared baking dish.
4. Transfer the dish in the Air Fryer basket and cook for about 7 minutes.
5. Dish out and serve warm.

Nutrition Facts Per Serving:
Calories: 250, Fat: 17.2g, Carbohydrates: 10g, Sugar: 2.7g, Protein: 15.2g, Sodium: 330mg

Chicken Omelet

Prep time: 15 minutes, cook time: 16 minutes; Serves 8

5 Ingredients:

- 1 teaspoon butter
- 1 onion, chopped
- ½ jalapeño pepper, seeded and chopped
- 3 eggs
- ¼ cup chicken, cooked and shredded

What you'll need from the store cupboard:

- Salt and black pepper, to taste

Instructions:

1. Preheat the Air fryer to 355 ° F and grease an Air Fryer pan.
2. Heat butter in a frying pan over medium heat and add onions.
3. Sauté for about 5 minutes and add jalapeño pepper.
4. Sauté for about 1 minute and stir in the chicken.
5. Remove from the heat and keep aside.
6. Meanwhile, whisk together the eggs, salt, and black pepper in a bowl.
7. Place the chicken mixture into the prepared pan and top with the egg mixture.
8. Cook for about 10 minutes until completely done and serve hot.

Nutrition Facts Per Serving:
Calories: 161, Fat: 3.4g, Carbohydrates: 5.9g, Sugar: 3g, Protein: 14.1g, Sodium: 197mg

Bacon and Hot Dogs Omelet

Prep time: 10 minutes, cook time: 10 minutes; Serves 2

5 Ingredients:

- 4 eggs
- 1 bacon slice, chopped
- 2 hot dogs, chopped
- 2 small onions, chopped
- 2 tablespoons milk

What you'll need from the store cupboard:

- Salt and black pepper, to taste

Instructions:

1. Preheat the Air fryer to 325 ° F and grease an Air Fryer pan.
2. Whisk together eggs and stir in the remaining ingredients.
3. Stir well to combine and place in the Air fryer.
4. Cook for about 10 minutes and serve hot.

Nutrition Facts Per Serving:
Calories: 418, Fat: 31.5g, Carbohydrates: 9.7g, Sugar: 5.6g, Protein: 23.4g, Sodium: 1000mg

Tofu and Mushroom Omelet

Prep time: 15 minutes, cook time: 28 minutes; Serves 2

5 Ingredients:
- ¼ of onion, chopped
- 8 ounces silken tofu, pressed and sliced
- 3½ ounces fresh mushrooms, sliced
- 3 eggs, beaten
- 2 tablespoons milk

What you' ll need from the store cupboard:
- 2 teaspoons canola oil
- 1 garlic clove, minced
- Salt and black pepper, to taste

Instructions:
1. Preheat the Air fryer to 360 º F and grease an Air Fryer pan.
2. Heat oil in the Air Fryer pan and add garlic and onion.
3. Cook for about 3 minutes and stir in the tofu and mushrooms.
4. Season with salt and black pepper and top with the beaten eggs.
5. Cook for about 25 minutes, poking the eggs twice in between.
6. Dish out and serve warm.

Nutrition Facts Per Serving:
Calories: 224, Fat: 14.5g, Carbohydrates: 6.6g, Sugar: 3.4g, Protein: 17.9g, Sodium: 214mg

Eggs, Mushrooms and Tomatoes Scramble

Prep time: 15 minutes, cook time: 11 minutes; Serves 4

5 Ingredients:
- ¾ cup milk
- 4 eggs
- 8 grape tomatoes, halved
- ½ cup mushrooms, sliced
- 1 tablespoon chives, chopped

What you' ll need from the store cupboard:
- Salt and black pepper, to taste

Instructions:
1. Preheat the Air fryer to 360 º F and grease an Air Fryer pan.
2. Whisk eggs with milk, salt, and black pepper in a bowl.
3. Transfer the egg mixture into the Air Fryer pan and cook for about 6 minutes.
4. Add mushrooms, grape tomatoes and chives and cook for about 5 minutes.
5. Dish out and serve warm.

Nutrition Facts Per Serving:
Calories: 132, Fat: 5.8g, Carbohydrates: 12.5g, Sugar: 9g, Protein: 9.5g, Sodium: 96mg

Bok Choy and Egg Frittata

Prep time: 15 minutes, cook time: 8 minutes; Serves 2

5 Ingredients:
- 1 cup bok choy, chopped
- 2 eggs
- 2 tablespoons milk
- 1 tablespoon cheddar cheese, grated
- 1 tablespoon feta cheese, grated

What you' ll need from the store cupboard:
- Salt and black pepper, to taste
- 1 tablespoon olive oil

Instructions:
1. Preheat the Air fryer to 360 º F and grease an Air Fryer pan.
2. Whisk together eggs with milk, salt and black pepper in a bowl.
3. Heat olive oil in the Air Fryer pan and add bok choy.
4. Cook for about 3 minutes and stir in the whisked eggs.
5. Top with cheese and cook for about 5 minutes.
6. Dish out and serve hot.

Nutrition Facts Per Serving:
Calories: 186, Fats: 11.7g, Carbohydrates: 6.8g, Sugar: 1.7g, Proteins: 13.2g, Sodium: 498mg

Spinach and Egg Cups

Prep time: 15 minutes, cook time: 23 minutes; Serves 4

5 Ingredients:

- 1 tablespoon unsalted butter, melted
- 1 pound fresh baby spinach
- 4 eggs
- 7 ounces ham, sliced
- 4 teaspoons milk

What you'll need from the store cupboard:

- 1 tablespoon olive oil
- Salt and black pepper, to taste

Instructions:

1. Preheat the Air fryer at 365 ° F and grease 4 ramekins with butter.
2. Heat olive oil in a pan and add spinach.
3. Sauté for about 3 minutes and drain the liquid completely from the spinach.
4. Divide the spinach equally into the prepared ramekins and add ham slices.
5. Crack 1 egg over ham in each ramekin and pour milk evenly over eggs.
6. Season with salt and black pepper and transfer the ramekins in the Air fryer.
7. Cook for about 20 minutes and serve warm.

Nutrition Facts Per Serving:
Calories: 228, Fat: 15.8g, Carbohydrates: 6.6g, Sugar: 1.1g, Protein: 17.2g, Sodium: 821mg

Sausage Frittata

Prep time: 15 minutes, cook time: 11 minutes; Serves 2

5 Ingredients:

- ½ of chorizo sausage, sliced
- ½ cup frozen corn
- 1 large potato, boiled, peeled and cubed
- 3 jumbo eggs
- 2 tablespoons feta cheese, crumbled

What you'll need from the store cupboard:

- 1 tablespoon olive oil
- Salt and black pepper, to taste

Instructions:

1. Preheat the Air fryer to 355 ° F and grease an Air Fryer pan.
2. Whisk together eggs with salt and black pepper in a bowl.
3. Heat olive oil in the Air Fryer pan and add sausage, corn and potato.
4. Cook for about 6 minutes and stir in the whisked eggs.
5. Top with cheese and cook for about 5 minutes.
6. Dish out and serve hot.

Nutrition Facts Per Serving:
Calories: 327, Fat: 20.2g, Carbohydrates: 23.3g, Sugar: 2.8g, Protein: 15.3g, Sodium: 316mg

Trout Frittata

Prep time: 15 minutes, cook time: 23 minutes; Serves 4

5 Ingredients:

- 1 onion, sliced
- 6 eggs
- 2 hot-smoked trout fillets, chopped
- ¼ cup fresh dill, chopped
- 1 tomato, chopped

What you'll need from the store cupboard:

- 2 tablespoons olive oil
- ½ tablespoon horseradish sauce
- 2 tablespoons crème fraiche

Instructions:

1. Preheat the Air fryer to 325 ° F and grease a baking dish lightly.
2. Whisk together eggs with horseradish sauce and crème fraiche in a bowl.
3. Heat olive oil in a pan and add onions.
4. Sauté for about 3 minutes and transfer into a baking dish.
5. Stir in the whisked eggs, trout, tomato and dill.
6. Arrange the baking dish into an air fryer basket and cook for about 20 minutes.
7. Dish out and serve hot.

Nutrition Facts Per Serving:
Calories: 429, Fat: 38.1g, Carbohydrates: 5.5g, Sugar: 2.1g, Protein: 17.3g, Sodium: 252mg

Mushroom and Tomato Frittata

Prep time: 15 minutes, cook time: 14 minutes; Serves 2

5 Ingredients:
- 1 bacon slice, chopped
- 6 cherry tomatoes, halved
- 6 fresh mushrooms, sliced
- 3 eggs
- ½ cup Parmesan cheese, grated

What you' ll need from the store cupboard:
- 1 tablespoon olive oil
- Salt and black pepper, to taste

Instructions:
1. Preheat the Air fryer to 390 º F and grease a baking dish lightly.
2. Mix together bacon, mushrooms, tomatoes, salt and black pepper in the baking dish.
3. Arrange the baking dish into the Air Fryer basket and cook for about 6 minutes.
4. Whisk together eggs in a small bowl and add cheese.
5. Mix well and pour over the bacon mixture.
6. Place the baking dish in the Air Fryer basket and cook for about 8 minutes.
7. Dish out and serve hot.

Nutrition Facts Per Serving:
Calories: 397, Fat: 26.2g, Carbohydrates: 23.3g, Sugar: 11.2g, Protein: 27.3g, Sodium: 693mg

Breakfast Zucchini

Prep time: 5 minutes, cook time: 35 minutes; Serves 4

5 Ingredients:
- 4 zucchinis, diced into 1-inch pieces, drained
- 2 small bell pepper, chopped medium
- 2 small onion, chopped medium

What you' ll need from the store cupboard:
- Cooking oil spray
- Pinch salt and black pepper

Instructions:
1. Preheat the Air fryer to 350 º F and grease the Air fryer basket with cooking spray.
2. Season the zucchini with salt and black pepper and place in the Air fryer basket.
3. Select Roasting mode and cook for about 20 minutes, stirring occasionally.
4. Add onion and bell pepper and cook for 5 more minutes.
5. Remove from the Air fryer and mix well to serve warm.

Nutrition Facts Per Serving:
Calories: 146, Fat: 0.5g, Carbohydrates: 3.8g, Sugar: 5.5g, Protein: 4g, Sodium: 203mg

Mini Tomato Quiche

Prep time: 15 minutes, cook time: 30 minutes; Serves 2

5 Ingredients:
- 4 eggs
- ¼ cup onion, chopped
- ½ cup tomatoes, chopped
- ½ cup milk
- 1 cup Gouda cheese, shredded

What you' ll need from the store cupboard:
- Salt, to taste

Instructions:
1. Preheat the Air fryer to 340 º F and grease a large ramekin with cooking spray.
2. Mix together all the ingredients in a ramekin and transfer into the air fryer basket.
3. Cook for about 30 minutes and dish out to serve hot.

Nutrition Facts Per Serving:
Calories: 345, Fat: 23.8g, Carbohydrates: 7.9g, Sugar: 6.3g, Protein: 26.1g, Sodium: 640mg

Chicken and Broccoli Quiche

Prep time: 15 minutes, cook time: 12 minutes; Serves 8

5 Ingredients:

- 1 frozen ready-made pie crust
- 1 egg
- 1/3 cup cheddar cheese, grated
- ¼ cup boiled broccoli, chopped
- ¼ cup cooked chicken, chopped

What you' ll need from the store cupboard:

- ½ tablespoon olive oil
- 3 tablespoons whipping cream
- Salt and black pepper, to taste

Instructions:

1. Preheat the Air fryer to 390 º F and grease 2 small pie pans with olive oil.
2. Whisk egg with whipping cream, cheese, salt and black pepper in a bowl.
3. Cut 2 (5-inch) rounds from the pie crust and arrange in each pie pan.
4. Press in the bottom and sides gently and pour the egg mixture over pie crust.
5. Top evenly with chicken and broccoli and place the pie pans into an Air Fryer basket.
6. Cook for about 12 minutes and dish out to serve hot.

Nutrition Facts Per Serving:
Calories: 166, Fat: 10.3g, Carbohydrates: 14.6g, Sugar: 8.5g, Protein: 4.2g, Sodium: 186mg

Eggless Spinach and Bacon Quiche

Prep time: 15 minutes, cook time: 10 minutes; Serves 2

5 Ingredients:

- 1 cup fresh spinach, chopped
- 4 slices of bacon, cooked and chopped
- ½ cup mozzarella cheese, shredded
- 4 tablespoons milk
- 1 cup Parmesan cheese, shredded

What you' ll need from the store cupboard:

- 4 dashes Tabasco sauce
- Salt and black pepper, to taste

Instructions:

1. Preheat the Air fryer to 325 º F and grease a baking dish lightly.
2. Mix together all the ingredients in a bowl and transfer the mixture into prepared baking dish.
3. Place in the Air fryer and cook for about 10 minutes.
4. Dish out and serve warm.

Nutrition Facts Per Serving:
Calories: 72, Fat: 5.2g, Carbohydrates: 0.9g, Sugar: 0.4g, Protein: 5.5g, Sodium: 271mg

Air Fryer Breakfast Frittata

Prep time: 15 minutes, cook time: 20 minutes; Serves 2

5 Ingredients:

- ¼ pound breakfast sausage, fully cooked and crumbled
- 4 eggs, lightly beaten
- ½ cup Monterey Jack cheese, shredded
- 2 tablespoons red bell pepper, diced
- 1 green onion, chopped

What you' ll need from the store cupboard:

- 1 pinch cayenne pepper

Instructions:

1. Preheat the Air fryer to 365 º F and grease a nonstick 6x2-inch cake pan.
2. Whisk together eggs with sausage, green onion, bell pepper, cheese and cayenne in a bowl.
3. Transfer the egg mixture in the prepared cake pan and place in the Air fryer.
4. Cook for about 20 minutes and serve warm.

Nutrition Facts Per Serving:
Calories: 464, Fat: 33.7g, Carbohydrates: 10.4g, Sugar: 7g, Protein: 30.4g, Sodium: 704mg

Breakfast Pockets

Prep time: 15 minutes, cook time: 30 minutes; Serves 4

5 Ingredients:
- 2 sheets (17.25 oz) almond flour puff pastry, cut into 4 equal sized pieces
- 1 package (6 oz.) ground breakfast sausage, crumbled
- 2 eggs, lightly beaten
- 1 cup cheddar cheese, shredded

What you'll need from the store cupboard:
- 1 teaspoon kosher salt
- ½ teaspoon ground black pepper
- 2 tablespoons canola oil

Instructions:
1. Preheat the Air fryer to 375 ° F and grease the Air fryer basket.
2. Arrange the sausages in the basket and roast for about 15 minutes.
3. Place the eggs into the basket and cook for about 5 minutes.
4. Season with salt and black pepper and divide the egg sausages mixture over the 4 puff pastry rectangles.
5. Top with shredded cheddar cheese and drizzle with canola oil.
6. Place 1 egg pocket in the basket and cook for 6 minutes at 400 ° F.
7. Remove from the Air fryer and repeat with the remaining pockets.
8. Serve warm and enjoy.

Nutrition Facts Per Serving:
Calories: 197, Fats: 15.4g, Carbs: 8.5g, Sugar: 1.1g, Proteins: 7.9g, Sodium: 203mg

Ham and Egg Toast Cups

Prep time: 5 minutes, cook time: 5 minutes; Serves 2

5 Ingredients:
- 2 eggs
- 2 slices of ham
- 2 tablespoons butter
- Cheddar cheese, for topping

What you'll need from the store cupboard:
- Salt, to taste
- Black pepper, to taste

Instructions:
1. Preheat the Air fryer to 400 ° F and grease both ramekins with melted butter.
2. Place each ham slice in the greased ramekins and crack each egg over ham slices.
3. Sprinkle with salt, black pepper and cheddar cheese and transfer into the Air fryer basket.
4. Cook for about 5 minutes and remove the ramekins from the basket.
5. Serve warm.

Nutrition Facts Per Serving:
Calories: 202, Fat: 13.7g, Carbs: 7.4g, Sugar: 3.3g, Protein: 10.2g, Sodium: 203mg

Sausage Solo

Prep time: 5 minutes, cook time: 22 minutes; Serves 4

5 Ingredients:
- 6 eggs
- 4 cooked sausages, sliced
- 2 bread slices, cut into sticks
- ½ cup mozzarella cheese, grated

What you'll need from the store cupboard:
- ½ cup cream

Instructions:
1. Preheat the Air fryer to 355 ° F and grease 4 ramekins lightly.
2. Whisk together eggs and cream in a bowl and beat well.
3. Transfer the egg mixture into ramekins and arrange the bread sticks and sausage slices around the edges.
4. Top with mozzarella cheese evenly and place the ramekins in Air fryer basket.
5. Cook for about 22 minutes and dish out to serve warm.

Nutrition Facts Per Serving:
Calories: 180, Fat: 12.7g, Carbs: 3.9g, Sugar: 1.3g, Protein: 12.4g, Sodium: 251mg

Cauliflower Hash Brown

Prep time: 20 minutes, cook time: 10 minutes; Serves 4

5 Ingredients:
- 2 cups cauliflower, finely grated, soaked and drained
- 2 tablespoons xanthan gum

What you'll need from the store cupboard:
- Salt, to taste
- Pepper powder, to taste
- 2 teaspoons chili flakes
- 1 teaspoon garlic
- 1 teaspoon onion powder
- 2 teaspoons vegetable oil

Instructions:
1. Preheat the Air fryer to 300 º F and grease an Air fryer basket with oil.
2. Heat vegetable oil in a nonstick pan and add cauliflower.
3. Sauté for about 4 minutes and dish out the cauliflower in a plate.
4. Mix the cauliflower with xanthum gum, salt, chili flakes, garlic and onion powder.
5. Mix well and refrigerate the hash for about 20 minutes.
6. Place the hash in the Air fryer basket and cook for about 10 minutes.
7. Flip the hash after cooking half way through and dish out to serve warm.

Nutrition Facts Per Serving:
Calories: 291, Fat: 2.8g, Carbs: 6.5g, Sugar: 4.5g, Protein: 6.6g, Sodium: 62mg

French toast Sticks

Prep time: 10 minutes, cook time: 5 minutes; Serves 4

5 Ingredients:
- 4 bread, sliced into sticks
- 2 tablespoons soft butter or margarine
- 2 eggs, gently beaten

What you'll need from the store cupboard:
- Salt, to taste
- 1 pinch cinnamon
- 1 pinch nutmeg
- 1 pinch ground cloves

Instructions:
1. Preheat the Air fryer at 365 º F and grease an Air fryer pan with butter.
2. Whisk eggs with salt, cinnamon, nutmeg and ground cloves in a bowl.
3. Dip the bread sticks in the egg mixture and place in the pan.
4. Cook for about 5 minutes, flipping in between and remove from the Air fryer.
5. Dish out and serve warm.

Nutrition Facts Per Serving:
Calories: 186, Fat: 11.7g, Carbs: 6.8g, Sugar: 1.7g, Protein: 13.2g, Sodium: 498mg

Sausage Bacon Fandango

Prep time: 5 minutes, cook time: 20 minutes; Serves 4

5 Ingredients:
- 8 bacon slices
- 8 chicken sausages
- 4 eggs

What you'll need from the store cupboard:
- Salt and black pepper, to taste

Instructions:
1. Preheat the Air fryer to 320 º F and grease 4 ramekins lightly.
2. Place bacon slices and sausages in the Air fryer basket.
3. Cook for about 10 minutes and crack 1 egg in each prepared ramekin.
4. Season with salt and black pepper and cook for about 10 more minutes.
5. Divide bacon slices and sausages in serving plates.
6. Place 1 egg in each plate and serve warm.

Nutrition Facts Per Serving:
Calories: 287, Fat: 21.5g, Carbs: 0.9g, Sugar: 0.3g, Protein: 21.4g, Sodium: 1007mg

Creamy Parsley Soufflé

Prep time: 5 minutes, cook time: 10 minutes; Serves 2

5 Ingredients:
- 2 eggs
- 1 tablespoon fresh parsley, chopped
- 1 fresh red chili pepper, chopped

What you' ll need from the store cupboard:
- 2 tablespoons light cream
- Salt, to taste

Instructions:
1. Preheat the Air fryer to 390 º F and grease 2 soufflé dishes.
2. Mix together all the ingredients in a bowl until well combined.
3. Transfer the mixture into prepared soufflé dishes and place in the Air fryer.
4. Cook for about 10 minutes and dish out to serve warm.

Nutrition Facts Per Serving:
Calories: 108, Fat: 9g, Carbs: 1.1g, Sugar: 0.5g, Protein: 6g, Sodium: 146mg

Sweet Potato Hash

Prep time: 10 minutes, cook time: 15 minutes; Serves 6

5 Ingredients:
- 2 large sweet potato, cut into small cubes
- 2 slices bacon, cut into small pieces

What you' ll need from the store cupboard:
- 2 tablespoons olive oil
- 1 tablespoon smoked paprika
- 1 teaspoon sea salt
- 1 teaspoon ground black pepper
- 1 teaspoon dried dill weed

Instructions:
1. Preheat the Air Fryer to 400 º F and grease an Air fryer pan.
2. Mix together sweet potato, bacon, olive oil, paprika, salt, black pepper and dill in a large bowl.
3. Transfer the mixture into the preheated air fryer pan and cook for about 15 minutes, stirring in between.
4. Dish out and serve warm.

Nutrition Facts Per Serving:
Calories: 191, Fat: 6g, Carbohydrates: 31.4g, Sugar: 6g, Protein: 3.7g, Sodium: 447mg

Toad-in-the-Hole Tarts

Prep time: 5 minutes, cook time: 25 minutes; Serves 4

5 Ingredients:
- 1 sheet frozen puff pastry, thawed and cut into 4 squares
- 4 tablespoons cheddar cheese, shredded
- 4 tablespoons cooked ham, diced
- 4 eggs
- 2 tablespoons fresh chives, chopped

What you' ll need from the store cupboard:
- 1 tablespoon olive oil

Instructions:
1. Preheat the Air fryer to 400 º F and grease an Air fryer basket.
2. Place 2 pastry squares in the air fryer basket and cook for about 8 minutes.
3. Remove Air fryer basket from the Air fryer and press each square gently with a metal tablespoon to form an indentation.
4. Place 1 tablespoon of ham and 1 tablespoon of cheddar cheese in each hole and top with 1 egg each.
5. Return Air fryer basket to Air fryer and cook for about 6 more minutes.
6. Remove tarts from the Air fryer basket and allow to cool.
7. Repeat with remaining pastry squares, cheese, ham, and eggs.
8. Dish out and garnish tarts with chives.

Nutrition Facts Per Serving:
Calories: 175, Fat: 13.7g, Carbohydrates: 4.1g, Sugar: 0.5g, Protein: 9.3g, Sodium: 233mg

Tex-Mex Hash Browns

Prep time: 15 minutes, cook time: 30 minutes; Serves 4

5 Ingredients:

- 1½ pounds potatoes, peeled, cut into 1-inch cubes and soaked
- 1 red bell pepper, seeded and cut into 1-inch pieces
- 1 small onion, cut into 1-inch pieces
- 1 jalapeno, seeded and cut into 1-inch rings

What you' ll need from the store cupboard:

- 1 tablespoon olive oil
- ½ teaspoon taco seasoning mix
- ½ teaspoon ground cumin
- 1 pinch salt and ground black pepper, to taste

Instructions:

1. Preheat the Air fryer to 330 º F and grease an Air fryer basket.
2. Coat the potatoes with olive oil and transfer into the Air fryer basket.
3. Cook for about 18 minutes and dish out in a bowl.
4. Mix together bell pepper, onion, and jalapeno in the bowl and season with taco seasoning mix, cumin, salt and black pepper.
5. Toss to coat well and combine with the potatoes.
6. Transfer the seasoned vegetables into the Air fryer basket and cook for about 12 minutes, stirring in between.
7. Dish out and serve immediately.

Nutrition Facts Per Serving:
Calories: 186, Fat: 4.3g, Carbohydrates: 33.7g, Sugar: 3g, Protein: 4g, Sodium: 79mg

Puffed Egg Tarts

Prep time: 10 minutes, cook time: 42 minutes; Serves 4

5 Ingredients:

- 1 sheet frozen puff pastry half, thawed and cut into 4 squares
- ¾ cup Monterey Jack cheese, shredded and divided
- 4 large eggs
- 1 tablespoon fresh parsley, minced

What you' ll need from the store cupboard:

- 1 tablespoon olive oil

Instructions:

1. Preheat the Air fryer to 390 º F
2. Place 2 pastry squares in the air fryer basket and cook for about 10 minutes.
3. Remove Air fryer basket from the Air fryer and press each square gently with a metal tablespoon to form an indentation.
4. Place 3 tablespoons of cheese in each hole and top with 1 egg each.
5. Return Air fryer basket to Air fryer and cook for about 11 minutes.
6. Remove tarts from the Air fryer basket and sprinkle with half the parsley.
7. Repeat with remaining pastry squares, cheese and eggs.
8. Dish out and serve warm.

Nutrition Facts Per Serving:
Calories: 246, Fat: 19.4g, Carbohydrates: 5.9g, Sugar: 0.6g, Protein: 12.4g, Sodium: 213mg

Air Fryer Bacon

Prep time: 1 minutes, cook time: 9 minutes; Serves 6

5 Ingredients:

- 6 bacon strips

What you' ll need from the store cupboard:

- ½ tablespoon olive oil

Instructions:

1. Preheat the Air fryer to 350 º F and grease an Air fryer basket with olive oil.
2. Cook for about 9 minutes and flip the bacon.
3. Cook for 3 more minutes until crispy and serve warm.

Nutrition Facts Per Serving:
Calories: 245, Fat: 17.1g, Carbohydrates: 10.2g, Sugar: 2.7g, Protein: 12.8g, Sodium: 580mg

Broccoli Cheese Quiche

Prep time: 10 minutes, cook time: 40 minutes; Serves 2

5 Ingredients:
- 1 large broccoli, chopped into florets
- 3 large carrots, peeled and diced
- 1 cup cheddar cheese, grated
- ¼ cup feta cheese
- 2 large eggs

What you'll need from the store cupboard:
- 1 teaspoon dried rosemary
- 1 teaspoon dried thyme
- Salt and black pepper, to taste

Instructions:
1. Preheat the Air fryer to 360 º F and grease a quiche dish.
2. Place broccoli and carrots into a food steamer and cook for about 20 minutes until soft.
3. Whisk together eggs with milk, dried herbs, salt and black pepper in a bowl.
4. Place steamed vegetables at the bottom of the quiche pan and top with tomatoes and cheese.
5. Drizzle with the egg mixture and transfer the quiche dish in the Air fryer.
6. Cook for about 20 minutes and dish out to serve warm.

Nutrition Facts Per Serving:
Calories: 412, Fat: 28, Carbohydrates: 16.3g, Sugar: 7.5g, Protein: 25.3g, Sodium: 720mg

Bacon and Egg Bite Cups

Prep time: 15 minutes, cook time: 15 minutes; Serves 4

5 Ingredients:
- 6 large eggs
- ½ cup red peppers, chopped
- ¼ cup fresh spinach, chopped
- ¾ cup mozzarella cheese, shredded
- 3 slices bacon, cooked and crumbled

What you'll need from the store cupboard:
- 2 tablespoons heavy whipping cream
- Salt and black pepper, to taste

Instructions:
1. Preheat the Air fryer to 300 º F and grease 4 silicone molds.
2. Whisk together eggs with cream, salt and black pepper in a large bowl until combined.
3. Stir in rest of the ingredients and transfer the mixture into silicone molds.
4. Place in the Air fryer and cook for about 15 minutes.
5. Dish out and serve warm.

Nutrition Facts Per Serving:
Calories: 233, Fats: 17.2g, Carbohydrates: 2.9g, Sugar: 1.6g, Proteins: 16.8g, Sodium: 472mg

Bacon Grilled Cheese

Prep time: 5 minutes, cook time: 7 minutes; Serves 2

5 Ingredients:
- 4 slices of bread
- 1 tablespoon butter, softened
- 2 slices mild cheddar cheese
- 6 slices bacon, cooked
- 2 slices mozzarella cheese

What you'll need from the store cupboard:
- 1 tablespoon olive oil

Instructions:
1. Preheat the Air fryer to 370 º F and grease an Air fryer basket with olive oil.
2. Spread butter onto one side of each bread slice and place in the Air Fryer basket.
3. Layer with cheddar cheese slice, followed by bacon, mozzarella cheese and close with the other bread slice.
4. Place in the Air fryer and cook for about 4 minutes.
5. Flip the sandwich and cook for 3 more minutes.
6. Remove from the Air fryer and serve.

Nutrition Facts Per Serving:
Calories: 518, Fat: 34.9g, Carbohydrates: 20g, Sugar: 0.6g, Protein: 29.9g, Sodium: 1475mg

Air Fryer Breakfast Casserole

Prep time: 10 minutes, cook time: 25 minutes; Serves 2

5 Ingredients:

- 3 red potatoes
- 3 eggs
- 2 turkey sausage patties
- ¼ cup cheddar cheese
- 1 tablespoon milk

What you'll need from the store cupboard:

- Olive oil cooking spray

Instructions:

1. Preheat the Air fryer to 400 ° F and grease a baking dish with cooking spray.
2. Place the potatoes in the Air fryer basket and cook for about 10 minutes.
3. Whisk eggs with milk in a bowl.
4. Put the potatoes and sausage in the baking dish and pour egg mixture on top.
5. Sprinkle with cheddar cheese and arrange in the Air fryer.
6. Cook for about 15 minutes at 350 ° F and dish out to serve warm.

Nutrition Facts Per Serving:
Calories: 469, Fat: 16.3g, Carbohydrates: 51.9g, Sugar: 4.1g, Protein: 29.1g, Sodium: 623mg

Air Fryer Breakfast Bake

Prep time: 15 minutes, cook time: 25 minutes; Serves 2

5 Ingredients:

- 4 eggs
- 1 slice whole grain bread, torn into pieces
- 1½ cups baby spinach
- 1/3 cup cheddar cheese, shredded
- ½ cup bell pepper, diced

What you'll need from the store cupboard:

- ½ teaspoon kosher salt
- 1 teaspoon hot sauce

Instructions:

1. Preheat the Air fryer to 250 ° F and grease a 6-inch soufflé dish with nonstick cooking spray.
2. Whisk together eggs, salt and hot sauce in a bowl.
3. Dip the bread pieces, spinach, ¼ cup cheddar cheese and bell pepper in the whisked eggs.
4. Pour this mixture into prepared soufflé dish and sprinkle with remaining cheese.
5. Transfer into the Air fryer basket and cook for about 25 minutes.
6. Remove from the Air fryer basket and let it rest for 10 minutes before serving.

Nutrition Facts Per Serving:
Calories: 249, Fat: 15.7g, Carbohydrates: 10.3g, Sugar: 3.4g, Protein: 18.2g, Sodium: 979mg

Sausage Breakfast Casserole

Prep time: 10 minutes, cook time: 20 minutes; Serves 4

5 Ingredients:

- 1 pound hash browns
- 1 pound ground breakfast sausage
- 3 bell peppers, diced
- ¼ cup sweet onion, diced
- 4 eggs

What you' ll need from the store cupboard:

- 1 tablespoon olive oil
- Salt and black pepper, to taste

Instructions:

1. Preheat the Air fryer to 355 º F and grease the casserole dish with olive oil.
2. Place the hash browns on the bottom of the casserole dish and top with sausages, bell peppers and onions.
3. Transfer into the Air fryer and cook for about 10 minutes.
4. Crack eggs into the casserole dish and cook for 10 more minutes.
5. Season with salt and black pepper and serve warm.

Nutrition Facts Per Serving:
Calories: 472, Fat: 25g, Carbohydrates: 47.6g, Sugar: 6.8g, Protein: 15.6g, Sodium: 649mg

Egg Veggie Frittata

Prep time: 10 minutes, cook time: 18 minutes; Serves 2

5 Ingredients:

- 4 eggs
- ½ cup milk
- 2 green onions, chopped
- ¼ cup baby Bella mushrooms, chopped
- ¼ cup spinach, chopped

What you' ll need from the store cupboard:

- ½ teaspoon salt
- ½ teaspoon black pepper
- Dash of hot sauce

Instructions:

1. Preheat the Air fryer to 365 º F and grease 6x3 inch square pan with butter.
2. Whisk eggs with milk in a large bowl and stir in green onions, mushrooms and spinach.
3. Sprinkle with salt, black pepper and hot sauce and pour this mixture into the prepared pan.
4. Place in the Air fryer and cook for about 18 minutes.
5. Dish out in a platter and serve warm.

Nutrition Facts Per Serving:
Calories: 166, Fat: 10.1g, Carbohydrates: 5.8g, Sugar: 4g, Protein: 13.8g, Sodium: 748mg

Chapter 3 Fish and Seafood Recipes

Delicious Prawns and Sweet Potatoes

Prep time: 20 minutes, cook time: 20 minutes; Serves 4

5 Ingredients:

- 1 shallot, chopped
- 1 red chili pepper, seeded and chopped finely
- 12 king prawns, peeled and deveined
- 5 large sweet potatoes, peeled and cut into slices
- 4 lemongrass stalks

What you' ll need from the store cupboard:

- 2 tablespoons dried rosemary
- 1/3 cup olive oil, divided
- 4 garlic cloves, minced
- Smoked paprika, to taste
- 1 tablespoon honey

Instructions:

1. Preheat the Air fryer to 355 º F and grease an Air fryer basket.
2. Mix ¼ cup of the olive oil, shallot, red chili pepper, garlic and paprika in a bowl.
3. Add prawns and coat evenly with the mixture.
4. Thread the prawns onto lemongrass stalks and refrigerate to marinate for about 3 hours.
5. Mix sweet potatoes, honey and rosemary in a bowl and toss to coat well.
6. Arrange the potatoes in the Air fryer basket and cook for about 15 minutes.
7. Remove the sweet potatoes from the Air fryer and set the Air fryer to 390 degrees F.
8. Place the prawns in the Air fryer basket and cook for about 5 minutes.
9. Dish out in a bowl and serve with sweet potatoes.

Nutrition Facts Per Serving:
Calories: 285, Fats: 3.8g, Carbohydrates: 51.6g, Sugar: 5.8g, Proteins: 10.5g, Sodium: 235mg

Nutritious Salmon and Veggie Patties

Prep time: 15 minutes, cook time: 7 minutes; Serves 6

5 Ingredients:

- 3 large russet potatoes, boiled and mashed
- 1 (6-ounce) salmon fillet
- 1 egg
- ¾ cup frozen vegetables, parboiled and drained
- 1 cup breadcrumbs

What you' ll need from the store cupboard:

- 2 tablespoons dried parsley, chopped
- 1 teaspoon dried dill, chopped
- Salt and freshly ground pepper, to taste
- ¼ cup olive oil

Instructions:

1. Preheat the Air fryer to 355 º F and line a pan with foil paper.
2. Place salmon in the Air fryer basket and cook for about 5 minutes.
3. Dish out the salmon in a large bowl and flake with a fork.
4. Mix potatoes, egg, parboiled vegetables, parsley, dill, salt and black pepper until well combined.
5. Make 6 equal sized patties from the mixture and coat the patties evenly with breadcrumbs.
6. Drizzle with the olive oil and arrange the patties in the pan.
7. Transfer into the Air fryer basket and cook for about 12 minutes, flipping once in between.

Nutrition Facts Per Serving:
Calories: 334, Fat: 12.1g, Carbohydrates: 45.1g, Sugar: 4g, Protein: 12.6g, Sodium: 175mg

Cod Cakes

Prep time: 15 minutes, cook time: 14 minutes; Serves 4

5 Ingredients:
- 1 pound cod fillets
- 1 egg
- 1/3 cup coconut, grated and divided
- 1 scallion, chopped finely
- 2 tablespoons fresh parsley, chopped

What you' ll need from the store cupboard:
- 1 teaspoon fresh lime zest, grated finely
- 1 teaspoon red chili paste
- Salt, to taste
- 1 tablespoon fresh lime juice

Instructions:
1. Preheat the Air fryer to 375 º F and grease an Air fryer basket.
2. Put cod filets, lime zest, egg, chili paste, salt and lime juice in a food processor and pulse until smooth.
3. Transfer the cod mixture to a bowl and add 2 tablespoons coconut, scallion and parsley.
4. Make 12 equal sized round cakes from the mixture.
5. Put the remaining coconut in a shallow dish and coat the cod cakes in it.
6. Arrange 6 cakes in the Air fryer basket and cook for about 7 minutes.
7. Repeat with the remaining cod cakes and serve warm.

Nutrition Facts Per Serving:
Calories: 171, Fat: 3.3g, Carbohydrates: 16.1g, Sugar: 13.2g, Protein: 19g, Sodium: 115mg

Ham-Wrapped Prawns with Roasted Pepper Chutney

Prep time: 15 minutes, cook time: 13 minutes; Serves 4

5 Ingredients:
- 1 large red bell pepper
- 8 king prawns, peeled and deveined
- 4 ham slices, halved

What you' ll need from the store cupboard:
- 1 garlic clove, minced
- 1 tablespoon olive oil
- ½ tablespoon paprika
- Salt and freshly ground black pepper, to taste

Instructions:
1. Preheat the Air fryer to 375 º F and grease an Air fryer basket.
2. Place the bell pepper in the Air fryer basket and cook for about 10 minutes.
3. Dish out the bell pepper into a bowl and keep aside, covered for about 15 minutes.
4. Now, peel the bell pepper and remove the stems and seeds and chop it.
5. Put the chopped bell pepper, garlic, paprika and olive oil in a blender and pulse until a puree is formed.
6. Wrap each ham slice around each prawn and transfer to the Air fryer basket.
7. Cook for about 3 minutes and serve with roasted pepper chutney.

Nutrition Facts Per Serving:
Calories: 353, Fat: 9.9g, Carbohydrates: 7.6g, Sugar: 1.8g, Protein: 55.4g, Sodium: 904mg

Super-Simple Scallops

Prep time: 10 minutes, cook time: 4 minutes; Serves 2

5 Ingredients:
- ¾ pound sea scallops
- 1 tablespoon butter, melted
- ½ tablespoon fresh thyme, minced

What you' ll need from the store cupboard:
- Salt and black pepper, to taste

Instructions:
1. Preheat the Air fryer to 390 º F and grease an Air fryer basket.
2. Mix all the ingredients in a bowl and toss to coat well.
3. Arrange the scallops in the Air fryer basket and cook for about 4 minutes.
4. Dish out and serve warm.

Nutrition Facts Per Serving:
Calories: 202, Fat: 7.1g, Carbohydrates: 4.4g, Sugar: 0g, Protein: 28.7g, Sodium: 315mg

Juicy Salmon and Asparagus Parcels

Prep time: 5 minutes, cook time: 13 minutes; Serves 2

5 Ingredients:

- 2 salmon fillets
- 4 asparagus stalks
- ¼ cup champagne

What you'll need from the store cupboard:

- Salt and black pepper, to taste
- ¼ cup white sauce
- 1 teaspoon olive oil

Instructions:

1. Preheat the Air fryer to 355 º F and grease an Air fryer basket.
2. Mix all the ingredients in a bowl and divide this mixture evenly over 2 foil papers.
3. Arrange the foil papers in the Air fryer basket and cook for about 13 minutes.
4. Dish out in a platter and serve hot.

Nutrition Facts Per Serving:
Calories: 328, Fat: 16.6g, Carbohydrates: 4.1g, Sugar: 1.8g, Protein: 36.6g, Sodium: 190mg

Appetizing Tuna Patties

Prep time: 15 minutes, cook time: 10 minutes; Serves 6

5 Ingredients:

- 2 (6-ounce) cans tuna, drained
- ½ cup panko bread crumbs
- 1 egg
- 2 tablespoons fresh parsley, chopped

What you'll need from the store cupboard:

- 2 teaspoons Dijon mustard
- Dash of Tabasco sauce
- Salt and black pepper, to taste
- 1 tablespoon fresh lemon juice
- 1 tablespoon olive oil

Instructions:

1. Preheat the Air fryer to 355 º F and line a baking tray with foil paper.
2. Mix all the ingredients in a large bowl until well combined.
3. Make equal sized patties from the mixture and refrigerate overnight.
4. Arrange the patties on the baking tray and transfer to an Air fryer basket.
5. Cook for about 10 minutes and dish out to serve warm.

Nutrition Facts Per Serving:
Calories: 130, Fat: 6.2g, Carbohydrates: 5.1g, Sugar: 0.5g, Protein: 13g, Sodium: 94mg

Quick and Easy Shrimp

Prep time: 10 minutes, cook time: 5 minutes; Serves 2

5 Ingredients:

- ½ pound tiger shrimp

What you'll need from the store cupboard:

- 1 tablespoon olive oil
- ½ teaspoon old bay seasoning
- ¼ teaspoon smoked paprika
- ¼ teaspoon cayenne pepper
- Salt, to taste

Instructions:

1. Preheat the Air fryer to 390 º F and grease an Air fryer basket.
2. Mix all the ingredients in a large bowl until well combined.
3. Place the shrimps in the Air fryer basket and cook for about 5 minutes.
4. Dish out and serve warm.

Nutrition Facts Per Serving:
Calories: 174, Fat: 8.3g, Carbohydrates: 0.3g, Sugar: 0g, Protein: 23.8g, Sodium: 492mg

Crispy Shrimp with Orange Marmalade Dip

Prep time: 25 minutes, cook time: 20 minutes; Serves 4

5 Ingredients:
- 8 large shrimp, peeled and deveined
- 8 ounces coconut milk
- ½ cup panko breadcrumbs

What you'll need from the store cupboard:
- Salt and black pepper, to taste
- ½ teaspoon cayenne pepper

For Dip:
- ½ cup orange marmalade
- 1 teaspoon mustard
- ¼ teaspoon hot sauce
- 1 tablespoon honey

Instructions:
1. Preheat the Air fryer to 350 º F and grease an Air fryer basket.
2. Mix coconut milk, salt and black pepper in a shallow dish.
3. Combine breadcrumbs, cayenne pepper, salt and black pepper in another shallow dish.
4. Coat the shrimps in coconut milk mixture and then roll into the breadcrumb mixture.
5. Arrange the shrimps in the Air fryer basket and cook for about 20 minutes.
6. Meanwhile, mix all the dip ingredients and serve with shrimp.

Nutrition Facts Per Serving:
Calories: 316, Fat: 14.7g, Carbohydrates: 44.3g, Sugar: 31.1g, Protein: 6g, Sodium: 165mg

Tuna-Stuffed Potato Boats

Prep time: 10 minutes, cook time: 16 minutes; Serves 4

5 Ingredients:
- 4 starchy potatoes, soaked for about 30 minutes and drain
- 1 (6-ounce) can tuna, drained
- 2 tablespoons plain Greek yogurt
- 1 scallion, chopped and divided
- 1 tablespoon capers

What you'll need from the store cupboard:
- ½ tablespoon olive oil
- 1 teaspoon red chili powder
- Salt and black pepper, to taste

Instructions:
1. Preheat the Air fryer to 355 º F and grease an Air fryer basket.
2. Arrange the potatoes in the Air fryer basket and cook for about 30 minutes.
3. Meanwhile, mix tuna, yogurt, red chili powder, salt, black pepper and half of scallion in a bowl and mash the mixture well.
4. Remove the potatoes from the Air fryer and halve the potatoes lengthwise carefully.
5. Stuff in the tuna mixture in the potatoes and top with capers and remaining scallion.
6. Dish out in a platter and serve immediately.

Nutrition Facts Per Serving:
Calories: 281, Fat: 13g, Carbohydrates: 15.4g, Sugar: 1.8g, Protein: 26.2g, Sodium: 249mg

Amazing Salmon Fillets

Prep time: 5 minutes, cook time: 7 minutes; Serves 2

5 Ingredients:
- 2 (7-ounce) (¾-inch thick) salmon fillets

What you'll need from the store cupboard:
- 1 tablespoon Italian seasoning
- 1 tablespoon fresh lemon juice

Instructions:
1. Preheat the Air fryer to 355 º F and grease an Air fryer grill pan.
2. Rub the salmon evenly with Italian seasoning and transfer into the Air fryer grill pan, skin-side up.
3. Cook for about 7 minutes and squeeze lemon juice on it to serve.

Nutrition Facts Per Serving:
Calories: 88, Fat: 4.1g, Carbohydrates: 0.1g, Sugar: 0g, Protein: 12.9g, Sodium: 55mg

Glazed Halibut Steak

Prep time: 30 minutes, cook time: 11 minutes; Serves 4

5 Ingredients:
- 1 pound haddock steak

What you'll need from the store cupboard:
- 1 garlic clove, minced
- ¼ teaspoon fresh ginger, grated finely
- ½ cup low-sodium soy sauce
- ¼ cup fresh orange juice
- 2 tablespoons lime juice
- ½ cup cooking wine
- ¼ cup sugar
- ¼ teaspoon red pepper flakes, crushed

Instructions:
1. Preheat the Air fryer to 390 ° F and grease an Air fryer basket.
2. Put all the ingredients except haddock steak in a pan and bring to a boil.
3. Cook for about 4 minutes, stirring continuously and remove from the heat.
4. Put the haddock steak and half of the marinade in a resealable bag and shake well.
5. Refrigerate for about 1 hour and reserve the remaining marinade.
6. Place the haddock steak in the Air fryer basket and cook for about 11 minutes.
7. Coat with the remaining glaze and serve hot.

Nutrition Facts Per Serving:
Calories: 219, Fats: 1.1g, Carbohydrates: 17.9g, Sugar: 16.2g, Proteins: 29.7g, Sodium: 1861mg

Steamed Salmon with Dill Sauce

Prep time: 15 minutes, cook time: 11 minutes; Serves 2

5 Ingredients:
- 1 cup water
- 2 (6-ounce) salmon fillets
- ½ cup Greek yogurt
- 2 tablespoons fresh dill, chopped and divided

What you'll need from the store cupboard:
- 2 teaspoons olive oil
- Salt, to taste
- ½ cup sour cream

Instructions:
1. Preheat the Air fryer to 285 ° F and grease an Air fryer basket.
2. Place water the bottom of the Air fryer pan.
3. Coat salmon with olive oil and season with a pinch of salt.
4. Arrange the salmon in the Air fryer and cook for about 11 minutes.
5. Meanwhile, mix remaining ingredients in a bowl to make dill sauce.
6. Serve the salmon with dill sauce.

Nutrition Facts Per Serving:
Calories: 224, Fat: 14.4g, Carbohydrates: 3.6g, Sugar: 1.5g, Protein: 21.2g, Sodium: 108mg

Best Cod Ever

Prep time: 15 minutes, cook time: 7 minutes; Serves 2

5 Ingredients:
- 2 (4-ounce) skinless codfish fillets, cut into rectangular pieces
- ½ cup flour
- 3 eggs
- 1 green chili, chopped finely
- 3 scallions, chopped finely

What you'll need from the store cupboard:
- 2 garlic cloves, minced
- 1 teaspoon light soy sauce
- Salt and black pepper, to taste

Instructions:
1. Preheat the Air fryer to 375 ° F and grease an Air fryer basket.
2. Place the flour in a shallow dish and mix remaining ingredients in another shallow dish except cod.
3. Coat each fillet with the flour and then dip into the egg mixture.
4. Place the cod in the Air fryer basket and cook for about 7 minutes.
5. Dish out in a platter and serve warm.

Nutrition Facts Per Serving:
Calories: 405, Fat: 8.4g, Carbohydrates: 28.2g, Sugar: 1.7g, Protein: 51.1g, Sodium: 439mg

Honey Glazed Salmon

Prep time: 10 minutes, cook time: 14 minutes; Serves 2

5 Ingredients:
- 1 teaspoon water
- 2 (3½-ounce) salmon fillets

What you'll need from the store cupboard:
- 1/3 cup soy sauce
- 1/3 cup honey
- 3 teaspoons rice wine vinegar

Instructions:
1. Preheat the Air fryer to 355 º F and grease an Air fryer grill pan.
2. Mix all the ingredients in a small bowl except salmon.
3. Reserve half of the mixture in a small bowl and coat the salmon in remaining mixture.
4. Refrigerate, covered for about 2 hours and place the salmon in the Air fryer grill pan.
5. Cook for about 13 minutes, flipping once in between and coat with reserved marinade.
6. Place the reserved marinade in a small pan and cook for about 1 minute.
7. Serve salmon with marinade sauce and enjoy.

Nutrition Facts Per Serving:
Calories: 331, Fat: 6.1g, Carbohydrates: 49.8g, Sugar: 47.1g, Protein: 22.1g, Sodium: 2442mg

Shrimp Magic

Prep time: 20 minutes, cook time: 5 minutes; Serves 3

5 Ingredients:
- 1½ pounds shrimps, peeled and deveined
- Lemongrass stalks

What you'll need from the store cupboard:
- 4 garlic cloves, minced
- 1 red chili pepper, seeded and chopped
- 2 tablespoons olive oil
- ½ teaspoon smoked paprika

Instructions:
1. Preheat the Air fryer to 390 º F and grease an Air fryer basket.
2. Mix all the ingredients in a large bowl and refrigerate to marinate for about 2 hours.
3. Thread the shrimps onto lemongrass stalks and transfer into the Air fryer basket.
4. Cook for about 5 minutes and dish out to serve warm.

Nutrition Facts Per Serving:
Calories: 367, Fat: 13.3g, Carbohydrates: 7.5g, Sugar: 0.2g, Protein: 52.2g, Sodium: 555mg

Tempting Seafood Platter with Shell Pasta

Prep time: 15 minutes, cook time: 18 minutes; Serves 4

5 Ingredients:
- 14-ounce shell pasta
- 4 (4-ounce) salmon steaks
- ½ pound cherry tomatoes, halved
- 8 large prawns, peeled and deveined
- 2 tablespoons fresh thyme, chopped

What you'll need from the store cupboard:
- 4 tablespoons pesto, divided
- 2 tablespoons olive oil
- 2 tablespoons fresh lemon juice

Instructions:
1. Preheat the Air fryer to 390 º F and grease a baking dish.
2. Cook pasta in a large pan of salted water for about 10 minutes.
3. Meanwhile, spread pesto in the bottom of a baking dish.
4. Arrange salmon steaks and cherry tomatoes over pesto and drizzle evenly with olive oil.
5. Top with prawns and sprinkle with lemon juice and thyme.
6. Transfer the baking dish in the Air fryer and cook for about 8 minutes.
7. Serve the seafood mixture with pasta and enjoy.

Nutrition Facts Per Serving:
Calories: 592, Fat: 23.2g, Carbohydrates: 58.7g, Sugar: 2.7g, Protein: 37.9g, Sodium: 203mg

Herbed Haddock

Prep time: 10 minutes, cook time: 8 minutes; Serves 2

5 Ingredients:
- 2 (6-ounce) haddock fillets
- 2 tablespoons pine nuts
- 3 tablespoons fresh basil, chopped
- 1 tablespoon Parmesan cheese, grated

What you'll need from the store cupboard:
- ½ cup extra-virgin olive oil
- Salt and black pepper, to taste

Instructions:
1. Preheat the Air fryer to 355 ° F and grease an Air fryer basket.
2. Coat the haddock fillets evenly with olive oil and season with salt and black pepper.
3. Place the haddock fillets in the Air fryer basket and cook for about 8 minutes.
4. Dish out the haddock fillets in serving plates.
5. Meanwhile, put remaining ingredients in a food processor and pulse until smooth.
6. Top this cheese sauce over the haddock fillets and serve hot.

Nutrition Facts Per Serving:
Calories: 751, Fat: 65.5g, Carbohydrates: 1.3g, Sugar: 0g, Protein: 43.5g, Sodium: 176mg

Paprika Shrimp

Prep time: 10 minutes, cook time: 10 minutes; Serves 2

5 Ingredients:
- 1 pound tiger shrimp

What you'll need from the store cupboard:
- 2 tablespoons olive oil
- ½ teaspoon smoked paprika
- Salt, to taste

Instructions:
1. Preheat the Air fryer to 390 ° F and grease an Air fryer basket.
2. Mix all the ingredients in a large bowl until well combined.
3. Place the shrimp in the Air fryer basket and cook for about 10 minutes.
4. Dish out and serve warm.

Nutrition Facts Per Serving:
Calories: 173, Fat: 8.3g, Carbohydrates: 0.1g, Sugar: 0g, Protein: 23.8g, Sodium: 332mg

Cod with Shrimps and Pasta

Prep time: 20 minutes, cook time: 18 minutes; Serves 4

5 Ingredients:
- 14 ounces pasta
- 4 (4-ounces) salmon steaks
- ½ pound mushrooms, chopped
- 8 large shrimps, peeled and deveined
- 2 tablespoons fresh parsley, chopped

What you'll need from the store cupboard:
- 4 tablespoons pesto, divided
- 2 tablespoons olive oil
- 2 tablespoons fresh lemon juice

Instructions:
1. Preheat the Air fryer to 385 ° F and grease a baking dish.
2. Cook pasta in a large pan of salted water for about 10 minutes.
3. Meanwhile, spread pesto in the bottom of a baking dish.
4. Arrange cod steaks and mushrooms over pesto and drizzle evenly with olive oil.
5. Top with shrimps and sprinkle with lemon juice and parsley.
6. Transfer the baking dish in the Air fryer and cook for about 8 minutes.
7. Serve the cod and shrimps with pasta and enjoy.

Nutrition Facts Per Serving:
Calories: 592, Fat: 23.2g, Carbohydrates: 58.7g, Sugar: 2.7g, Protein: 37.7g, Sodium: 203mg

Cajun Spiced Salmon

Prep time: 10 minutes, cook time: 8 minutes; Serves 2

5 Ingredients:

- 2 (7-ounces) (¾-inch thick) salmon fillets

What you' ll need from the store cupboard:

- 1 tablespoon Cajun seasoning
- ½ teaspoon sugar
- 1 tablespoon fresh lemon juice

Instructions:

1. Preheat the Air fryer to 365 º F and grease an Air fryer grill pan.
2. Season the salmon evenly with Cajun seasoning and sugar.
3. Arrange the salmon fillets into the Air fryer grill pan, skin-side up.
4. Cook for about 8 minutes and dish out the salmon fillets in the serving plates.
5. Drizzle with the lemon juice and serve hot.

Nutrition Facts Per Serving:
Calories: 268, Fats: 12.3g, Carbohydrates: 1.2g, Sugar: 1.2g, Proteins: 38.6g, Sodium: 164mg

Spicy Cod

Prep time: 10 minutes, cook time: 11 minutes; Serves 2

5 Ingredients:

- 2 (6-ounces) (1½-inch thick) cod fillets

What you' ll need from the store cupboard:

- 1 teaspoon smoked paprika
- 1 teaspoon cayenne pepper
- 1 teaspoon onion powder
- 1 teaspoon garlic powder
- Salt and ground black pepper, as required
- 2 teaspoons olive oil

Instructions:

1. Preheat the Air fryer to 390 º F and grease an Air fryer basket.
2. Drizzle the salmon fillets with olive oil and rub with the all the spices.
3. Arrange the salmon fillets into the Air fryer basket and cook for about 11 minutes.
4. Dish out the salmon fillets in the serving plates and serve hot.

Nutrition Facts Per Serving:
Calories: 277, Fat: 15.4g, Carbohydrates: 2.5g, Sugar: 0.9g, Protein: 33.5g, Sodium: 154mg

Zesty Mahi Mahi

Prep time: 10 minutes, cook time: 8 minutes; Serves 3

5 Ingredients:

- 1½ pounds Mahi Mahi fillets
- 1 lemon, cut into slices
- 1 tablespoon fresh dill, chopped

What you' ll need from the store cupboard:

- ½ teaspoon red chili powder
- Salt and ground black pepper, as required

Instructions:

1. Preheat the Air fryer to 375 º F and grease an Air fryer basket.
2. Season the Mahi Mahi fillets evenly with chili powder, salt, and black pepper.
3. Arrange the Mahi Mahi fillets into the Air fryer basket and top with the lemon slices.
4. Cook for about 8 minutes and dish out
5. Place the lemon slices over the salmon the salmon fillets in the serving plates.
6. Garnish with fresh dill and serve warm.

Nutrition Facts Per Serving:
Calories: 206, Fat: 9.5g, Carbohydrates: 1.3g, Sugar: 0.2g, Protein: 29.7g, Sodium: 124mg

Maple Glazed Salmon

Prep time: 10 minutes, cook time: 8 minutes; Serves 2

5 Ingredients:
- 2 (6-ounces) salmon fillets

What you'll need from the store cupboard:
- Salt, to taste
- 2 tablespoons maple syrup

Instructions:
1. Preheat the Air fryer to 355° F and grease an Air fryer basket.
2. Coat the salmon fillets evenly with maple syrup and season with salt.
3. Arrange the salmon fillets into the Air fryer basket and cook for about 8 minutes.
4. Remove from the Air fryer and dish out the salmon fillets to serve hot.

Nutrition Facts Per Serving:
Calories: 277, Fat: 10.5g, Carbohydrates: 13.4g, Sugar: 11.9g, Protein: 33g, Sodium: 154mg

Sweet and Sour Glazed Cod

Prep time: 20 minutes, cook time: 12 minutes; Serves 2

5 Ingredients:
- 1 teaspoon water
- 4 (3½-ounces) cod fillets

What you'll need from the store cupboard:
- 1/3 cup soy sauce
- 1/3 cup honey
- 3 teaspoons rice wine vinegar

Instructions:
1. Preheat the Air fryer to 355° F and grease an Air fryer basket.
2. Mix the soy sauce, honey, vinegar and water in a small bowl.
3. Reserve about half of the mixture in another bowl.
4. Stir the cod fillets in the remaining mixture until well coated.
5. Cover and refrigerate to marinate for about 3 hours.
6. Arrange the cod fillets into the Air fryer basket and cook for about 12 minutes, flipping once in between.
7. Coat with the reserved marinade and dish out the cod to serve hot.

Nutrition Facts Per Serving:
Calories: 462, Fat: 12.3g, Carbohydrates: 49.8g, Sugar: 47.1g, Protein: 41.3g, Sodium: 2000mg

Salmon with Broccoli

Prep time: 15 minutes, cook time: 12 minutes; Serves 2

5 Ingredients:
- 1½ cups small broccoli florets
- ¼ teaspoon cornstarch
- 2 (6-ounces) salmon fillets, skin-on
- 1 scallion, thinly sliced

What you'll need from the store cupboard:
- 2 tablespoons vegetable oil, divided
- Salt and black pepper, as required
- 1 (½-inch) piece fresh ginger, grated
- 1 tablespoon soy sauce
- 1 teaspoon rice vinegar
- 1 teaspoon light brown sugar

Instructions:
1. Preheat the Air fryer to 375° F and grease an Air fryer basket.
2. Mix the broccoli, 1 tablespoon of vegetable oil, salt, and black pepper.
3. Combine ginger, soy sauce, rice vinegar, sugar and cornstarch in another bowl.
4. Rub the salmon fillets evenly with remaining olive oil and the ginger mixture.
5. Place the broccoli florets into the Air fryer basket and top with salmon fillets.
6. Cook for about 12 minutes and dish out in serving plates.

Nutrition Facts Per Serving:
Calories: 385, Fat: 24.4g, Carbohydrates: 7.8g, Sugar: 3g, Protein: 35.6g, Sodium: 628mg

Cod with Asparagus

Prep time: 15 minutes, cook time: 11 minutes; Serves 2

5 Ingredients:
- 2 (6-ounces) boneless cod fillets
- 2 tablespoons fresh parsley, roughly chopped
- 2 tablespoons fresh dill, roughly chopped
- 1 bunch asparagus

What you'll need from the store cupboard:
- 1½ tablespoons fresh lemon juice
- 1 tablespoon olive oil
- Salt and black pepper, to taste

Instructions:
1. Preheat the Air fryer to 400 º F and grease an Air fryer basket.
2. Mix lemon juice, oil, herbs, salt, and black pepper in a small bowl.
3. Combine the cod and ¾ of the oil mixture in another bowl.
4. Coat asparagus with remaining oil mixture and transfer to the Air fryer basket.
5. Cook for about 3 minutes and arrange cod fillets on top of asparagus.
6. Cook for about 8 minutes and dish out in serving plates.

Nutrition Facts Per Serving:
Calories: 331, Fat: 18g, Carbohydrates: 8.8g, Sugar: 3.5g, Protein: 37.6g, Sodium: 167mg

Mahi Mahi with Green Beans

Prep time: 15 minutes, cook time: 12 minutes; Serves 4

5 Ingredients:
- 5 cups green beans
- 2 tablespoons fresh dill, chopped
- 4 (6-ounces) Mahi Mahi fillets

What you'll need from the store cupboard:
- 1 tablespoon avocado oil
- Salt, as required
- 2 garlic cloves, minced
- 2 tablespoons fresh lemon juice
- 1 tablespoon olive oil

Instructions:
1. Preheat the Air fryer to 375 º F and grease an Air fryer basket.
2. Mix the green beans, avocado oil and salt in a large bowl.
3. Arrange green beans into the Air fryer basket and cook for about 6 minutes.
4. Combine garlic, dill, lemon juice, salt and olive oil in a bowl.
5. Coat Mahi Mahi in this garlic mixture and place on the top of green beans.
6. Cook for 6 more minutes and dish out to serve warm.

Nutrition Facts Per Serving:
Calories: 310, Fat: 14.8g, Carbohydrates: 11.5g, Sugar: 2.1g, Protein: 326g, Sodium: 127mg

Simple Salmon

Prep time: 5 minutes, cook time: 10 minutes; Serves 2

5 Ingredients:
- 2 (6-ounces) salmon fillets

What you'll need from the store cupboard:
- Salt and black pepper, as required
- 1 tablespoon olive oil

Instructions:
1. Preheat the Air fryer to 390 º F and grease an Air fryer basket.
2. Season each salmon fillet with salt and black pepper and drizzle with olive oil.
3. Arrange salmon fillets into the Air fryer basket and cook for about 10 minutes.
4. Remove from the Air fryer and dish out the salmon fillets onto the serving plates.

Nutrition Facts Per Serving:
Calories: 285, Fat: 17.5g, Carbohydrates: 0g, Sugar: 0g, Protein: 33g, Sodium: 153mg

Tilapia Patties

Prep time: 20 minutes, cook time: 26 minutes; Serves 6

5 Ingredients:

- 3 large russet potatoes, peeled and cubed
- 1 (6-ounces) tilapia fillets
- 1 egg
- ¾ cup frozen vegetables (of your choice), parboiled and drained
- 1 cup breadcrumbs

What you' ll need from the store cupboard:

- ¼ cup olive oil
- 1 teaspoon dried dill, chopped
- Salt and black pepper, to taste

Instructions:

1. Preheat the Air fryer to 355 º F and grease an Air fryer basket.
2. Cook potatoes in a large pan of salted water for about 10 minutes and drain well.
3. Mash the potatoes and keep aside to completely cool.
4. Arrange the tilapia fillets into the Air fryer basket and cook for about 5 minutes.
5. Dish out the tilapia fillets and flake with fork.
6. Stir in the mashed potatoes, egg, vegetables, dill, salt, and black pepper and mix well.
7. Make 6 equal-sized patties from the mixture and coat evenly with breadcrumbs.
8. Drizzle with olive oil and transfer the patties into Air fryer basket.
9. Cook for about 12 minutes, flipping once in between.
10. Dish out the patties in serving plates and serve warm.

Nutrition Facts Per Serving:
Calories: 334, Fat: 12.1g, Carbohydrates: 45.2g, Sugar: 40g, Protein: 12.6g, Sodium: 202mg

Chinese Style Cod

Prep time: 20 minutes, cook time: 15 minutes; Serves 2

5 Ingredients:

- 2 (7-ounces) cod fillets
- 1 cup water
- 2 scallions (green part), sliced
- ¼ cup fresh cilantro, chopped

What you' ll need from the store cupboard:

- Salt and black pepper, to taste
- ¼ teaspoon sesame oil
- 5 little squares rock sugar
- 5 tablespoons light soy sauce
- 1 teaspoon dark soy sauce
- 3 tablespoons olive oil
- 5 ginger slices

Instructions:

1. Preheat the Air fryer to 355 º F and grease an Air fryer basket.
2. Season each cod fillet with salt and black pepper and drizzle with sesame oil.
3. Arrange the cod fillets into the Air fryer basket and cook for about 12 minutes.
4. Bring water to boil and add rock sugar and both soy sauces.
5. Cook until sugar is dissolved, continuously stirring and keep aside.
6. Dish out the cod fillets onto serving plates and top each fillet with cilantro and scallions.
7. Heat olive oil over medium heat in a small frying pan and add ginger slices.
8. Sauté for about 3 minutes and discard the ginger slices.
9. Drizzle the hot oil over cod fillets and top with the sauce mixture to serve.

Nutrition Facts Per Serving:
Calories: 433, Fat: 23.4g, Carbohydrates: 7.6g, Sugar: 4.2g, Protein: 48.2g, Sodium: 2001mg

Cod and Veggies

Prep time: 20 minutes, cook time: 15 minutes; Serves 4

5 Ingredients:

- 2 tablespoons butter, melted
- ½ cup red bell peppers, seeded and thinly sliced
- ½ cup carrots, peeled and julienned
- ½ cup fennel bulbs, julienned
- 2 (5-ounces) frozen cod fillets, thawed

What you' ll need from the store cupboard:

- 1 tablespoon fresh lemon juice
- ½ teaspoon dried tarragon
- Salt and ground black pepper, as required
- 1 tablespoon olive oil

Instructions:

1. Preheat the Air fryer to 350 º F and grease an Air fryer basket.
2. Mix butter, lemon juice, tarragon, salt, and black pepper in a large bowl.
3. Add the carrot, bell pepper and fennel bulb and generously coat with the butter mixture.
4. Coat the cod fillets with olive oil and season with salt and black pepper.
5. Arrange cod fillets in the Air fryer basket and top evenly with the vegetables.
6. Top with any remaining sauce from the bowl and cook for about 15 minutes.
7. Dish out the cod and veggies in the serving plates and serve warm.

Nutrition Facts Per Serving:
Calories: 344, Fats: 19.9g, Carbohydrates: 6.8g, Sugar: 3g, Proteins: 33.4g, Sodium: 225mg

Spicy Prawns

Prep time: 15 minutes, cook time: 5 minutes; Serves 3

5 Ingredients:

- 1 pound prawns, peeled and deveined

What you' ll need from the store cupboard:

- 2 tablespoons olive oil
- 1 teaspoon old bay seasoning
- ½ teaspoon red chili flakes
- ½ teaspoon smoked paprika
- ½ teaspoon cayenne pepper
- Salt, as required

Instructions:

1. Preheat the Air fryer to 390 º F and grease an Air fryer basket.
2. Mix shrimp with olive oil and seasonings in a large bowl.
3. Arrange the shrimp into the Air fryer basket in a single layer and cook for about 5 minutes.
4. Dish out the shrimp onto serving plates and serve hot.

Nutrition Facts Per Serving:
Calories: 262, Fat: 12g, Carbohydrates: 2.7g, Sugar: 0.1g, Protein: 34.5g, Sodium: 633mg

Crispy Cod Sticks

Prep time: 20 minutes, cook time: 7 minutes; Serves 2

5 Ingredients:

- 3 (4-ounces) skinless cod fillets, cut into rectangular pieces
- ¾ cup flour
- 4 eggs
- 1 green chili, finely chopped

What you' ll need from the store cupboard:

- 2 garlic cloves, minced
- 2 teaspoons light soy sauce
- Salt and ground black pepper, to taste

Instructions:

1. Preheat the Air fryer to 375 º F and grease an Air fryer basket.
2. Place flour in a shallow dish and whisk the eggs, garlic, green chili, soy sauce, salt, and black pepper in a second dish.
3. Coat the cod fillets evenly in flour and dip in the egg mixture.
4. Arrange the cod pieces in an Air fryer basket and cook for about 7 minutes.
5. Dish out and serve warm.

Nutrition Facts Per Serving:
Calories: 483, Fat: 10.7g, Carbohydrates: 38g, Sugar: 1.1g, Protein: 55.3g, Sodium: 634mg

Cod Cakes

Prep time: 20 minutes, cook time: 14 minutes; Serves 6

5 Ingredients:
- 1 pound cod fillet
- 1 egg
- 1/3 cup coconut, grated and divided
- 1 scallion, finely chopped
- 2 tablespoons fresh parsley, chopped

What you'll need from the store cupboard:
- 1 teaspoon fresh lime zest, finely grated
- 1 teaspoon red chili paste
- Salt, as required
- 1 tablespoon fresh lime juice

Instructions:
1. Preheat the Air fryer to 375 º F and grease an Air fryer basket.
2. Put the cod fillet, lime zest, egg, chili paste, salt and lime juice in a food processor and pulse until smooth.
3. Transfer the cod mixture into a bowl and add scallion, parsley and 2 tablespoons of coconut.
4. Mix until well combined and make 12 equal-sized round cakes from the mixture.
5. Place the remaining coconut in a shallow bowl and coat the cod cakes with coconut.
6. Arrange cod cakes into the Air fryer basket in 2 batches and cook for about 7 minutes.
7. Dish out in 2 serving plates and serve warm.

Nutrition Facts Per Serving:
Calories: 165, Fat: 4.5g, Carbohydrates: 2.1g, Sugar: 1g, Protein: 27.7g, Sodium: 161mg

Crispy Halibut Strips

Prep time: 20 minutes, cook time: 14 minutes; Serves 2

5 Ingredients:
- 2 eggs
- 1 tablespoon water
- ¾ cup plain panko breadcrumbs
- ¾ pound skinless halibut fillets, cut into 1-inch strips

What you'll need from the store cupboard:
- 4 tablespoons taco seasoning mix

Instructions:
1. Preheat the Air fryer to 350 º F and grease an Air fryer basket.
2. Put the taco seasoning mix in a shallow bowl and whisk together eggs and water in a second bowl.
3. Place the breadcrumbs in a third bowl.
4. Dredge the halibut with taco seasoning mix, then dip into the egg mixture and finally, coat evenly with the breadcrumbs.
5. Arrange halibut strips into the Air fryer basket and cook for about 14 minutes, flipping once in between.
6. Dish out the halibut strips onto serving plates and serve warm.

Nutrition Facts Per Serving:
Calories: 443, Fat: 11.2g, Carbohydrates: 15.5g, Sugar: 0.4g, Protein: 42.4g, Sodium: 961mg

(Note: Taco seasoning mix - Mix chili powder, garlic powder, onion powder, red pepper flakes, oregano, paprika, cumin, salt and pepper in a small bowl. Store in an airtight container.)

Spiced Catfish

Prep time: 10 minutes, cook time: 23 minutes; Serves 4

5 Ingredients:
- 4 (6-ounces) catfish fillets
- 1 tablespoon olive oil
- 2 tablespoons corn meal
- 2 tablespoons corn flour

What you'll need from the store cupboard:
- 2 tablespoons garlic
- 2 tablespoons salt

Instructions:
1. Preheat the Air fryer to 400 º F and grease an Air fryer basket.
2. Mix the catfish fillets with corn meal, corn flour, garlic and salt in a bowl.

3. Drizzle with olive oil and arrange catfish fillets into the Air fryer basket.
4. Cook for about 10 minutes and flip the side.
5. Cook for another 10 minutes and flip again.

6. Cook for about 3 more minutes and dish out the catfish fillets to serve hot.

Nutrition Facts Per Serving:
Calories: 294, Fat: 18.3g, Carbohydrates: 2.6g, Sugar: 0g, Protein: 28.7g, Sodium: 170mg

Breaded Flounder

Prep time: 15 minutes, cook time: 12 minutes; Serves 3

5 Ingredients:
- 1 egg
- 1 cup dry breadcrumbs
- 3 (6-ounces) flounder fillets
- 1 lemon, sliced

What you' ll need from the store cupboard:
- ¼ cup vegetable oil

Instructions:
1. Preheat the Air fryer to 360 º F and grease an Air fryer basket.
2. Whisk the egg in a shallow bowl and mix breadcrumbs and oil in another bowl.

3. Dip flounder fillets into the whisked egg and coat with the breadcrumb mixture.
4. Arrange flounder fillets into the Air fryer basket and cook for about 12 minutes.
5. Dish out the flounder fillets onto serving plates and garnish with the lemon slices to serve.

Nutrition Facts Per Serving:
Calories: 524, Fat: 24.4g, Carbohydrates: 26.5g, Sugar: 2.5g, Protein: 47.8g, Sodium: 463mg

Southern Style Catfish

Prep time: 15 minutes, cook time: 15 minutes; Serves 5

5 Ingredients:
- 5 (6-ounces) catfish fillets
- 1 cup milk
- ½ cup cornmeal
- ¼ cup all-purpose flour
- Olive oil cooking spray

What you' ll need from the store cupboard:
- 2 teaspoons fresh lemon juice
- ½ cup yellow mustard
- 2 tablespoons dried parsley flakes
- ¼ teaspoon red chili powder
- ¼ teaspoon cayenne pepper
- ¼ teaspoon onion powder
- ¼ teaspoon garlic powder
- Salt and ground black pepper, as required

Instructions:
1. Preheat the Air fryer to 400 º F and grease an Air fryer basket.

2. Mix catfish, milk, and lemon juice in a large bowl and refrigerate for about 30 minutes.
3. Put the mustard in a shallow bowl and mix the cornmeal, flour, parsley flakes, and spices in another bowl.
4. Remove the catfish fillets from milk mixture and coat each fish fillet with mustard.
5. Roll evenly into the cornmeal mixture and arrange in the Air fryer basket.
6. Spray with the olive oil cooking spray and cook for about 10 minutes.
7. Flip the side and cook for about 5 more minutes.
8. Dish out the catfish fillets onto serving plates and serve hot.

Nutrition Facts Per Serving:
Calories: 340, Fat: 15.5g, Carbohydrates: 18.3g, Sugar: 2.7g, Protein: 30.9g, Sodium: 435mg

Sesame Seeds Coated Haddock

Prep time: 15 minutes, cook time: 14 minutes; Serves 4

5 Ingredients:
- 4 tablespoons plain flour
- 2 eggs
- ½ cup sesame seeds, toasted
- ½ cup breadcrumbs
- 4 (6-ounces) frozen haddock fillets

What you' ll need from the store cupboard:
- 1/8 teaspoon dried rosemary, crushed
- Salt and ground black pepper, as required
- 3 tablespoons olive oil

Instructions:
1. Preheat the Air fryer to 390 ⁰ F and grease an Air fryer basket.
2. Place the flour in a shallow bowl and whisk the eggs in a second bowl.
3. Mix sesame seeds, breadcrumbs, rosemary, salt, black pepper and olive oil in a third bowl until a crumbly mixture is formed.
4. Coat each fillet with flour, dip into whisked eggs and finally, dredge into the breadcrumb mixture
5. Arrange haddock fillets into the Air fryer basket in a single layer and cook for about 14 minutes, flipping once in between.
6. Dish out the haddock fillets onto serving plates and serve hot.

Nutrition Facts Per Serving:
Calories: 497, Fat: 24g, Carbohydrates: 20.1g, Sugar: 1.1g, Protein: 49.8g, Sodium: 319mg

Breaded Hake

Prep time: 15 minutes, cook time: 12 minutes; Serves 2

5 Ingredients:
- 1 egg
- 4 ounces breadcrumbs
- 4 (6-ounces) hake fillets
- 1 lemon, cut into wedges

What you' ll need from the store cupboard:
- 2 tablespoons vegetable oil

Instructions:
1. Preheat the Air fryer to 350 ⁰ F and grease an Air fryer basket.
2. Whisk the egg in a shallow bowl and mix breadcrumbs and oil in another bowl.
3. Dip hake fillets into the whisked egg and then, dredge in the breadcrumb mixture.
4. Arrange the hake fillets into the Air fryer basket in a single layer and cook for about 12 minutes.
5. Dish out the hake fillets onto serving plates and serve, garnished with lemon wedges.

Nutrition Facts Per Serving:
Calories: 300, Fats: 10.6g, Carbohydrates: 23g, Sugar: 2.2g, Proteins: 29.3g, Sodium: 439mg

Cajun Coated Catfish

Prep time: 15 minutes, cook time: 14 minutes; Serves 4

5 Ingredients:
- 2 tablespoons cornmeal polenta
- 2 (6-ounces) catfish fillets

What you' ll need from the store cupboard:
- 2 teaspoons Cajun seasoning
- ½ teaspoon paprika
- ½ teaspoon garlic powder
- Salt, as required
- 1 tablespoon olive oil

Instructions:
1. Preheat the Air fryer to 400 ⁰ F and grease an Air fryer basket.
2. Mix the cornmeal, Cajun seasoning, paprika, garlic powder, and salt in a bowl.
3. Stir in the catfish fillets and coat evenly with the mixture.
4. Drizzle each fillet with olive oil and transfer the catfish fillets into the Air fryer basket.
5. Cook for about 14 minutes, flipping once in between and dish out in serving plates to serve hot.

Nutrition Facts Per Serving:
Calories: 321, Fat: 20.3g, Carbohydrates: 6.7g, Sugar: 0.3g, Protein: 27.3g, Sodium: 221mg

Ranch Tilapia

Prep time: 15 minutes, cook time: 13 minutes; Serves 4

5 Ingredients:
- ¾ cup cornflakes, crushed
- 2 eggs
- 4 (6-ounces) tilapia fillets

What you'll need from the store cupboard:
- 2½ tablespoons vegetable oil

Ranch Dressing
- ½ cup dry buttermilk powder
- 1 tablespoon dried parsley
- 2 teaspoons dried dill weed
- 1 teaspoon freeze dried chives
- 1 tablespoon garlic powder
- 1 tablespoon onion powder
- 1 teaspoon sea salt
- ½ teaspoon ground black pepper

Instructions:

1. Preheat the Air fryer to 360 º F and grease an Air fryer basket.
2. Whisk the eggs in a shallow bowl.
3. Mix cornflakes, ranch dressing and olive oil in another bowl until a crumbly mixture is formed.
4. Dip the tilapia fillets into whisked eggs and dredge into the breadcrumb mixture.
5. Arrange tilapia fillets into the Air fryer basket in a single layer and cook for about 13 minutes, flipping once in between.
6. Dish out the tilapia fillets onto serving plates and serve hot.

Nutrition Facts Per Serving:
Calories: 532, Fat: 41.8g, Carbohydrates: 4.9g, Sugar: 0.7g, Protein: 34.8g, Sodium: 160mg

Sesame Seeds Coated Tuna

Prep time: 15 minutes, cook time: 6 minutes; Serves 2

5 Ingredients:
- ¼ cup white sesame seeds
- 1 tablespoon black sesame seeds
- 1 egg white
- 2 (6-ounces) tuna steaks

What you'll need from the store cupboard:
- Salt and black pepper, as required

Instructions:

1. Preheat the Air fryer to 400 º F and grease an Air fryer basket.
2. Whisk the egg white in a shallow bowl.
3. Mix the sesame seeds, salt, and black pepper in another bowl.
4. Dip the tuna steaks into the whisked egg white and dredge into the sesame seeds mixture.
5. Arrange the tuna steaks into the Air fryer basket in a single layer and cook for about 6 minutes, flipping once in between.
6. Dish out the tuna steaks onto serving plates and serve hot.

Nutrition Facts Per Serving:
Calories: 450, Fat: 21.9g, Carbohydrates: 5.4g, Sugar: 0.2g, Protein: 56.7g, Sodium: 182mg

Lemon Garlic Shrimps

Prep time: 15 minutes, cook time: 8 minutes; Serves 2

5 Ingredients:
- ¾ pound medium shrimp, peeled and deveined

What you'll need from the store cupboard:
- 1½ tablespoons fresh lemon juice
- 1 tablespoon olive oil
- 1 teaspoon lemon pepper
- ¼ teaspoon paprika
- ¼ teaspoon garlic powder

Instructions:

1. Preheat the Air fryer to 400 º F and grease an Air fryer basket.
2. Mix lemon juice, olive oil, lemon pepper, paprika and garlic powder in a large bowl.
3. Stir in the shrimp and toss until well combined.
4. Arrange shrimp into the Air fryer basket in a single layer and cook for about 8 minutes.
5. Dish out the shrimp in serving plates and serve warm.

Nutrition Facts Per Serving:
Calories: 260, Fat: 12.4g, Carbohydrates: 0.3g, Sugar: 0.1g, Protein: 35.6g, Sodium: 619mg

Tuna and Potato Cakes

Prep time: 20 minutes, cook time: 12 minutes; Serves 4

5 Ingredients:

- 1 onion, chopped
- 1 green chili, seeded and finely chopped
- 2 (6-ounces) cans tuna, drained
- 1 medium boiled potato, mashed
- 1 cup breadcrumbs

What you'll need from the store cupboard:

- ½ tablespoon olive oil
- 1 tablespoon fresh ginger, grated
- Salt, as required

Instructions:

1. Preheat the Air fryer to 390 º F and grease an Air fryer basket.
2. Heat olive oil in a frying pan and add onions, ginger, and green chili.
3. Sauté for about 30 seconds and add the tuna.
4. Stir fry for about 3 minutes and dish out the tuna mixture onto a large bowl.
5. Add mashed potato, celery, and salt and mix well.
6. Make 4 equal-sized patties from the mixture.
7. Place the breadcrumbs in a shallow bowl and whisk the egg in another bowl.
8. Dredge each patty with breadcrumbs, then dip into egg and coat again with the breadcrumbs.
9. Arrange tuna cakes into the Air fryer basket and cook for about 3 minutes.
10. Flip the side and cook for about 5 minutes.
11. 1Dish out the tuna cakes onto serving plates and serve warm.

Nutrition Facts Per Serving:
Calories: 353, Fat: 11.3g, Carbohydrates: 32.6g, Sugar: 3.5g, Protein: 29.1g, Sodium: 302mg

Creamy Tuna Cakes

Prep time: 15 minutes, cook time: 15 minutes; Serves 4

5 Ingredients:

- 2 (6-ounces) cans tuna, drained
- 1½ tablespoon almond flour

What you'll need from the store cupboard:

- 1½ tablespoons mayonnaise
- 1 tablespoon fresh lemon juice
- 1 teaspoon dried dill
- 1 teaspoon garlic powder
- ½ teaspoon onion powder
- Pinch of salt and ground black pepper

Instructions:

1. Preheat the Air fryer to 400 º F and grease an Air fryer basket.
2. Mix the tuna, mayonnaise, almond flour, lemon juice, dill, and spices in a large bowl.
3. Make 4 equal-sized patties from the mixture and arrange in the Air fryer basket.
4. Cook for about 10 minutes and flip the sides.
5. Cook for 5 more minutes and dish out the tuna cakes in serving plates to serve warm.

Nutrition Facts Per Serving:
Calories: 200, Fat: 10.1g, Carbohydrates: 2.9g, Sugar: 0.8g, Protein: 23.4g, Sodium: 122mg

Buttered Scallops

Prep time: 15 minutes, cook time: 4 minutes; Serves 2

5 Ingredients:

- ¾ pound sea scallops, cleaned and patted very dry
- 1 tablespoon butter, melted
- ½ tablespoon fresh thyme, minced

What you'll need from the store cupboard:

- Salt and black pepper, as required

Instructions:

1. Preheat the Air fryer to 390 º F and grease an Air fryer basket.
2. Mix scallops, butter, thyme, salt, and black pepper in a bowl.
3. Arrange scallops in the Air fryer basket and cook for about 4 minutes.
4. Dish out the scallops in a platter and serve hot.

Nutrition Facts Per Serving:
Calories: 202, Fat: 7.1g, Carbohydrates: 4.4g, Sugar: 0g, Protein: 28.7g, Sodium: 393mg

Creamy Breaded Shrimp

Prep time: 15 minutes, cook time: 20 minutes; Serves 3

5 Ingredients:
- ¼ cup all-purpose flour
- 1 cup panko breadcrumbs
- 1 pound shrimp, peeled and deveined

What you'll need from the store cupboard:
- ½ cup mayonnaise
- ¼ cup sweet chili sauce
- 1 tablespoon Sriracha sauce

Instructions:
1. Preheat the Air fryer to 400 º F and grease an Air fryer basket.
2. Place flour in a shallow bowl and mix the mayonnaise, chili sauce, and Sriracha sauce in another bowl.
3. Place the breadcrumbs in a third bowl.
4. Coat each shrimp with the flour, dip into mayonnaise mixture and finally, dredge in the breadcrumbs.
5. Arrange half of the coated shrimps into the Air fryer basket and cook for about 10 minutes.
6. Dish out the coated shrimps onto serving plates and repeat with the remaining mixture.

Nutrition Facts Per Serving:
Calories: 540, Fat: 18.2g, Carbohydrates: 33.1g, Sugar: 10.6g, Protein: 36.8g, Sodium: 813mg

Breaded Shrimp with Lemon

Prep time: 15 minutes, cook time: 14 minutes; Serves 3

5 Ingredients:
- ½ cup plain flour
- 2 egg whites
- 1 cup breadcrumbs
- 1 pound large shrimp, peeled and deveined

What you'll need from the store cupboard:
- Salt and ground black pepper, as required
- ¼ teaspoon lemon zest
- ¼ teaspoon cayenne pepper
- ¼ teaspoon red pepper flakes, crushed
- 2 tablespoons vegetable oil

Instructions:
1. Preheat the Air fryer to 400 º F and grease an Air fryer basket.
2. Mix flour, salt, and black pepper in a shallow bowl.
3. Whisk the egg whites in a second bowl and mix the breadcrumbs, lime zest and spices in a third bowl.
4. Coat each shrimp with the flour, dip into egg whites and finally, dredge in the breadcrumbs.
5. Drizzle the shrimp evenly with olive oil and arrange half of the coated shrimps into the Air fryer basket.
6. Cook for about 7 minutes and dish out the coated shrimps onto serving plates.
7. Repeat with the remaining mixture and serve hot.

Nutrition Facts Per Serving:
Calories: 432, Fat: 11.3g, Carbohydrates: 44.8g, Sugar: 2.5g, Protein: 37.7g, Sodium: 526mg

Rice in Crab Shell

Prep time: 20 minutes, cook time: 8 minutes; Serves 2

5 Ingredients:
- 1 bowl cooked rice
- 4 tablespoons crab meat
- 2 tablespoons butter
- 2 tablespoons Parmesan cheese, shredded
- 2 crab shells

What you'll need from the store cupboard:
- Paprika, to taste

Instructions:
1. Preheat the Air fryer to 390 º F and grease an Air fryer basket.
2. Mix rice, crab meat, butter and paprika in a bowl.
3. Fill crab shell with rice mixture and top with Parmesan cheese.
4. Arrange the crab shell in the Air fryer basket and cook for about 8 minutes.
5. Sprinkle with more paprika and serve hot.

Nutrition Facts Per Serving:
Calories: 285, Fat: 33g, Carbohydrates: 0g, Sugar: 0g, Protein: 33g, Sodium: 153mg

Coconut Crusted Shrimp

Prep time: 15 minutes, cook time: 40 minutes; Serves 3

5 Ingredients:

- 8 ounces coconut milk
- ½ cup sweetened coconut, shredded
- ½ cup panko breadcrumbs
- 1 pound large shrimp, peeled and deveined

What you' ll need from the store cupboard:

- Salt and black pepper, to taste

Instructions:

1. Preheat the Air fryer to 350 º F and grease an Air fryer basket.
2. Place the coconut milk in a shallow bowl.
3. Mix coconut, breadcrumbs, salt, and black pepper in another bowl.
4. Dip each shrimp into coconut milk and finally, dredge in the coconut mixture.
5. Arrange half of the shrimps into the Air fryer basket and cook for about 20 minutes.
6. Dish out the shrimps onto serving plates and repeat with the remaining mixture to serve.

Nutrition Facts Per Serving:
Calories: 408, Fats: 23.7g, Carbohydrates: 11.7g, Sugar: 3.4g, Proteins: 31g, Sodium: 253mg

Shrimp Scampi

Prep time: 15 minutes, cook time: 7 minutes; Serves 6

5 Ingredients:

- 4 tablespoons salted butter
- 1 pound shrimp, peeled and deveined
- 2 tablespoons fresh basil, chopped
- 1 tablespoon fresh chives, chopped

What you' ll need from the store cupboard:

- 1 tablespoon fresh lemon juice
- 1 tablespoon garlic, minced
- 2 teaspoons red pepper flakes, crushed
- 2 tablespoons dry white wine

Instructions:

1. Preheat the Air fryer to 325 º F and grease an Air fryer pan.
2. Heat butter, lemon juice, garlic, and red pepper flakes in a pan and return the pan to Air fryer basket.
3. Cook for about 2 minutes and stir in shrimp, basil, chives and wine.
4. Cook for about 5 minutes and dish out the mixture onto serving plates.
5. Serve hot.

Nutrition Facts Per Serving:
Calories: 250, Fat: 13.7g, Carbohydrates: 3.3g, Sugar: 0.3g, Protein: 26.3g, Sodium: 360mg

Rice Flour Coated Shrimp

Prep time: 20 minutes, cook time: 20 minutes; Serves 3

5 Ingredients:

- 3 tablespoons rice flour
- 1 pound shrimp, peeled and deveined

What you' ll need from the store cupboard:

- 2 tablespoons olive oil
- 1 teaspoon powdered sugar
- Salt and black pepper, as required

Instructions:

1. Preheat the Air fryer to 325 º F and grease an Air fryer basket.
2. Mix rice flour, olive oil, sugar, salt, and black pepper in a bowl.
3. Stir in the shrimp and transfer half of the shrimp to the Air fryer basket.
4. Cook for about 10 minutes, flipping once in between.
5. Dish out the mixture onto serving plates and repeat with the remaining mixture.

Nutrition Facts Per Serving:
Calories: 299, Fat: 12g, Carbohydrates: 11.1g, Sugar: 0.8g, Protein: 35g, Sodium: 419mg

Shrimp Kebabs

Prep time: 15 minutes, cook time: 10 minutes; Serves 2

5 Ingredients:
- ¾ pound shrimp, peeled and deveined
- 1 tablespoon fresh cilantro, chopped
- Wooden skewers, presoaked

What you'll need from the store cupboard:
- 2 tablespoons fresh lemon juice
- 1 teaspoon garlic, minced
- ½ teaspoon paprika
- ½ teaspoon ground cumin
- Salt and ground black pepper, as required

Instructions:
1. Preheat the Air fryer to 350 º F and grease an Air fryer basket.
2. Mix lemon juice, garlic, and spices in a bowl.
3. Stir in the shrimp and mix to coat well.
4. Thread the shrimp onto presoaked wooden skewers and transfer to the Air fryer basket.
5. Cook for about 10 minutes, flipping once in between.
6. Dish out the mixture onto serving plates and serve garnished with fresh cilantro.

Nutrition Facts Per Serving:
Calories: 212, Fat: 3.2g, Carbohydrates: 3.9g, Sugar: 0.4g, Protein: 39.1g, Sodium: 497mg

Garlic Parmesan Shrimp

Prep time: 20 minutes, cook time: 10 minutes; Serves 2

5 Ingredients:
- 1 pound shrimp, deveined and peeled
- ½ cup parmesan cheese, grated
- ¼ cup cilantro, diced

What you'll need from the store cupboard:
- 1 tablespoon olive oil
- 1 teaspoon salt
- 1 teaspoon fresh cracked pepper
- 1 tablespoon lemon juice
- 6 garlic cloves, diced

Instructions:
1. Preheat the Air fryer to 350 º F and grease an Air fryer basket.
2. Drizzle shrimp with olive oil and lemon juice and season with garlic, salt and cracked pepper.
3. Cover the bowl with plastic wrap and refrigerate for about 3 hours.
4. Stir in the parmesan cheese and cilantro to the bowl and transfer to the Air fryer basket.
5. Cook for about 10 minutes and serve immediately.

Nutrition Facts Per Serving:
Calories: 602, Fat: 23.9g, Carbohydrates: 46.5g, Sugar: 2.9g, Protein: 11.3g, Sodium: 886mg

Cheesy Shrimp

Prep time: 20 minutes, cook time: 20 minutes; Serves 4

5 Ingredients:
- 2/3 cup Parmesan cheese, grated
- 2 pounds shrimp, peeled and deveined

What you'll need from the store cupboard:
- 4 garlic cloves, minced
- 2 tablespoons olive oil
- 1 teaspoon dried basil
- ½ teaspoon dried oregano
- 1 teaspoon onion powder
- ½ teaspoon red pepper flakes, crushed
- Ground black pepper, as required
- 2 tablespoons fresh lemon juice

Instructions:
1. Preheat the Air fryer to 350 º F and grease an Air fryer basket.
2. Mix Parmesan cheese, garlic, olive oil, herbs, and spices in a large bowl.
3. Arrange half of the shrimp into the Air fryer basket in a single layer and cook for about 10 minutes.
4. Dish out the shrimps onto serving plates and drizzle with lemon juice to serve hot.

Nutrition Facts Per Serving:
Calories: 386, Fat: 14.2g, Carbohydrates: 5.3g, Sugar: 0.4g, Protein: 57.3g, Sodium: 670mg

Prawn Burgers

Prep time: 20 minutes, cook time: 6 minutes; Serves 2

5 Ingredients:

- ½ cup prawns, peeled, deveined and finely chopped
- ½ cup breadcrumbs
- 2-3 tablespoons onion, finely chopped
- 3 cups fresh baby greens

What you'll need from the store cupboard:

- ½ teaspoon ginger, minced
- ½ teaspoon garlic, minced
- ½ teaspoon red chili powder
- ½ teaspoon ground cumin
- ¼ teaspoon ground turmeric
- Salt and ground black pepper, as required

Instructions:

1. Preheat the Air fryer to 390 ° F and grease an Air fryer basket.
2. Mix the prawns, breadcrumbs, onion, ginger, garlic, and spices in a bowl.
3. Make small-sized patties from the mixture and transfer to the Air fryer basket.
4. Cook for about 6 minutes and dish out in a platter.
5. Serve immediately warm alongside the baby greens.

Nutrition Facts Per Serving:
Calories: 240, Fat: 2.7g, Carbohydrates: 37.4g, Sugar: 4g, Protein: 18g, Sodium: 371mg

Scallops with Capers Sauce

Prep time: 15 minutes, cook time: 6 minutes; Serves 2

5 Ingredients:

- 10 (1-ounce) sea scallops, cleaned and patted very dry
- 2 tablespoons fresh parsley, finely chopped
- 2 teaspoons capers, finely chopped

What you'll need from the store cupboard:

- Salt and ground black pepper, as required
- ¼ cup extra-virgin olive oil
- 1 teaspoon fresh lemon zest, finely grated
- ½ teaspoon garlic, finely chopped

Instructions:

1. Preheat the Air fryer to 390 ° F and grease an Air fryer basket.
2. Season the scallops evenly with salt and black pepper.
3. Arrange the scallops in the Air fryer basket and cook for about 6 minutes.
4. Mix parsley, capers, olive oil, lemon zest and garlic in a bowl.
5. Dish out the scallops in a platter and top with capers sauce.

Nutrition Facts Per Serving:
Calories: 344, Fat: 26.3g, Carbohydrates: 4.2g, Sugar: 0.1g, Protein: 24g, Sodium: 393mg

Crispy Scallops

Prep time: 15 minutes, cook time: 6 minutes; Serves 4

5 Ingredients:

- 18 sea scallops, cleaned and patted very dry
- 1/8 cup all-purpose flour
- 1 tablespoon 2% milk
- ½ egg
- ¼ cup cornflakes, crushed

What you'll need from the store cupboard:

- ½ teaspoon paprika
- Salt and black pepper, as required

Instructions:

1. Preheat the Air fryer to 400 ° F and grease an Air fryer basket.
2. Mix flour, paprika, salt, and black pepper in a bowl.
3. Whisk egg with milk in another bowl and place the cornflakes in a third bowl.
4. Coat each scallop with the flour mixture, dip into the egg mixture and finally, dredge in the cornflakes.
5. Arrange scallops in the Air fryer basket and cook for about 6 minutes.
6. Dish out the scallops in a platter and serve hot.

Nutrition Facts Per Serving:
Calories: 150, Fat: 1.7g, Carbohydrates: 8g, Sugar: 0.4g, Protein: 24g, Sodium: 278mg

Scallops with Spinach

Prep time: 20 minutes, cook time: 10 minutes; Serves 2

5 Ingredients:
- 1 (12-ounces) package frozen spinach, thawed and drained
- 8 jumbo sea scallops
- Olive oil cooking spray
- 1 tablespoon fresh basil, chopped

What you' ll need from the store cupboard:
- Salt and ground black pepper, as required
- ¾ cup heavy whipping cream
- 1 tablespoon tomato paste
- 1 teaspoon garlic, minced

Instructions:
1. Preheat the Air fryer to 350 ° F and grease an Air fryer pan.
2. Season the scallops evenly with salt and black pepper.
3. Mix cream, tomato paste, garlic, basil, salt, and black pepper in a bowl.
4. Place spinach at the bottom of the Air fryer pan, followed by seasoned scallops and top with the cream mixture.
5. Transfer into the Air fryer and cook for about 10 minutes.
6. Dish out in a platter and serve hot.

Nutrition Facts Per Serving:
Calories: 203, Fat: 18.3g, Carbohydrates: 12.3g, Sugar: 1.7g, Protein: 26.4g, Sodium: 101mg

Bacon Wrapped Scallops

Prep time: 15 minutes, cook time: 12 minutes; Serves 4

5 Ingredients:
- 5 center-cut bacon slices, cut each in 4 pieces
- 20 sea scallops, cleaned and patted very dry
- Olive oil cooking spray

What you' ll need from the store cupboard:
- 1 teaspoon lemon pepper seasoning
- ½ teaspoon paprika
- Salt and ground black pepper, to taste

Instructions:
1. Preheat the Air fryer to 400 ° F and grease an Air fryer basket.
2. Wrap each scallop with a piece of bacon and secure each with a toothpick.
3. Season the scallops evenly with lemon pepper seasoning and paprika.
4. Arrange half of the scallops into the Air fryer basket and spray with cooking spray.
5. Season with salt and black pepper and cook for about 6 minutes.
6. Repeat with the remaining half and serve warm.

Nutrition Facts Per Serving:
Calories: 330, Fat: 16.3g, Carbohydrates: 4.5g, Sugar: 0g, Protein: 38.7g, Sodium: 1118mg

Crab Cakes

Prep time: 20 minutes, cook time: 20 minutes; Serves 4

5 Ingredients:
- 1 pound lump crab meat
- 1/3 cup panko breadcrumbs
- ¼ cup scallion, finely chopped
- 2 large eggs

What you' ll need from the store cupboard:
- 2 tablespoons mayonnaise
- 1 teaspoon Dijon mustard
- 1 teaspoon Worcestershire sauce
- 1½ teaspoons Old Bay seasoning
- Ground black pepper, as required

Instructions:
1. Preheat the Air fryer to 375 ° F and grease an Air fryer basket.
2. Mix all the ingredients in a large bowl and cover to refrigerate for about 1 hour.
3. Make 8 equal-sized patties from the mixture and transfer 4 patties into the Air fryer.
4. Cook for about 10 minutes, flipping once in between and repeat with the remaining patties.
5. Dish out and serve warm.

Nutrition Facts Per Serving:
Calories: 183, Fat: 14.8g, Carbohydrates: 5.9g, Sugar: 1.1g, Protein: 20.1g, Sodium: 996mg

Glazed Calamari

Prep time: 20 minutes, cook time: 13 minutes; Serves 3

5 Ingredients:

- ½ pound calamari tubes, cut into ¼ inch rings
- 1 cup club soda
- 1 cup flour

What you' ll need from the store cupboard:

- ½ tablespoon red pepper flakes, crushed
- Salt and black pepper, to taste

For Sauce

- ½ cup honey
- 2 tablespoons Sriracha sauce
- ¼ teaspoon red pepper flakes, crushed

Instructions:

1. Preheat the Air fryer to 375 º F and grease an Air fryer basket.
2. Soak the calamari in the club soda in a bowl and keep aside for about 10 minutes.
3. Mix flour, red pepper flakes, salt, and black pepper in another bowl.
4. Drain the club soda from calamari and coat the calamari rings evenly with flour mixture.
5. Arrange calamari rings into the Air fryer basket and cook for about 11 minutes.
6. Meanwhile, mix the honey, Sriracha sauce and red pepper flakes in a bowl.
7. Coat the calamari rings with the honey sauce and cook for 2 more minutes.
8. Dish out the calamari rings onto serving plates and serve hot.

Nutrition Facts Per Serving:
Calories: 307, Fats: 1.4g, Carbohydrates: 62.1g, Sugar: 35g, Proteins: 12g, Sodium: 131mg

Buttered Crab Shells

Prep time: 20 minutes, cook time: 10 minutes; Serves 4

5 Ingredients:

- 4 soft crab shells, cleaned
- 1 cup buttermilk
- 3 eggs
- 2 cups panko breadcrumb
- 2 tablespoons butter, melted

What you' ll need from the store cupboard:

- 2 teaspoons seafood seasoningo
- 1½ teaspoons lemon zest, grated

Instructions:

1. Preheat the Air fryer to 375 º F and grease an Air fryer basket.
2. Place the buttermilk in a shallow bowl and whisk the eggs in a second bowl.
3. Mix the breadcrumbs, seafood seasoning, and lemon zest in a third bowl.
4. Soak the crab shells into the buttermilk for about 10 minutes, then dip in the eggs.
5. Dredge in the breadcrumb mixture and arrange the crab shells into the Air fryer basket.
6. Cook for about 10 minutes and dish out in a platter.
7. Drizzle melted butter over the crab shells and immediately serve.

Nutrition Facts Per Serving:
Calories: 521, Fat: 16.8g, Carbohydrates: 11.5g, Sugar: 3.3g, Protein: 47.8g, Sodium: 1100mg
(**Note: Seafood Seasoning** - Mix the salt, celery seed, dry mustard powder, red pepper, black pepper, bay leaves, paprika, cloves, allspice, ginger, cardamom, and cinnamon together in a bowl until thoroughly combined. Or, you can buy at your local store or on Amazon.)

Wasabi Crab Cakes

Prep time: 20 minutes, cook time: 24 minutes; Serves 6

5 Ingredients:

- 3 scallions, finely chopped
- 1 celery rib, finely chopped
- 1/3 cup plus ½ cup dry breadcrumbs, divided
- 2 large egg whites
- 1½ cups lump crab meat, drained

What you'll need from the store cupboard:

- 3 tablespoons mayonnaise
- 1 medium sweet red pepper, finely chopped
- ¼ teaspoon prepared wasabi
- Salt, to taste

Instructions:

1. Preheat the Air fryer to 375 ° F and grease an Air fryer basket.
2. Mix scallions, red pepper, celery, 1/3 cup of breadcrumbs, egg whites, mayonnaise, wasabi, and salt in a large bowl.
3. Fold in the crab meat gently and mix well.
4. Place the remaining breadcrumbs in another bowl.
5. Make ¾-inch thick patties from the mixture and arrange half of the patties into the Air fryer.
6. Cook for about 12 minutes, flipping once halfway through and repeat with the remaining patties.
7. Dish out and serve warm.

Nutrition Facts Per Serving:
Calories: 112, Fat: 4g, Carbohydrates: 15.5g, Sugar: 2.7g, Protein: 4.9g, Sodium: 253mg

Lemony Tuna

Prep time: 15 minutes, cook time: 12 minutes; Serves 8

5 Ingredients:

- 4 tablespoons fresh parsley, chopped
- 4 (6-ounce) cans water packed plain tuna
- 1 cup breadcrumbs
- 2 eggs

What you'll need from the store cupboard:

- 4 teaspoons Dijon mustard
- 2 tablespoons fresh lime juice
- 6 tablespoons canola oil
- Dash of hot sauce
- Salt and black pepper, to taste

Instructions:

1. Preheat the Air fryer to 360 ° F and grease an Air fryer basket.
2. Mix tuna fish, breadcrumbs, mustard, parsley, hot sauce, canola oil, eggs, salt and lime juice in a large bowl.
3. Make equal-sized patties from the mixture and refrigerate for about 3 hours.
4. Transfer the patties into the Air fryer basket and cook for about 12 minutes.
5. Dish out and serve warm.

Nutrition Facts Per Serving:
Calories: 388, Fat: 21.8g, Carbohydrates: 31.7g, Sugar: 1.2g, Protein: 14.2g, Sodium: 680mg

Haddock with Cheese Sauce

Prep time: 15 minutes, cook time: 8 minutes; Serves 4

5 Ingredients:

- 4 (6-ounce) haddock fillets
- 6 tablespoons fresh basil, chopped
- 4 tablespoons pine nuts
- 2 tablespoons Parmesan cheese, grated

What you'll need from the store cupboard:

- 2 tablespoons olive oil
- Salt and black pepper, to taste

Instructions:

1. Preheat the Air fryer to 360 ° F and grease an Air fryer basket.
2. Season the haddock fillets with salt and black pepper and coat evenly with olive oil.
3. Transfer the haddock fillets in the Air fryer basket and cook for about 8 minutes.

4. Meanwhile, put rest of the ingredients in a food processor and pulse until smooth to make cheese sauce.
5. Dish out the haddock fillets in the bowl and top with cheese sauce to serve.

Nutrition Facts Per Serving:
Calories: 354, Fat: 17.5g, Carbohydrates: 1.7g, Sugar: 0.3g, Protein: 47g, Sodium: 278mg

Crumbed Cod

Prep time: 15 minutes, cook time: 7 minutes; Serves 4

5 Ingredients:
- 1 cup flour
- 4 (4-ounce) skinless codfish fillets, cut into rectangular pieces
- 6 eggs
- 2 green chilies, finely chopped
- 6 scallions, finely chopped

What you' ll need from the store cupboard:
- 4 garlic cloves, minced
- Salt and black pepper, to taste
- 2 teaspoons soy sauce

Instructions:

1. Preheat the Air fryer to 375 º F and grease an Air fryer basket.
2. Place the flour in a shallow dish and mix remaining ingredients except cod in another shallow dish.
3. Coat each cod fillet into the flour and then dip in the egg mixture.
4. Arrange the cod fillets in the Air fryer basket and cook for about 7 minutes.
5. Dish out and serve warm.

Nutrition Facts Per Serving:
Calories: 462, Fat: 16.9g, Carbohydrates: 51.3g, Sugar: 3.3g, Protein: 24.4g, Sodium: 646mg

Lemony and Spicy Coconut Crusted Salmon

Prep time: 10 minutes, cook time: 6 minutes; Serves 4

5 Ingredients:
- 1 pound salmon
- ½ cup flour
- 2 egg whites
- ½ cup breadcrumbs
- ½ cup unsweetened coconut, shredded

What you' ll need from the store cupboard:
- ¼ teaspoon lemon zest
- Salt and freshly ground black pepper, to taste
- ¼ teaspoon cayenne pepper
- ¼ teaspoon red pepper flakes, crushed
- Vegetable oil, as required

Instructions:
1. Preheat the Air fryer to 400 º F and grease an Air fryer basket.

2. Mix the flour, salt and black pepper in a shallow dish.
3. Whisk the egg whites in a second shallow dish.
4. Mix the breadcrumbs, coconut, lime zest, salt and cayenne pepper in a third shallow dish.
5. Coat salmon in the flour, then dip in the egg whites and then into the breadcrumb mixture evenly.
6. Place the salmon in the Air fryer basket and drizzle with vegetable oil.
7. Cook for about 6 minutes and dish out to serve warm.

Nutrition Facts Per Serving:
Calories: 558, Fat: 22.2g, Carbohydrates: 18.6g, Sugar: 8.7g, Protein: 43g, Sodium: 3456mg

Chapter 4 Poultry Recipes

Cornish Game Hens

Prep time: 20 minutes, cook time: 16 minutes; Serves 4

5 Ingredients:
- 1 teaspoon fresh rosemary, chopped
- 1 teaspoon fresh thyme, chopped
- 2 pounds Cornish game hen, backbone removed and halved

What you' ll need from the store cupboard:
- ½ cup olive oil
- ¼ teaspoon sugar
- ¼ teaspoon red pepper flakes, crushed
- Salt and black pepper, to taste
- 1 teaspoon fresh lemon zest, finely grated

Instructions:

1. Preheat the Air fryer to 390 º F and grease an Air fryer basket.
2. Mix olive oil, herbs, lemon zest, sugar, and spices in a bowl.
3. Stir in the Cornish game hen and refrigerate to marinate well for about 24 hours.
4. Transfer the Cornish game hen to the Air fryer and cook for about 16 minutes.
5. Dish out the hen portions onto serving plates and serve hot.

Nutrition Facts Per Serving:
Calories: 523, Fats: 34.1g, Carbohydrates: 0.8g, Sugar: 0.6g, Proteins: 52.9g, Sodium: 143mg

Deliciously Crisp Chicken

Prep time: 10 minutes, cook time: 12 minutes; Serves 4

5 Ingredients:
- 1 egg, beaten
- ½ cup breadcrumbs
- 8 skinless, boneless chicken tenderloins

What you' ll need from the store cupboard:
- 2 tablespoons vegetable oil

Instructions:
1. Preheat the Air fryer to 355 º F and grease an Air fryer basket.
2. Whisk the egg in a shallow dish and mix vegetable oil and breadcrumbs in another shallow dish.
3. Dip the chicken tenderloins in egg and then coat in the breadcrumb mixture.
4. Arrange the chicken tenderloins in the Air fryer basket and cook for about 12 minutes.
5. Dish out and serve warm.

Nutrition Facts Per Serving:
Calories: 271, Fat: 11.5g, Carbohydrates: 9.8g, Sugar: 0.9g, Protein: 30.4g, Sodium: 113mg

Roasted Chicken with Potatoes

Prep time: 15 minutes, cook time: 1 hour; Serves 2

5 Ingredients:
- 1 (1½-pounds) whole chicken
- ½ pound small potatoes

What you' ll need from the store cupboard:
- Salt and black pepper, as required
- 1 tablespoon olive oil

Instructions:
1. Preheat the Air fryer to 355 º F and grease an Air fryer basket.
2. Season the chicken and potatoes with salt and black pepper and drizzle with olive oil.
3. Transfer the chicken into the Air fryer basket and cook for about 45 minutes.
4. Dish out in a serving platter and transfer the potatoes in the Air fryer basket.
5. Cook for about 15 minutes and serve alongside the chicken.

Nutrition Facts Per Serving:
Calories: 271, Fat: 11.5g, Carbohydrates: 9.8g, Sugar: 0.9g, Protein: 30.4g, Sodium: 113mg

Juicy Herbed Drumsticks

Prep time: 10 minutes, cook time: 22 minutes; Serves 4

5 Ingredients:
- ½ tablespoon fresh rosemary, minced
- 1 tablespoon fresh thyme, minced
- 4 boneless chicken drumsticks

What you'll need from the store cupboard:
- ¼ cup Dijon mustard
- 1 tablespoon honey
- 2 tablespoons olive oil
- Salt and freshly ground black pepper, to taste

Instructions:
1. Preheat the Air fryer to 320 º F and grease an Air fryer basket.
2. Mix all the ingredients in a bowl except the drumsticks until well combined.
3. Stir in the drumsticks and coat generously with the mixture.
4. Cover and refrigerate to marinate overnight.
5. Transfer into the Air fryer basket and cook for about 12 minutes.
6. Set the Air fryer to 355 degrees F and cook for about 10 minutes.
7. Dish out and serve warm.

Nutrition Facts Per Serving:
Calories: 167, Fat: 10.4g, Carbohydrates: 5.8g, Sugar: 4.4g, Protein: 13.4g, Sodium: 215mg

Glazed Chicken Wings

Prep time: 10 minutes, cook time: 19 minutes; Serves 4

5 Ingredients:
- 8 chicken wings
- 2 tablespoons all-purpose flour

What you'll need from the store cupboard:
- 1 teaspoon garlic, chopped finely
- 1 tablespoon fresh lemon juice
- 1 tablespoon soy sauce
- ½ teaspoon dried oregano, crushed
- Salt and freshly ground black pepper, to taste

Instructions:
1. Preheat the Air fryer to 355 º F and grease an Air fryer basket.
2. Mix all the ingredients except wings in a large bowl.
3. Coat wings generously with the marinade and refrigerate for about 2 hours.
4. Remove the chicken wings from marinade and sprinkle with flour evenly.
5. Transfer the wings in the Air fryer tray and cook for about 6 minutes, flipping once in between.
6. Dish out the chicken wings in a platter and serve hot.

Nutrition Facts Per Serving:
Calories: 350, Fat: 12.7g, Carbohydrates: 5.5g, Sugar: 1.8g, Protein: 50.1g, Sodium: 510mg

Crispy Herbed Turkey Breast

Prep time: 5 minutes, cook time: 30 minutes; Serves 2

5 Ingredients:
- ½ tablespoon fresh rosemary, chopped
- ½ tablespoon fresh parsley, chopped
- 2 turkey breasts

What you'll need from the store cupboard:
- 1 garlic clove, minced
- 1 tablespoon ginger, minced
- 1 teaspoon five spice powder
- Salt and black pepper, to taste

Instructions:
1. Preheat the Air fryer to 340 º F and grease an Air fryer basket.
2. Mix garlic, herbs, five spice powder, salt and black pepper in a bowl.
3. Brush the turkey breasts generously with garlic mixture and transfer into the Air fryer.
4. Cook for about 25 minutes and set the Air fryer to 390 º F.
5. Cook for about 5 more minutes and dish out to serve warm.

Nutrition Facts Per Serving:
Calories: 138, Fat: 4.5g, Carbohydrates: 1g, Sugar: 0g, Protein: 22g, Sodium: 82mg

Sweet and Salty Chicken Kebobs

Prep time: 20 minutes, cook time: 12 minutes; Serves 4

5 Ingredients:

- 4 (4-ounce) skinless, boneless chicken thighs, cubed into 1-inch size
- 5 scallions, cut into 1-inch pieces lengthwise
- Wooden skewers, presoaked

What you' ll need from the store cupboard:

- ¼ cup light soy sauce
- 1 tablespoon mirin
- 1 teaspoon garlic salt
- 1 teaspoon sugar

Instructions:

1. Preheat the Air fryer to 355 º F and grease an Air fryer pan.
2. Mix soy sauce, mirin, garlic salt and sugar in a large baking dish.
3. Thread green onions and chicken onto pre-soaked wooden skewers.
4. Coat the skewers generously with marinade and place the skewers in the Air fryer pan.
5. Cook for about 12 minutes until golden brown and serve warm.

Nutrition Facts Per Serving:
Calories: 161, Fat: 4.1g, Carbohydrates: 6.9g, Sugar: 4g, Protein: 26.2g, Sodium: 781mg

Original Chicken Chilaquiles

Prep time: 15 minutes, cook time: 30 minutes; Serves 4

5 Ingredients:

- 1 (8-ounce) skinless, boneless chicken breast
- 2 (14½-ounce) can diced tomatoes
- 10 corn tortillas, cut into diamond slices
- 4 tablespoons feta cheese, crumbled
- 3 red onions, sliced

What you' ll need from the store cupboard:

- 3 garlic cloves, chopped
- ½ of poblano pepper
- Salt, to taste
- 1 tablespoon olive oil
- ¼ cup sour cream

Instructions:

1. Preheat the Air fryer to 400 º F and grease an Air fryer basket.
2. Add half of tortilla slices, half of olive oil in a bowl and salt and toss to coat well.
3. Cook chicken breasts for about 20 minutes in a pan of water.
4. Dish out the chicken and shred with 2 forks.
5. Put onion, garlic, poblano pepper and tomato in a food processor and pulse till smooth.
6. Transfer the onion mixture into a skillet and bring to a boil on medium-high heat.
7. Reduce the heat to medium-low and let it simmer for about 10 minutes.
8. Season with salt and dish out to keep aside.
9. Arrange the tortilla slices in an Air fryer basket in 2 batches and cook for about 10 minutes.
10. Dish out the tortillas into the serving bowl and top with chicken and onion sauce.

Nutrition Facts Per Serving:
Calories: 363, Fat: 12.8g, Carbohydrates: 44.8g, Sugar: 10.2g, Protein: 20.8g, Sodium: 212mg

Air Fried Chicken Fillets with Coconut Rice

Prep time: 15 minutes, cook time: 15 minutes; Serves 4

5 Ingredients:

- 4 (4-ounce) skinless, boneless chicken breasts
- 2¼ cups water
- 1 (14-ounce) can coconut milk
- 1 cup rice

What you' ll need from the store cupboard:

- ½ cup coconut cream
- 1 garlic clove, minced
- 1 teaspoon fresh lime zest, grated finely
- 3 teaspoons avocado oil
- 2 tablespoons fresh lime juice
- 2 teaspoons soy sauce
- 2 teaspoons pure maple syrup
- ¼ teaspoon chile paste
- 2 teaspoons curry powder
- 1½ teaspoons ground coriander
- 1 teaspoon ground cumin
- ¼ teaspoons dried cilantro, crushed
- Pinch of cayenne pepper

- Salt, to taste

Instructions:

1. Preheat the Air fryer to 370 º F and grease an Air fryer basket.
2. Put all the ingredients in a large bowl except chicken and mix until well combined.
3. Stir in the chicken and coat generously with marinade.
4. Cover the bowl and refrigerate for about 24 hours.
5. Arrange the chicken in the Air fryer basket and cook for about 15 minutes.
6. Meanwhile, mix water, coconut cream, rice and salt in a pan and bring to a boil.
7. Lower the heat, cover and let it simmer for about 15 minutes.
8. Serve chicken with coconut rice.

Nutrition Facts Per Serving:
Calories: 705, Fat: 40.2g, Carbohydrates: 48.6g, Sugar: 6.6g, Protein: 39.6g, Sodium: 314mg

Traditional Mongolian Chicken

Prep time: 15 minutes, cook time: 16 minutes; Serves 4

5 Ingredients:

- 1 pound boneless chicken, cubed
- ½ tablespoon corn starch
- 1 egg
- 1 medium yellow onion, sliced thinly
- ½ cup evaporated milk

What you' ll need from the store cupboard:

- 1 tablespoon light soy sauce
- 2 tablespoons olive oil
- 3 teaspoons garlic, minced
- 1 teaspoon fresh ginger, grated
- 5 curry leaves
- ½ teaspoon curry powder
- 1 tablespoon chili sauce
- 1 teaspoon sugar
- ½ teaspoon salt
- Pinch of black pepper

Instructions:

1. Preheat the Air fryer to 390 º F and grease an Air fryer basket.
2. Mix chicken, egg, soy sauce and corn starch in a bowl.
3. Cover and marinate for about 1 hour.
4. Arrange the chicken in the Air fryer basket and cook for about 10 minutes.
5. Heat olive oil in a skillet on medium heat and add onion, garlic and ginger.
6. Sauté for about 2 minutes and stir in the chicken, curry powder, chili sauce, sugar, salt and black pepper.
7. Mix until well combined and whisk in evaporated milk.
8. Cook for about 4 minutes and dish out to serve warm.

Nutrition Facts Per Serving:
Calories: 363, Fat: 19g, Carbohydrates: 10g, Sugar: 5.8g, Protein: 37.1g, Sodium: 789mg

Yummy Stuffed Chicken Breast

Prep time: 15 minutes, cook time: 15 minutes; Serves 4

5 Ingredients:

- 2 (8-ounce) chicken fillets, skinless and boneless, each cut into 2 pieces
- 4 brie cheese slices
- 1 tablespoon chive, minced
- 4 cured ham slices

What you' ll need from the store cupboard:

- Salt and black pepper, to taste

Instructions:

1. Preheat the Air fryer to 355 º F and grease an Air fryer basket.
2. Make a slit in each chicken piece horizontally and season with the salt and black pepper.
3. Insert cheese slice in the slits and sprinkle with chives.
4. Wrap each chicken piece with one ham slice and transfer into the Air fryer basket.
5. Cook for about 15 minutes and dish out to serve warm.

Nutrition Facts Per Serving:
Calories: 376, Fat: 20.2g, Carbohydrates: 1.5g, Sugar: 0g, Protein: 44.5g, Sodium: 639mg

Marinated Duck Breasts

Prep time: 15 minutes, cook time: 16 minutes; Serves 4

5 Ingredients:
- 1 teaspoon fresh rosemary, chopped
- 1 teaspoon fresh thyme, chopped
- 2 pounds

What you' ll need from the store cupboard:
- ½ cup olive oil
- 1 teaspoon fresh lemon zest, duck breasts grated finely
- ¼ teaspoon sugar
- ¼ teaspoon red pepper flakes, crushed
- Salt and black pepper, to taste

Instructions:

1. Preheat the Air fryer to 390 º F and grease an Air fryer basket.
2. Mix all the ingredients in a large bowl except duck breasts.
3. Stir in the duck breasts and refrigerate to marinate well for about 24 hours.
4. Transfer the duck breasts to the Air fryer and cook for about 16 minutes.
5. Dish out the duck breasts onto serving plates and serve hot.

Nutrition Facts Per Serving:
Calories: 523, Fat: 34.1g, Carbohydrates: 0.8g, Sugar: 0g, Protein: 52.9g, Sodium: 143mg

Succulent Duck Breast with Balsamic Vinaigrette

Prep time: 15 minutes, cook time: 20 minutes; Serves 2

5 Ingredients:
- 1 tablespoon fresh thyme, chopped
- 1 (10½-ounce) duck breast
- 4 cherry tomatoes
- ¼ cup black olives

What you' ll need from the store cupboard:
- 1 tablespoon olive oil
- 1 teaspoon mustard
- 1 cup beer
- Salt and freshly ground black pepper, to taste
- 1 tablespoon balsamic vinegar

Instructions:
1. Preheat the Air fryer to 390 º F and grease an Air fryer basket.
2. Mix olive oil, mustard, thyme, beer, salt and black pepper in a bowl.
3. Add duck breast and coat generously with marinade.
4. Cover the duck breast with foil paper and refrigerate for about 4 hours.
5. Arrange the duck breast in the Air fryer basket and cook for about 15 minutes.
6. Remove the foil paper from the breast and set the Air fryer to 355 º F.
7. Add tomatoes in the Air fryer basket and cook for about 5 minutes.
8. Drizzle with vinegar and serve topped with olives.

Nutrition Facts Per Serving:
Calories: 380, Fat: 15.8g, Carbohydrates: 16.4g, Sugar: 6.6g, Protein: 36.1g, Sodium: 164mg

Sausage Stuffed Chicken

Prep time: 10 minutes, cook time: 15 minutes; Serves 4

5 Ingredients:
- 4 (4-ounce) skinless, boneless chicken breasts
- 4 sausages, casing removed

What you' ll need from the store cupboard:
- 2 tablespoons mustard sauce

Instructions:
1. Preheat the Air fryer to 375 º F and grease an Air fryer basket.
2. Roll each chicken breast with a rolling pin for about 1 minute.
3. Arrange 1 sausage over each chicken breast and roll up.
4. Secure with toothpicks and transfer into the Air fryer basket.
5. Cook for about 15 minutes and dish out to serve warm.

Nutrition Facts Per Serving:
Calories: 345, Fat: 21.1g, Carbohydrates: 0g, Sugar: 0g, Protein: 37g, Sodium: 490mg

Sweet Garlicky Chicken

Prep time: 15 minutes, cook time: 14 minutes; Serves 4

5 Ingredients:
- 4 scallions, chopped
- 2 teaspoons sesame seeds, toasted
- 1 pound chicken tenders
- Wooden skewers, as required

What you'll need from the store cupboard:
- 1 tablespoon fresh ginger, grated finely
- 4 garlic cloves, minced
- ½ cup pineapple juice
- ½ cup soy sauce
- ¼ cup sesame oil
- Pinch of black pepper

Instructions:
1. Preheat the Air fryer to 390 º F and grease an Air fryer basket.
2. Mix all the ingredients in a large baking dish except chicken.
3. Thread chicken onto skewer and transfer the skewers on the baking dish.
4. Coat evenly with marinade and cover to refrigerate for about 3 hours.
5. Transfer half of the chicken skewers into the Air fryer basket and cook for about 7 minutes.
6. Repeat with the remaining skewers and dish out to serve warm.

Nutrition Facts Per Serving:
Calories: 392, Fats: 23g, Carbohydrates: 9.9g, Sugar: 4.1g, Proteins: 35.8g, Sodium: 1899mg

Appetizing Chicken

Prep time: 15 minutes, cook time: 19 minutes; Serves 2

5 Ingredients:
- ¾ pound chicken pieces
- 1 tablespoon fresh rosemary, chopped
- 1 lemon, cut into wedges

What you'll need from the store cupboard:
- 1 teaspoon ginger, minced
- 1 tablespoon soy sauce
- ½ tablespoon olive oil
- 1 tablespoon oyster sauce
- 3 tablespoons brown sugar

Instructions:
1. Preheat the Air fryer to 390 º F and grease an Air fryer basket.
2. Mix chicken, ginger, soy sauce and olive oil in a bowl.
3. Marinate and refrigerate for about 30 minutes and transfer the chicken in the Air fryer pan.
4. Cook for about 6 minutes and dish out.
5. Meanwhile, mix the remaining ingredients in a small bowl and spread over the chicken.
6. Squeeze juice from lemon wedges over chicken and top with the wedges.
7. Transfer into the Air fryer and cook for about 13 minutes.
8. Dish out and serve warm.

Nutrition Facts Per Serving:
Calories: 353, Fat: 9g, Carbohydrates: 16.2g, Sugar: 13.4g, Protein: 50g, Sodium: 618mg

Surprisingly Tasty Chicken

Prep time: 10 minutes, cook time: 1 hour; Serves 4

5 Ingredients:
- 1 (1½ pound) whole chicken
- 1 pound small potatoes

What you'll need from the store cupboard:
- Salt and black pepper, to taste
- 1 tablespoon olive oil, scrubbed

Instructions:
1. Preheat the Air fryer to 390 º F and grease an Air fryer basket.
2. Season the chicken with salt and black pepper and transfer into the Air fryer.
3. Cook for about 40 minutes and dish out in a plate, covering with a foil paper.
4. Mix potato, oil, salt and black pepper in a bowl and toss to coat well
5. Arrange the potatoes into the Air fryer basket and cook for 20 minutes.
6. Dish out and serve warm.

Nutrition Facts Per Serving:
Calories: 431, Fat: 16.2g, Carbohydrates: 17.8g, Sugar: 1.3g, Protein: 51.1g, Sodium: 153mg

Mouthwatering Turkey Roll

Prep time: 20 minutes, cook time: 40 minutes; Serves 4

5 Ingredients:

- 1 pound turkey breast fillet, deep slit cut lengthwise with knife
- 3 tablespoons fresh parsley, chopped finely
- 1 small red onion, chopped finely

What you'll need from the store cupboard:

- 1 garlic clove, crushed
- 1½ teaspoons ground cumin
- 1 teaspoon ground cinnamon
- ½ teaspoon red chili powder
- Salt, to taste
- 2 tablespoons olive oil

Instructions:

1. Preheat the Air fryer to 355 º F and grease an Air fryer basket.
2. Mix garlic, parsley, onion, spices and olive oil in a bowl.
3. Coat the open side of fillet with onion mixture and roll the fillet tightly.
4. Coat the outer side of roll with remaining spice mixture and transfer into the Air fryer.
5. Cook for about 40 minutes and dish out to serve warm.

Nutrition Facts Per Serving:
Calories: 193, Fat: 9.2g, Carbohydrates: 7.8g, Sugar: 4.8g, Protein: 19.9g, Sodium: 1197mg

Crunchy Stuffed Chicken Breast

Prep time: 20 minutes, cook time: 45 minutes; Serves 2

5 Ingredients:

- 1 medium eggplant, halved lengthwise
- ¼ cup pomegranate seeds
- 2 (4-ounce) chicken breasts, skinless and boneless
- 2 egg whites
- ¼ cup breadcrumbs

What you'll need from the store cupboard:

- Salt, to taste
- Freshly ground black pepper, to taste
- ½ tablespoon olive oil

Instructions:

1. Preheat the Air fryer to 390 º F and grease an Air fryer basket.
2. Season the eggplant halves with some salt and keep aside for about 20 minutes.
3. Arrange the eggplant halves in the Air fryer basket, cut side up and cook for about 20 minutes.
4. Dish out and scoop out the flesh from each eggplant half.
5. Put the eggplant pulp and a pinch of salt and black pepper in the food processor and pulse until a puree is formed.
6. Dish out the eggplant puree into a bowl and stir in the pomegranate seeds.
7. Cut the chicken breasts lengthwise to make a pocket and stuff in the eggplant mixture.
8. Whisk together egg whites, a pinch of salt and black pepper in a shallow dish.
9. Mix breadcrumbs, thyme and olive oil in another dish.
10. Dip the chicken breasts in the egg white mixture and then coat with flour.
11. Set the Air fryer to 355 º F and transfer the chicken breasts into the Air fryer.
12. Cook for about 25 minutes and dish out to serve warm.

Nutrition Facts Per Serving:
Calories: 386, Fat: 13.1g, Carbohydrates: 26.5g, Sugar: 9.4g, Protein: 40.6g, Sodium: 312mg

Herbed Roasted Chicken

Prep time: 15 minutes, cook time: 1 hour; Serves 7

5 Ingredients:

- 1 (5-pounds) whole chicken

What you'll need from the store cupboard:

- 3 garlic cloves, minced
- 1 teaspoon fresh lemon zest, finely grated
- 1 teaspoon dried thyme, crushed
- 1 teaspoon dried oregano, crushed
- 1 teaspoon dried rosemary, crushed
- 1 teaspoon smoked paprika

- Salt and ground black pepper, as required
- 2 tablespoons fresh lemon juice
- 2 tablespoons olive oil

Instructions:
1. Preheat the Air fryer to 360 º F and grease an Air fryer basket.
2. Mix the garlic, lemon zest, herbs and spices in a bowl.
3. Rub the herb mixture over the chicken and drizzle with lemon juice and oil.
4. Keep aside for about 2 hours at room temperature and transfer into the Air fryer.
5. Cook for about 50 minutes and carefully flip the chicken.
6. Cook for 10 more minutes and dish out in a plate.
7. Cut into desired size pieces with a knife and serve warm.

Nutrition Facts Per Serving:
Calories: 860, Fat: 50g, Carbohydrates: 1.3g, Sugar: 0.2g, Protein: 71.1g, Sodium: 299mg

Spicy Chicken Legs

Prep time: 15 minutes, cook time: 25 minutes; Serves 3

5 Ingredients:
- 3 (8-ounces) chicken legs
- 1 cup buttermilk
- 2 cups white flour

What you' ll need from the store cupboard:
- 1 teaspoon garlic powder
- 1 teaspoon onion powder
- 1 teaspoon ground cumin
- 1 teaspoon paprika
- Salt and ground black pepper, as required
- 1 tablespoon olive oil

Instructions:
1. Preheat the Air fryer to 360 º F and grease an Air fryer basket.
2. Mix the chicken legs, and buttermilk in a bowl and refrigerate for about 2 hours.
3. Combine the flour and spices in another bowl and dredge the chicken legs into this mixture.
4. Now, dip the chicken into the buttermilk and coat again with the flour mixture.
5. Arrange the chicken legs into the Air fryer basket and drizzle with the oil
6. Cook for about 25 minutes and dish out in a serving platter to serve hot.

Nutrition Facts Per Serving:
Calories: 781, Fats: 7.6g, Carbohydrates: 69.5g, Sugar: 4.7g, Proteins: 55.9g, Sodium: 288mg

Spiced Roasted Chicken

Prep time: 15 minutes, cook time: 14 minutes; Serves 2

5 Ingredients:
- 1 (5-pounds) whole chicken, necks and giblets removed

What you' ll need from the store cupboard:
- 2 teaspoons dried thyme
- 2 teaspoons paprika
- 1 teaspoon cayenne pepper
- 1 teaspoon ground white pepper
- 1 teaspoon onion powder
- 1 teaspoon garlic powder
- Salt and ground black pepper, as required
- 3 tablespoons olive oil

Instructions:
1. Preheat the Air fryer to 350 º F and grease an Air fryer basket.
2. Mix the thyme and spices in a bowl.
3. Coat the chicken generously with olive oil and rub with spice mixture.
4. Arrange the chicken into the Air Fryer basket, breast side down and cook for about 30 minutes.
5. Flip the chicken and cook for 30 more minutes.
6. Dish out the chicken in a platter and cut into desired size pieces to serve.

Nutrition Facts Per Serving:
Calories: 871, Fat: 60g, Carbohydrates: 1.7g, Sugar: 0.4g, Protein: 70.6g, Sodium: 296mg

Tandoori Chicken Legs

Prep time: 15 minutes, cook time: 20 minutes; Serves 4

5 Ingredients:
- 4 chicken legs
- 4 tablespoons hung curd

What you'll need from the store cupboard:
- 3 tablespoons fresh lemon juice
- 3 teaspoons ginger paste
- 3 teaspoons garlic paste
- Salt, as required
- 2 tablespoons tandoori masala powder
- 2 teaspoons red chili powder
- 1 teaspoon garam masala powder
- 1 teaspoon ground cumin
- 1 teaspoon ground coriander
- 1 teaspoon ground turmeric
- Ground black pepper, as required
- Pinch of orange food color

Instructions:
1. Preheat the Air fryer to 445 ° F and grease an Air fryer basket.
2. Mix chicken legs, lemon juice, ginger paste, garlic paste, and salt in a bowl.
3. Combine the curd, spices, and food color in another bowl.
4. Add the chicken legs into bowl and coat generously with the spice mixture.
5. Cover the bowl of chicken and refrigerate for at least 12 hours.
6. Arrange the chicken legs into the Air fryer basket and cook for about 20 minutes.
7. Dish out the chicken legs onto serving plates and serve hot.

Nutrition Facts Per Serving:
Calories: 356, Fat: 13.9g, Carbohydrates: 3.7g, Sugar: 0.5g, Protein: 51.5g, Sodium: 259mg

(Note: Hung curd - Hung curd is nothing but yogurt drained of all its water. It can be made very easily at home.)

Gingered Chicken Drumsticks

Prep time: 10 minutes, cook time: 25 minutes; Serves 3

5 Ingredients:
- ¼ cup full-fat coconut milk
- 3 (6-ounces) chicken drumsticks

What you'll need from the store cupboard:
- 2 teaspoons fresh ginger, minced
- 2 teaspoons galangal, minced
- 2 teaspoons ground turmeric
- Salt, to taste

Instructions:
1. Preheat the Air fryer to 375 ° F and grease an Air fryer basket.
2. Mix the coconut milk, galangal, ginger, and spices in a bowl.
3. Add the chicken drumsticks and coat generously with the marinade.
4. Refrigerate to marinate for at least 8 hours and transfer into the Air fryer basket.
5. Cook for about 25 minutes and dish out the chicken drumsticks onto a serving platter.

Nutrition Facts Per Serving:
Calories: 338, Fat: 13.9g, Carbohydrates: 2.6g, Sugar: 0.4g, Protein: 47.4g, Sodium: 192mg

Simple Chicken Wings

Prep time: 10 minutes, cook time: 25 minutes; Serves 2

5 Ingredients:
- 1 pound chicken wings

What you'll need from the store cupboard:
- Salt and black pepper, to taste

Instructions:
1. Preheat the Air fryer to 380 ° F and grease an Air fryer basket.
2. Season the chicken wings evenly with salt and black pepper.
3. Arrange the drumsticks into the Air Fryer basket and cook for about 25 minutes.
4. Dish out the chicken drumsticks onto a serving platter and serve hot.

Nutrition Facts Per Serving:
Calories: 431, Fats: 16.8g, Carbohydrates: 0g, Sugar: 0g, Proteins: 65.6g, Sodium: 273mg

Sweet and Spicy Chicken Drumsticks

Prep time: 15 minutes, cook time: 20 minutes; Serves 4

5 Ingredients:
- 4 (6-ounces) chicken drumsticks

What you'll need from the store cupboard:
- 1 garlic clove, crushed
- 1 tablespoon mustard
- 2 teaspoons brown sugar
- 1 teaspoon cayenne pepper
- 1 teaspoon red chili powder
- Salt and ground black pepper, as required
- 1 tablespoon vegetable oil

Instructions:
1. Preheat the Air fryer to 375 º F and grease an Air fryer basket.
2. Mix garlic, mustard, brown sugar, oil, and spices in a bowl.
3. Rub the chicken drumsticks with marinade and refrigerate for about 30 minutes.
4. Arrange the drumsticks into the Air Fryer basket in a single layer and cook for about 10 minutes.
5. Set the Air fryer to 300 º F and cook for 10 more minutes.
6. Dish out the chicken drumsticks onto a serving platter and serve hot.

Nutrition Facts Per Serving:
Calories: 341, Fat: 14.1g, Carbohydrates: 3.3g, Sugar: 1.8g, Protein: 47.7g, Sodium: 182mg

Chinese Chicken Drumsticks

Prep time: 15 minutes, cook time: 20 minutes; Serves 4

5 Ingredients:
- 4 (6-ounces) chicken drumsticks
- 1 cup corn flour

What you'll need from the store cupboard:
- 1 tablespoon oyster sauce
- 1 teaspoon light soy sauce
- ½ teaspoon sesame oil
- 1 teaspoon Chinese five spice powder
- Salt and white pepper, as required

Instructions:
1. Preheat the Air fryer to 390 º F and grease an Air fryer basket.
2. Mix the sauces, oil, five spice powder, salt, and black pepper in a bowl.
3. Rub the chicken drumsticks with marinade and refrigerate for about 40 minutes.
4. Arrange the drumsticks into the Air Fryer basket in a single layer and cook for about 20 minutes.
5. Dish out the chicken drumsticks onto a serving platter and serve hot.

Nutrition Facts Per Serving:
Calories: 400, Fat: 11.4g, Carbohydrates: 22.7g, Sugar: 0.2g, Protein: 48.9g, Sodium: 279mg

Cheese Stuffed Turkey Breasts

Prep time: 15 minutes, cook time: 18 minutes; Serves 4

5 Ingredients:
- 2 (8-ounces) turkey breast fillets, skinless and boneless, each cut into 2 pieces
- 4 cheddar cheese slices
- 1 tablespoon fresh parsley, minced
- 4 bacon slices

What you'll need from the store cupboard:
- Salt and black pepper, to taste

Instructions:
1. Preheat the Air fryer to 365 º F and grease an Air fryer basket.
2. Make a slit in each turkey piece horizontally and season with salt and black pepper.
3. Insert cheddar cheese slice into the slits and sprinkle with parsley.
4. Wrap each turkey piece with one bacon slice and transfer into the Air fryer basket.
5. Cook for about 18 minutes and dish out to serve warm.

Nutrition Facts Per Serving:
Calories: 376, Fat: 20.2g, Carbohydrates: 1.5g, Sugar: 0g, Protein: 44.5g, Sodium: 639mg

Honey Glazed Chicken Drumsticks

Prep time: 15 minutes, cook time: 22 minutes; Serves 4

5 Ingredients:
- ½ tablespoon fresh rosemary, minced
- 1 tablespoon fresh thyme, minced
- 4 (6-ounces) boneless chicken drumsticks

What you'll need from the store cupboard:
- ¼ cup Dijon mustard
- 1 tablespoon honey
- 2 tablespoons olive oil
- Salt and black pepper, to taste

Instructions:
1. Preheat the Air fryer to 320 º F and grease an Air fryer basket.
2. Mix mustard, honey, oil, herbs, salt, and black pepper in a bowl.
3. Rub the chicken drumsticks with marinade and refrigerate overnight.
4. Arrange the drumsticks into the Air Fryer basket in a single layer and cook for about 12 minutes.
5. Set the Air fryer to 355 º F and cook for 10 more minutes.
6. Dish out the chicken drumsticks onto a serving platter and serve hot.

Nutrition Facts Per Serving:
Calories: 377, Fat: 3.6g, Carbohydrates: 5.9g, Sugar: 4.5g, Protein: 47.6g, Sodium: 353mg

Crispy Chicken Drumsticks

Prep time: 15 minutes, cook time: 20 minutes; Serves 2

5 Ingredients:
- 4 (4-ounces) chicken drumsticks
- ½ cup buttermilk
- ½ cup all-purpose flour
- ½ cup panko breadcrumbs
- 3 tablespoons butter, melted

What you'll need from the store cupboard:
- ¼ teaspoon baking powder
- ¼ teaspoon dried oregano
- ¼ teaspoon dried thyme
- ¼ teaspoon celery salt
- ¼ teaspoon garlic powder
- ¼ teaspoon ground ginger
- ¼ teaspoon cayenne pepper
- ¼ teaspoon paprika
- Salt and ground black pepper, as required

Instructions:
1. Preheat the Air fryer to 390 º F and grease an Air fryer basket.
2. Put the chicken drumsticks and buttermilk in a resealable plastic bag.
3. Seal the bag tightly and refrigerate for about 3 hours.
4. Mix the flour, breadcrumbs, baking powder, herbs and spices in a bowl.
5. Remove the chicken drumsticks from bag and coat chicken drumsticks evenly with the seasoned flour mixture.
6. Transfer the chicken drumsticks into the Air fryer basket and cook for about 20 minutes, flipping once in between.
7. Dish out and serve hot.

Nutrition Facts Per Serving:
Calories: 771, Fat: 33.1g, Carbohydrates: 32.1g, Sugar: 3.2g, Protein: 68.7g, Sodium: 449mg

Chicken and Veggie Kabobs

Prep time: 20 minutes, cook time: 30 minutes; Serves 3

5 Ingredients:
- 1 lb. skinless, boneless chicken thighs, cut into cubes
- ½ cup plain Greek yogurt
- 2 small tomatoes, seeded and cut into large chunks
- 1 large red onion, cut into large chunks
- Wooden skewers, presoaked

What you'll need from the store cupboard:
- 1 tablespoon olive oil
- 2 teaspoons curry powder
- ½ teaspoon smoked paprika
- ¼ teaspoon cayenne pepper

- Salt, to taste

Instructions:
1. Preheat the Air fryer to 360 ° F and grease an Air fryer pan.
2. Mix the chicken, oil, yogurt, and spices in a large baking dish.
3. Thread chicken cubes, tomatoes and onion onto presoaked wooden skewers.
4. Coat the skewers generously with marinade and refrigerate for about 3 hours.
5. Transfer half of the skewers in the Air fryer pan and cook for about 15 minutes.
6. Repeat with the remaining mixture and dish out to serve warm.

Nutrition Facts Per Serving:
Calories: 222, Fat: 8.2g, Carbohydrates: 8.7g, Sugar: 5.3g, Protein: 27.9g, Sodium: 104mg

Sweet and Sour Chicken Thighs

Prep time: 15 minutes, cook time: 20 minutes; Serves 2

5 Ingredients:
- 1 scallion, finely chopped
- 2 (4-ounces) skinless, boneless chicken thighs
- ½ cup corn flour

What you'll need from the store cupboard:
- 1 garlic clove, minced
- ½ tablespoon soy sauce
- ½ tablespoon rice vinegar
- 1 teaspoon sugar
- Salt and black pepper, as required

Instructions:
1. Preheat the Air fryer to 390 ° F and grease an Air fryer basket.
2. Mix all the ingredients except chicken and corn flour in a bowl.
3. Place the corn flour in another bowl.
4. Coat the chicken thighs into the marinade and then dredge into the corn flour.
5. Arrange the chicken thighs into the Air Fryer basket, skin side down and cook for about 10 minutes.
6. Set the Air fryer to 355 ° F and cook for 10 more minutes.
7. Dish out the chicken thighs onto a serving platter and serve hot.

Nutrition Facts Per Serving:
Calories: 264, Fat: 5.2g, Carbohydrates: 25.3g, Sugar: 2.8g, Protein: 27.8g, Sodium: 347mg

Parmesan Chicken Cutlets

Prep time: 15 minutes, cook time: 30 minutes; Serves 4

5 Ingredients:
- ¾ cup all-purpose flour
- 2 large eggs
- 1½ cups panko breadcrumbs
- ¼ cup Parmesan cheese, grated
- 4 (6-ounces) (¼-inch thick) skinless, boneless chicken cutlets

What you'll need from the store cupboard:
- 1 tablespoon mustard powder
- Salt and black pepper, to taste

Instructions:
1. Preheat the Air fryer to 355 ° F and grease an Air fryer basket.
2. Place the flour in a shallow bowl and whisk the eggs in a second bowl.
3. Mix the breadcrumbs, cheese, mustard powder, salt, and black pepper in a third bowl.
4. Season the chicken with salt and black pepper and coat the chicken with flour.
5. Dip the chicken into whisked eggs and finally dredge into the breadcrumb mixture.
6. Arrange the chicken cutlets into the Air fryer basket and cook for about 30 minutes.
7. Dish out in a platter and immediately serve.

Nutrition Facts Per Serving:
Calories: 503, Fat: 42.3g, Carbohydrates: 42g, Sugar: 1.3g, Protein: 49.3g, Sodium: 226mg

Cajun Chicken Thighs

Prep time: 15 minutes, cook time: 25 minutes; Serves 4

5 Ingredients:
- ½ cup all-purpose flour
- 1 egg
- 4 (4-ounces) skin-on chicken thighs

What you'll need from the store cupboard:
- 1½ tablespoons Cajun seasoning
- 1 teaspoon seasoning salt

Instructions:
1. Preheat the Air fryer to 355 º F and grease an Air fryer basket.
2. Mix the flour, Cajun seasoning and salt in a bowl.
3. Whisk the egg in another bowl and coat the chicken thighs with the flour mixture.
4. Dip into the egg and dredge again into the flour mixture.
5. Arrange the chicken thighs into the Air Fryer basket, skin side down and cook for about 25 minutes.
6. Dish out the chicken thighs onto a serving platter and serve hot.

Nutrition Facts Per Serving:
Calories: 353, Fat: 18.8g, Carbohydrates: 12g, Sugar: 0.1g, Protein: 31.5g, Sodium: 749mg

Spiced Chicken Breasts

Prep time: 20 minutes, cook time: 23 minutes; Serves 4

5 Ingredients:
- 2 tablespoons butter, melted
- 4 (6-ounces) boneless, skinless chicken breasts

What you'll need from the store cupboard:
- ¼ teaspoon garlic powder
- ¼ teaspoon onion powder
- ¼ teaspoon smoked paprika
- Salt and black pepper, as required

Instructions:
1. Preheat the Air fryer to 350 º F and grease an Air fryer basket.
2. Mix butter and spices in a bowl and coat the chicken with this mixture.
3. Transfer into the Air fryer and cook for about 23 minutes, flipping once in between.
4. Dish out the chicken into a serving platter and serve hot.

Nutrition Facts Per Serving:
Calories: 376, Fat: 49.3g, Carbohydrates: 0.3g, Sugar: 0.1g, Protein: 49.3g, Sodium: 226mg

Buffalo Chicken Tenders

Prep time: 20 minutes, cook time: 12 minutes; Serves 3

5 Ingredients:
- 1 tablespoon water
- 1 large egg
- 16 ounces boneless, skinless chicken breasts, sliced into tenders
- ½ cup pork rinds, crushed
- 2 tablespoons butter, melted

What you'll need from the store cupboard:
- ½ cup unflavored whey protein powder
- ½ teaspoon garlic powder
- Salt and ground black pepper, as required
- ¼ cup buffalo wing sauce

Instructions:
1. Preheat the Air fryer to 400 º F and grease an Air fryer basket.
2. Whisk the egg and water in a bowl and coat the chicken with it.
3. Mix the pork rinds, protein powder, garlic powder, salt, and black pepper in another bowl.
4. Coat the chicken tenders with the pork rinds mixture and arrange into the Air Fryer basket.
5. Drizzle with the melted butter and cook for about 12 minutes.
6. Dish out the chicken tenders into a bowl and top with the buffalo sauce to serve hot.

Nutrition Facts Per Serving:
Calories: 292, Fat: 12.9g, Carbohydrates: 0.9g, Sugar: 0.2g, Protein: 43.6g, Sodium: 261mg

Breaded Chicken Tenderloins

Prep time: 15 minutes, cook time: 12 minutes; Serves 4

5 Ingredients:
- 1 egg, beaten
- ½ cup breadcrumbs
- 8 skinless, boneless chicken tenderloins

What you'll need from the store cupboard:
- 2 tablespoons vegetable oil

Instructions:
1. Preheat the Air fryer to 355 º F and grease an Air fryer basket.
2. Whisk the egg in a bowl and mix vegetable oil and breadcrumbs in another bowl.
3. Dip the chicken tenderloins into the whisked egg and then coat with the breadcrumb mixture.
4. Arrange the chicken tenderloins into the Air Fryer basket and cook for about 12 minutes.
5. Dish out the chicken tenderloins into a platter and serve hot.

Nutrition Facts Per Serving:
Calories: 271, Fats: 11.5g, Carbohydrates: 12g, Sugar: 0.9g, Proteins: 30.4g, Sodium: 113mg

Oats Crusted Chicken Breasts

Prep time: 20 minutes, cook time: 12 minutes; Serves 2

5 Ingredients:
- 2 (6-ounces) chicken breasts
- ¾ cup oats
- 1 tablespoon fresh parsley
- 2 medium eggs

What you'll need from the store cupboard:
- Salt and black pepper, to taste
- 2 tablespoons mustard powder

Instructions:
1. Preheat the Air fryer to 350 º F and grease an Air fryer grill pan.
2. Season the chicken pieces with salt and black pepper and keep aside.
3. Put the oats, mustard powder, parsley, salt and black pepper in a blender and pulse until coarse.
4. Place the oat mixture into a shallow bowl and whisk the eggs in another bowl.
5. Dredge the chicken in the oat mixture and dip into the whisked eggs.
6. Arrange the chicken breasts into the Air fryer grill pan and cook for about 12 minutes, flipping once in between.
7. Dish out the chicken into a serving platter and serve hot.

Nutrition Facts Per Serving:
Calories: 556, Fat: 22.2g, Carbohydrates: 25.1g, Sugar: 1.4g, Protein: 61.6g, Sodium: 289mg

Cheesy Chicken Breasts

Prep time: 20 minutes, cook time: 22 minutes; Serves 2

5 Ingredients:
- 2 (6-ounces) chicken breasts
- 1 egg, beaten
- 4 ounces breadcrumbs
- 1 tablespoon fresh basil
- ¼ cup Parmesan cheese, grated

What you'll need from the store cupboard:
- 2 tablespoons vegetable oil
- ¼ cup pasta sauce

Instructions:
1. Preheat the Air fryer to 350 º F and grease an Air fryer basket.
2. Whisk egg in a bowl and mix breadcrumbs, vegetable oil and basil in another bowl.
3. Dip the chicken breasts into the egg and then coat with the breadcrumb mixture.
4. Arrange the chicken breasts into the Air fryer basket and cook for about 15 minutes.
5. Top the chicken breasts with pasta sauce and Parmesan cheese.
6. Cook for about 7 more minutes and dish out in a serving platter.

Nutrition Facts Per Serving:
Calories: 623, Fat: 25.8g, Carbohydrates: 44.3g, Sugar: 6.2g, Protein: 51g, Sodium: 739mg

Spinach Stuffed Chicken Breasts

Prep time: 15 minutes, cook time: 29 minutes; Serves 2

5 Ingredients:
- 1¾ ounces fresh spinach
- ¼ cup ricotta cheese, shredded
- 2 (4-ounces) skinless, boneless chicken breasts
- 2 tablespoons cheddar cheese, grated

What you' ll need from the store cupboard:
- 1 tablespoon olive oil
- Salt and ground black pepper, as required
- ¼ teaspoon paprika

Instructions:
1. Preheat the Air fryer to 390 º F and grease an Air fryer basket.
2. Heat olive oil in a medium skillet over medium heat and cook spinach for about 4 minutes.
3. Add the ricotta and cook for about 1 minute.
4. Cut the slits in each chicken breast horizontally and stuff with the spinach mixture.
5. Season each chicken breast evenly with salt and black pepper and top with cheddar cheese and paprika.
6. Arrange chicken breasts into the Air fryer basket in a single layer and cook for about 25 minutes.
7. Dish out and serve hot.

Nutrition Facts Per Serving:
Calories: 279, Fat: 16g, Carbohydrates: 2.7g, Sugar: 0.3g, Protein: 31.4g, Sodium: 220mg

Chicken with Veggies

Prep time: 20 minutes, cook time: 45 minutes; Serves 2

5 Ingredients:
- 4 small artichoke hearts, quartered
- 4 fresh large button mushrooms, quartered
- ½ small onion, cut in large chunks
- 2 skinless, boneless chicken breasts
- 2 tablespoons fresh parsley, chopped

What you' ll need from the store cupboard:
- 2 garlic cloves, minced
- 2 tablespoons chicken broth
- 2 tablespoons red wine vinegar
- 2 tablespoons olive oil
- 1 tablespoon Dijon mustard
- 1/8 teaspoon dried thyme
- 1/8 teaspoon dried basil
- Salt and black pepper, as required

Instructions:
1. Preheat the Air fryer to 350 º F and grease a baking dish lightly.
2. Mix the garlic, broth, vinegar, olive oil, mustard, thyme, and basil in a bowl.
3. Place the artichokes, mushrooms, onions, salt, and black pepper in the baking dish.
4. Layer with the chicken breasts and spread half of the mustard mixture evenly on it.
5. Transfer the baking dish into the Air fryer basket and cook for about 23 minutes.
6. Coat the chicken breasts with the remaining mustard mixture and flip the side.
7. Cook for about 22 minutes and serve garnished with parsley.

Nutrition Facts Per Serving:
Calories: 448, Fat: 19.1g, Carbohydrates: 39.1g, Sugar: 5g, Protein: 38.5g, Sodium: 566mg

Air Fried Crispy Chicken Tenders

Prep time: 20 minutes, cook time: 30 minutes; Serves 3

5 Ingredients:
- 2 (6-ounces) boneless, skinless chicken breasts, pounded into ½-inch thickness and cut into tenders
- ½ cup all-purpose flour
- 1½ cups panko breadcrumbs
- ¼ cup Parmesan cheese, finely grated
- 2 large eggs

What you' ll need from the store cupboard:
- 1½ teaspoons Worcestershire sauce, divided
- ¾ cup buttermilk

- ½ teaspoon smoked paprika, divided
- Salt and ground black pepper, as required

Instructions:

1. Preheat the Air fryer to 400 º F and grease an Air fryer basket.
2. Mix buttermilk, ¾ teaspoon of Worcestershire sauce, ¼ teaspoon of paprika, salt, and black pepper in a bowl.
3. Combine the flour, remaining paprika, salt, and black pepper in another bowl.
4. Whisk the egg and remaining Worcestershire sauce in a third bowl.
5. Mix the panko breadcrumbs and Parmesan cheese in a fourth bowl.
6. Put the chicken tenders into the buttermilk mixture and refrigerate overnight.
7. Remove the chicken tenders from the buttermilk mixture and dredge into the flour mixture.
8. Dip into the egg and coat with the breadcrumb mixture.
9. Arrange half of the chicken tenders into the Air Fryer basket and cook for about 15 minutes, flipping once in between.
10. Repeat with the remaining mixture and dish out to serve hot.

Nutrition Facts Per Serving:
Calories: 537, Fat: 15.5g, Carbohydrates: 50.1g, Sugar: 4.8g, Protein: 48.2g, Sodium: 597mg

Bacon Wrapped Chicken Breasts

Prep time: 20 minutes, cook time: 23 minutes; Serves 4

5 Ingredients:
- 6-7 Fresh basil leaves
- 2 tablespoons water
- 2 (8-ounces) chicken breasts, cut each breast in half horizontally
- 12 bacon strips

What you' ll need from the store cupboard:
- 2 tablespoons fish sauce
- 1 tablespoon palm sugar
- Salt and ground black pepper, as required
- 1½ teaspoons honey

Instructions:

1. Preheat the Air fryer to 365 º F and grease an Air fryer basket.
2. Cook the palm sugar in a small heavy-bottomed pan over medium-low heat for about 3 minutes until caramelized.
3. Stir in the basil, fish sauce and water and dish out in a bowl.
4. Season each chicken breast with salt and black pepper and coat with the palm sugar mixture.
5. Refrigerate to marinate for about 6 hours and wrap each chicken piece with 3 bacon strips.
6. Dip into the honey and arrange into the Air Fryer basket.
7. Cook for about 20 minutes, flipping once in between.
8. Dish out in a serving platter and serve hot.
9. Refrigerate to marinate for about 4-6 hours.

Nutrition Facts Per Serving:
Calories: 365, Fat: 24.8g, Carbohydrates: 2.7g, Sugar: 2.1g, Protein: 30.2g, Sodium: 1300mg

BBQ Chicken Wings

Prep time: 10 minutes, cook time: 30 minutes; Serves 4

5 Ingredients:
- 2 pounds chicken wings, cut into drumettes and flats

What you' ll need from the store cupboard:
- ½ cup BBQ sauce

Instructions:

1. Preheat the Air fryer to 380 º F and grease an Air fryer basket.
2. Arrange the chicken wings into the Air Fryer basket and cook for about 6 minutes.
3. Dish out the chicken wings onto a serving platter and drizzle with the BBQ sauce to serve.

Nutrition Facts Per Serving:
Calories: 478, Fat: 16.9g, Carbohydrates: 11.3g, Sugar: 8.1g, Protein: 65.6g, Sodium: 545mg

Chicken and Scallion Kabobs

Prep time: 20 minutes, cook time: 24 minutes; Serves 4

5 Ingredients:
- 4 (4-ounces) skinless, boneless chicken thighs, cubed into 1-inch size
- 2 bell peppers, cut into 1-inch pieces lengthwise
- Wooden skewers, presoaked

What you' ll need from the store cupboard:
- ¼ cup light soy sauce
- 1 tablespoon mirin
- 1 teaspoon garlic salt
- 1 teaspoon sugar

Instructions:
1. Preheat the Air fryer to 355 º F and grease an Air fryer pan.
2. Mix the soy sauce, mirin, garlic salt, and sugar in a large baking dish.
3. Thread chicken and bell peppers onto presoaked wooden skewers.
4. Coat the skewers generously with marinade and refrigerate for about 3 hours.
5. Transfer the skewers in the Air fryer pan in a single layer and cook for about 12 minutes.
6. Dish out in a platter and serve warm.

Nutrition Facts Per Serving:
Calories: 161, Fat: 4.1g, Carbohydrates: 6.9g, Sugar: 4g, Protein: 26.2g, Sodium: 781mg

Chicken with Broccoli and Rice

Prep time: 20 minutes, cook time: 15 minutes; Serves 3

5 Ingredients:
- 1 pound boneless, skinless chicken breasts, sliced
- 1½ cups instant white rice
- 1/3 cup cream soup
- 1½ cups small broccoli florets
- 1/6 cup butter

What you' ll need from the store cupboard:
- 1½ tablespoons dried parsley, crushed
- ½ tablespoon onion powder
- ½ tablespoon garlic powder
- ¼ teaspoon red chili powder
- ¼ teaspoon paprika

Instructions:
1. Preheat the Air fryer to 390 º F and grease an Air fryer basket.
2. Mix the parsley and spices in a bowl.
3. Coat the chicken slices generously with the spice mixture.
4. Arrange 3 large pieces of foil and put ½ cup of rice over each foil piece.
5. Layer with 1/6 of chicken, 1 tablespoon of butter, ½ cup of broccoli, 2 tablespoons of cream soup and ½ cup of water.
6. Fold the foil tightly and transfer into the Air Fryer basket.
7. Cook for about 15 minutes and dish out to serve hot.

Nutrition Facts Per Serving:
Calories: 583, Fat: 23.1g, Carbohydrates: 65.6g, Sugar: 1.6g, Protein: 42.7g, Sodium: 374mg

Simple Turkey Breast

Prep time: 20 minutes, cook time: 40 minutes; Serves 10

5 Ingredients:
- 1 (8-pounds) bone-in turkey breast

What you' ll need from the store cupboard:
- Salt and black pepper, as required
- 2 tablespoons olive oil

Instructions:
1. Preheat the Air fryer to 360 º F and grease an Air fryer basket.
2. Season the turkey breast with salt and black pepper and drizzle with oil.
3. Arrange the turkey breast into the Air Fryer basket, skin side down and cook for about 20 minutes.
4. Flip the side and cook for another 20 minutes.
5. Dish out in a platter and cut into desired size slices to serve.

Nutrition Facts Per Serving:
Calories: 719, Fat: 35.9g, Carbohydrates: 0g, Sugar: 0g, Protein: 97.2g, Sodium: 386mg

Crunchy Chicken Wings

Prep time: 20 minutes, cook time: 25 minutes; Serves 2

5 Ingredients:
- 2 lemongrass stalk (white portion), minced
- 1 onion, finely chopped
- 1 pound chicken wings, rinsed and trimmed
- ½ cup cornstarch

What you'll need from the store cupboard:
- 1 tablespoon soy sauce
- 1½ tablespoons honey
- Salt and white pepper, as required

Instructions:
1. Preheat the Air fryer to 355 º F and grease an Air fryer basket.
2. Mix the lemongrass, onion, soy sauce, honey, salt, and white pepper in a bowl.
3. Coat the wings generously with marinade and refrigerate, covered to marinate overnight.
4. Arrange the chicken wings into the Air Fryer basket and cook for about 25 minutes.
5. Dish out the chicken wings onto a serving platter and serve hot.

Nutrition Facts Per Serving:
Calories: 724, Fat: 36.2g, Carbohydrates: 56.9g, Sugar: 15.4g, Protein: 43.5g, Sodium: 702mg

Herbed Turkey Breast

Prep time: 15 minutes, cook time: 35 minutes; Serves 3

5 Ingredients:
- 1 (2½-pounds) bone-in, skin-on turkey breast

What you'll need from the store cupboard:
- 1 teaspoon dried thyme, crushed
- 1 teaspoon dried rosemary, crushed
- ½ teaspoon dried sage, crushed
- ½ teaspoon dark brown sugar
- ½ teaspoon garlic powder
- ½ teaspoon paprika
- 1 tablespoon olive oil

Instructions:
1. Preheat the Air fryer to 360 º F and grease an Air fryer basket.
2. Mix the herbs, brown sugar, and spices in a bowl.
3. Drizzle the turkey breast with oil and season with the herb mixture.
4. Arrange the turkey breast into the Air Fryer basket, skin side down and cook for about 35 minutes, flipping once in between.
5. Dish out in a platter and cut into desired size slices to serve.

Nutrition Facts Per Serving:
Calories: 688, Fat: 31.8g, Carbohydrates: 1.6g, Sugar: 0.8g, Protein: 81.2g, Sodium: 473mg

Buffalo Chicken Wings

Prep time: 20 minutes, cook time: 22 minutes; Serves 6

5 Ingredients:
- 2 pounds chicken wings, cut into drumettes and flats

What you'll need from the store cupboard:
- 1 teaspoon chicken seasoning
- 1 teaspoon garlic powder
- Ground black pepper, to taste
- 1 tablespoon olive oil
- ¼ cup red hot sauce
- 2 tablespoons low-sodium soy sauce

Instructions:
1. Preheat the Air fryer to 400 º F and grease an Air fryer basket.
2. Season each chicken wing evenly with chicken seasoning, garlic powder, and black pepper.
3. Arrange the chicken wings into the Air Fryer basket and drizzle with olive oil.
4. Cook for about 10 minutes and dish out the chicken wings onto a serving platter.
5. Pour the red hot sauce and soy sauce on the chicken wings and toss to coat well.
6. Cook for about 12 minutes and dish out to serve hot.

Nutrition Facts Per Serving:
Calories: 311, Fat: 13.6g, Carbohydrates: 0.6g, Sugar: 0.3g, Protein: 44g, Sodium: 491mg

Sweet Chicken Kabobs

Prep time: 20 minutes, cook time: 14 minutes; Serves 3

5 Ingredients:
- 4 scallions, chopped
- 2 teaspoons sesame seeds, toasted
- 1 pound chicken tenders
- Wooden skewers, pres oaked

What you' ll need from the store cupboard:
- 1 tablespoon fresh ginger, finely grated
- 4 garlic cloves, minced
- ½ cup pineapple juice
- ½ cup soy sauce
- ¼ cup sesame oil
- A pinch of black pepper

Instructions:
1. Preheat the Air fryer to 390 º F and grease an Air fryer pan.
2. Mix scallion, ginger, garlic, pineapple juice, soy sauce, oil, sesame seeds, and black pepper in a large baking dish.
3. Thread chicken tenders onto pre-soaked wooden skewers.
4. Coat the skewers generously with marinade and refrigerate for about 2 hours.
5. Transfer half of the skewers in the Air fryer pan and cook for about 7 minutes.
6. Repeat with the remaining mixture and dish out to serve warm.

Nutrition Facts Per Serving:
Calories: 392, Fat: 23g, Carbohydrates: 9.9g, Sugar: 4.1g, Protein: 35.8g, Sodium: 1800mg

Chicken with Apple

Prep time: 10 minutes, cook time: 20 minutes; Serves 8

5 Ingredients:
- 1 shallot, thinly sliced
- 1 teaspoon fresh thyme, minced
- 2 (4-ounces) boneless, skinless chicken thighs, sliced into chunks
- 1 large apple, cored and cubed

What you' ll need from the store cupboard:
- 1 tablespoon fresh ginger, finely grated
- ½ cup apple cider
- 2 tablespoons maple syrup
- Salt and black pepper, as required

Instructions:
1. Preheat the Air fryer to 390 º F and grease an Air fryer basket.
2. Mix the shallot, ginger, thyme, apple cider, maple syrup, salt, and black pepper in a bowl.
3. Coat the chicken generously with the marinade and refrigerate to marinate for about 8 hours.
4. Arrange the chicken pieces and cubed apples into the Air Fryer basket and cook for about 20 minutes, flipping once halfway.
5. Dish out the chicken mixture into a serving bowl to serve.

Nutrition Facts Per Serving:
Calories: 299, Fat: 26.2g, Carbohydrates: 39.9g, Sugar: 30.4g, Protein: 26.2g, Sodium: 125mg

Jerk Chicken, Pineapple and Veggie Kabobs

Prep time: 20 minutes, cook time: 18 minutes; Serves 8

5 Ingredients:
- 8 (4-ounces) boneless, skinless chicken thigh fillets, trimmed and cut into cubes
- 2 large zucchinis, sliced
- 8 ounces white mushrooms, stems removed
- 1 (20-ounces) can pineapple chunks, drained
- Wooden skewers, presoaked

What you' ll need from the store cupboard:
- 1 tablespoon jerk seasoning
- Salt and black pepper, to taste
- 1 tablespoon jerk sauce

Instructions:
1. Preheat the Air fryer to 370 º F and grease an Air fryer pan.
2. Mix the chicken cubes and jerk seasoning in a bowl.
3. Season the zucchini slices and mushrooms evenly with salt and black pepper.

4. Thread chicken, zucchinis, mushrooms and pineapple chunks onto presoaked wooden skewers.
5. Transfer half of the skewers in the Air fryer pan and cook for about 9 minutes.
6. Repeat with the remaining mixture and dish out to serve hot.

Nutrition Facts Per Serving:
Calories: 274, Fat: 8.7g, Carbohydrates: 14.1g, Sugar: 9.9g, Protein: 35.1g, Sodium: 150mg

Curried Chicken

Prep time: 15 minutes, cook time: 18 minutes; Serves 3

5 Ingredients:
- 1 pound boneless chicken, cubed
- ½ tablespoon cornstarch
- 1 egg
- 1 medium yellow onion, thinly sliced
- ½ cup evaporated milk

What you'll need from the store cupboard:
- 1 tablespoon light soy sauce
- 2 tablespoons olive oil
- 3 teaspoons garlic, minced
- 1 teaspoon fresh ginger, grated
- 5 curry leaves
- 1 teaspoon curry powder
- 1 tablespoon chili sauce
- 1 teaspoon sugar
- Salt and black pepper, as required

Instructions:

1. Preheat the Air fryer to 390 º F and grease an Air fryer basket.
2. Mix the chicken cubes, soy sauce, cornstarch and egg in a bowl and keep aside for about 1 hour.
3. Arrange the chicken cubes into the Air Fryer basket and cook for about 10 minutes.
4. Heat olive oil in a medium skillet and add onion, green chili, garlic, ginger, and curry leaves.
5. Sauté for about 4 minutes and stir in the chicken cubes, curry powder, chili sauce, sugar, salt, and black pepper.
6. Mix well and add the evaporated milk.
7. Cook for about 4 minutes and dish out the chicken mixture into a serving bowl to serve.

Nutrition Facts Per Serving:
Calories: 363, Fat: 19g, Carbohydrates: 10g, Sugar: 0.8g, Protein: 37.1g, Sodium: 789mg

Glazed Turkey Breast

Prep time: 15 minutes, cook time: 55 minutes; Serves 8

5 Ingredients:
- 1 (5-pounds) boneless turkey breast
- 1 tablespoon butter, softened

What you'll need from the store cupboard:
- 1 teaspoon dried thyme, crushed
- ½ teaspoon dried sage, crushed
- ½ teaspoon smoked paprika
- Salt and ground black pepper, as required
- 2 teaspoons olive oil
- ¼ cup maple syrup
- 2 tablespoons Dijon mustard

Instructions:
1. Preheat the Air fryer to 350 º F and grease an Air fryer basket.
2. Mix the herbs, paprika, salt, and black pepper in a bowl.
3. Drizzle the turkey breast with oil and season with the herb mixture.
4. Arrange the turkey breast into the Air Fryer basket and cook for about 50 minutes, flipping twice in between.
5. Meanwhile, mix the maple syrup, mustard, and butter in a bowl.
6. Coat the turkey evenly with maple glaze and cook for about 5 minutes.
7. Dish out the turkey breast onto a cutting board and cut into desired size slices to serve.

Nutrition Facts Per Serving:
Calories: 302, Fat: 3.3g, Carbohydrates: 5.6g, Sugar: 4.7g, Protein: 56.2g, Sodium: 170mg

Chicken with Carrots

Prep time: 15 minutes, cook time: 25 minutes; Serves 2

5 Ingredients:
- 1 carrot, peeled and thinly sliced
- 2 tablespoons butter
- 2 (4-ounces) chicken breast halves
- 1 tablespoon fresh rosemary, chopped

What you' ll need from the store cupboard:
- Salt and black pepper, as required
- 2 tablespoons fresh lemon juice

Instructions:
1. Preheat the Air fryer to 375 ° F and grease an Air fryer basket.
2. Place 2 square-shaped parchment papers onto a smooth surface and arrange carrot slices evenly in the center of each parchment paper.
3. Drizzle ½ tablespoon of butter over carrot slices and season with salt and black pepper.
4. Layer with chicken breasts and top with rosemary, lemon juice and remaining butter.
5. Fold the parchment paper on all sides and transfer into the Air fryer.
6. Cook for about 25 minutes and dish out in a serving platter to serve.

Nutrition Facts Per Serving:
Calories: 339, Fats: 20.3g, Carbohydrates: 4.4g, Sugar: 1.8g, Proteins: 33.4g, Sodium: 2822mg

Citrus Turkey Legs

Prep time: 15 minutes, cook time: 30 minutes; Serves 2

5 Ingredients:
- 1 tablespoon fresh rosemary, minced
- 2 turkey legs

What you' ll need from the store cupboard:
- 2 garlic cloves, minced
- 1 teaspoon fresh lime zest, finely grated
- 2 tablespoons olive oil
- 1 tablespoon fresh lime juice
- Salt and black pepper, as required

Instructions:
1. Preheat the Air fryer to 350 ° F and grease an Air fryer basket.
2. Mix the garlic, rosemary, lime zest, oil, lime juice, salt, and black pepper in a bowl.
3. Coat the turkey legs with marinade and refrigerate to marinate for about 8 hours.
4. Arrange the turkey legs into the Air Fryer basket and cook for about 30 minutes, flipping once in between.
5. Dish out the turkey legs into serving plates.

Nutrition Facts Per Serving:
Calories: 458, Fat: 29.5g, Carbohydrates: 2.3g, Sugar: 0.1g, Protein: 44.6g, Sodium: 247mg

Chicken with Veggies and Rice

Prep time: 15 minutes, cook time: 20 minutes; Serves 3

5 Ingredients:
- 3 cups cold boiled white rice
- 1 cup cooked chicken, diced
- ½ cup frozen carrots
- ½ cup frozen peas
- ½ cup onion, chopped

What you' ll need from the store cupboard:
- 6 tablespoons soy sauce
- 1 tablespoon vegetable oil

Instructions:
1. Preheat the Air fryer to 360 ° F and grease a 7" nonstick pan.
2. Mix the rice, soy sauce, and vegetable oil in a bowl.
3. Stir in the remaining ingredients and mix until well combined.
4. Transfer the rice mixture into the pan and place in the Air fryer.
5. Cook for about 20 minutes and dish out to serve immediately.

Nutrition Facts Per Serving:
Calories: 405, Fat: 6.4g, Carbohydrates: 63g, Sugar: 3.5g, Protein: 21.7g, Sodium: 1500mg

Delicious Chicken Burgers

Prep time: 20 minutes, cook time: 30 minutes; Serves 4

5 Ingredients:
- 4 boneless, skinless chicken breasts
- 1¾ ounces plain flour
- 2 eggs
- 4 hamburger buns, split and toasted
- 4 mozzarella cheese slices

What you' ll need from the store cupboard:
- 1 teaspoon mustard powder
- ½ teaspoon paprika
- 1 teaspoon Worcestershire sauce
- ¼ teaspoon dried parsley
- ¼ teaspoon dried tarragon
- ¼ teaspoon dried oregano
- 1 teaspoon dried garlic
- 1 teaspoon chicken seasoning
- ½ teaspoon cayenne pepper
- Salt and black pepper, as required

Instructions:
1. Preheat the Air fryer to 355 º F and grease an Air fryer basket.
2. Put the chicken breasts, mustard, paprika, Worcestershire sauce, salt, and black pepper in a food processor and pulse until minced.
3. Make 4 equal-sized patties from the mixture.
4. Place the flour in a shallow bowl and whisk the egg in a second bowl.
5. Combine dried herbs and spices in a third bowl.
6. Coat each chicken patty with flour, dip into whisked egg and then coat with breadcrumb mixture.
7. Arrange the chicken patties into the Air fryer basket in a single layer and cook for about 30 minutes, flipping once in between.
8. Place half bun in a plate, layer with lettuce leaf, patty and cheese slice.
9. Cover with bun top and dish out to serve warm.

Nutrition Facts Per Serving:
Calories: 562, Fat: 20.3g, Carbohydrates: 33g, Sugar: 3.3g, Protcin: 58.7g, Sodium: 560mg

Duck Breast with Figs

Prep time: 20 minutes, cook time: 45 minutes; Serves 2

5 Ingredients:
- 1 pound boneless duck breast
- 6 fresh figs, halved
- 1 tablespoon fresh thyme, chopped

What you' ll need from the store cupboard:
- 2 cups fresh pomegranate juice
- 2 tablespoons lemon juice
- 3 tablespoons brown sugar
- 1 teaspoon olive oil
- Salt and black pepper, as required

Instructions:
1. Preheat the Air fryer to 400 º F and grease an Air fryer basket.
2. Put the pomegranate juice, lemon juice, and brown sugar in a medium saucepan over medium heat.
3. Bring to a boil and simmer on low heat for about 25 minutes.
4. Season the duck breasts generously with salt and black pepper.
5. Arrange the duck breasts into the Air fryer basket, skin side up and cook for about 14 minutes, flipping once in between.
6. Dish out the duck breasts onto a cutting board for about 10 minutes.
7. Meanwhile, put the figs, olive oil, salt, and black pepper in a bowl until well mixed.
8. Set the Air fryer to 400 º F and arrange the figs into the Air fryer basket.
9. Cook for about 5 more minutes and dish out in a platter.
10. Put the duck breast with the roasted figs and drizzle with warm pomegranate juice mixture.
11. Garnish with fresh thyme and serve warm.

Nutrition Facts Per Serving:
Calories: 699, Fat: 12.1g, Carbohydrates: 90g, Sugar: 74g, Protein: 519g, Sodium: 110mg

Buttermilk Brined Turkey Breast

Prep time: 15 minutes, cook time: 20 minutes; Serves 8

5 Ingredients:
- ¾ cup brine from a can of olives
- 3½ pounds boneless, skinless turkey breast
- 2 fresh thyme sprigs
- 1 fresh rosemary sprig

What you' ll need from the store cupboard:
- ½ cup buttermilk

Instructions:
1. Preheat the Air fryer to 350 º F and grease an Air fryer basket.
2. Mix olive brine and buttermilk in a bowl until well combined.
3. Place the turkey breast, buttermilk mixture and herb sprigs in a resealable plastic bag.
4. Seal the bag and refrigerate for about 12 hours.
5. Remove the turkey breast from bag and arrange the turkey breast into the Air fryer basket.
6. Cook for about 20 minutes, flipping once in between.
7. Dish out the turkey breast onto a cutting board and cut into desired size slices to serve.

Nutrition Facts Per Serving:
Calories: 215, Fat: 3.5g, Carbohydrates: 9.4g, Sugar: 7.7g, Protein: 34.4g, Sodium: 2000mg

Herbed Duck Legs

Prep time: 10 minutes, cook time: 30 minutes; Serves 2

5 Ingredients:
- ½ tablespoon fresh thyme, chopped
- ½ tablespoon fresh parsley, chopped
- 2 duck legs

What you' ll need from the store cupboard:
- 1 garlic clove, minced
- 1 teaspoon five spice powder
- Salt and black pepper, as required

Instructions:
1. Preheat the Air fryer to 340 º F and grease an Air fryer basket.
2. Mix the garlic, herbs, five spice powder, salt, and black pepper in a bowl.
3. Rub the duck legs with garlic mixture generously and arrange into the Air fryer basket.
4. Cook for about 25 minutes and set the Air fryer to 390 º F.
5. Cook for 5 more minutes and dish out to serve hot.

Nutrition Facts Per Serving:
Calories: 138, Fat: 4.5g, Carbohydrates: 1g, Sugar: 0g, Protein: 25g, Sodium: 82mg

Delightful Turkey Wings

Prep time: 10 minutes, cook time: 26 minutes; Serves 4

5 Ingredients:
- 2 pounds turkey wings

What you' ll need from the store cupboard:
- 4 tablespoons chicken rub
- 3 tablespoons olive oil

Instructions:
1. Preheat the Air fryer to 380 º F and grease an Air fryer basket.
2. Mix the turkey wings, chicken rub, and olive oil in a bowl until well combined.
3. Arrange the turkey wings into the Air fryer basket and cook for about 26 minutes, flipping once in between.
4. Dish out the turkey wings in a platter and serve hot.

Nutrition Facts Per Serving:
Calories: 204, Fat: 15.5g, Carbohydrates: 3g, Sugar: 0g, Protein: 12g, Sodium: 465mg

Duck Rolls

Prep time: 20 minutes, cook time: 40 minutes; Serves 3

5 Ingredients:

- 1 pound duck breast fillet, each cut into 2 pieces
- 3 tablespoons fresh parsley, finely chopped
- 1 small red onion, finely chopped

What you'll need from the store cupboard:

- 1 garlic clove, crushed
- 1½ teaspoons ground cumin
- 1 teaspoon ground cinnamon
- ½ teaspoon red chili powder
- Salt, to taste
- 2 tablespoons olive oil

Instructions:

1. Preheat the Air fryer to 355 º F and grease an Air fryer basket.
2. Mix the garlic, parsley, onion, spices, and 1 tablespoon of olive oil in a bowl.
3. Make a slit in each duck piece horizontally and coat with onion mixture.
4. Roll each duck piece tightly and transfer into the Air fryer basket.
5. Cook for about 40 minutes and cut into desired size slices to serve.

Nutrition Facts Per Serving:
Calories: 239, Fats: 8.2g, Carbohydrates: 3.2g, Sugar: 0.9g, Proteins: 37.5g, Sodium: 46mg

Turkey Meatloaf

Prep time: 20 minutes, cook time: 20 minutes; Serves 4

5 Ingredients:

- 1 pound ground turkey
- 1 cup kale leaves, trimmed and finely chopped
- 1 cup onion, chopped
- ½ cup fresh breadcrumbs
- 1 cup Monterey Jack cheese, grated

What you'll need from the store cupboard:

- 2 garlic cloves, minced
- ¼ cup salsa verde
- 1 teaspoon red chili powder
- ½ teaspoon ground cumin
- ½ teaspoon dried oregano, crushed
- Salt and ground black pepper, as required

Instructions:

1. Preheat the Air fryer to 400 º F and grease an Air fryer basket.
2. Mix all the ingredients in a bowl and divide the turkey mixture into 4 equal-sized portions.
3. Shape each into a mini loaf and arrange the loaves into the Air fryer basket.
4. Cook for about 20 minutes and dish out to serve warm.

Nutrition Facts Per Serving:
Calories: 435, Fat: 23.1g, Carbohydrates: 18.1g, Sugar: 3.6g, Protein: 42.2g, Sodium: 641mg

Spicy Green Crusted Chicken

Prep time: 10 minutes, cook time: 40 minutes; Serves 6

5 Ingredients:

- 6 eggs, beaten
- 6 teaspoons parsley
- 4 teaspoons thyme
- 1 pound chicken pieces

What you'll need from the store cupboard:

- 6 teaspoons oregano
- Salt and freshly ground black pepper, to taste
- 4 teaspoons paprika

Instructions:

1. Preheat the Air fryer to 360 º F and grease an Air fryer basket.
2. Whisk eggs in a bowl and mix all the ingredients in another bowl except chicken pieces.
3. Dip the chicken in eggs and then coat generously with the dry mixture.
4. Arrange half of the chicken pieces in the Air fryer basket and cook for about 20 minutes.
5. Repeat with the remaining mixture and dish out to serve hot.

Nutrition Facts Per Serving:
Calories: 218, Fat: 10.4g, Carbohydrates: 2.6g, Sugar: 0.6g, Protein: 27.9g, Sodium: 128mg

Buttered Duck Breasts

Prep time: 15 minutes, cook time: 22 minutes; Serves 4

5 Ingredients:

- 2 (12-ounces) duck breasts
- 3 tablespoons unsalted butter, melted

What you' ll need from the store cupboard:

- Salt and ground black pepper, as required
- ½ teaspoon dried thyme, crushed
- ¼ teaspoon star anise powder

Instructions:

1. Preheat the Air fryer to 390 ° F and grease an Air fryer basket.
2. Season the duck breasts generously with salt and black pepper.
3. Arrange the duck breasts into the prepared Air fryer basket and cook for about 10 minutes.
4. Dish out the duck breasts and drizzle with melted butter.
5. Season with thyme and star anise powder and place the duck breasts again into the Air fryer basket.
6. Cook for about 12 more minutes and dish out to serve warm.

Nutrition Facts Per Serving:
Calories: 296, Fat: 15.5g, Carbohydrates: 0.1g, Sugar: 0g, Protein: 37.5g, Sodium: 100mg

Beer Coated Duck Breast

Prep time: 15 minutes, cook time: 20 minutes; Serves 2

5 Ingredients:

- 1 tablespoon fresh thyme, chopped
- 1 cup beer
- 1 (10½-ounces) duck breast
- 6 cherry tomatoes

What you' ll need from the store cupboard:

- 1 tablespoon olive oil
- 1 teaspoon mustard
- Salt and ground black pepper, as required
- 1 tablespoon balsamic vinegar

Instructions:

1. Preheat the Air fryer to 390 ° F and grease an Air fryer basket.
2. Mix the olive oil, mustard, thyme, beer, salt, and black pepper in a bowl.
3. Coat the duck breasts generously with marinade and refrigerate, covered for about 4 hours.
4. Cover the duck breasts and arrange into the Air fryer basket.
5. Cook for about 15 minutes and remove the foil from breast.
6. Set the Air fryer to 355 ° F and place the duck breast and tomatoes into the Air Fryer basket.
7. Cook for about 5 minutes and dish out the duck breasts and cherry tomatoes.
8. Drizzle with vinegar and serve immediately.

Nutrition Facts Per Serving:
Calories: 332, Fat: 13.7g, Carbohydrates: 9.2g, Sugar: 2.5g, Protein: 34.6g, Sodium: 88mg

Fried Chicken Thighs

Prep time: 10 minutes, cook time: 25 minutes; Serves 4

5 Ingredients:

- ½ cup almond flour
- 1 egg beaten
- 4 small chicken thighs

What you' ll need from the store cupboard:

- 1½ tablespoons Old Bay Cajun Seasoning
- 1 teaspoon seasoning salt

Instructions:

1. Preheat the Air fryer to 400 ° F for 3 minutes and grease an Air fryer basket.
2. Whisk the egg in a shallow bowl and place the old bay, flour and salt in another bowl.
3. Dip the chicken in the egg and coat with the flour mixture.
4. Arrange the chicken thighs in the Air fryer basket and cook for about 25 minutes.
5. Dish out in a platter and serve warm.

Nutrition Facts Per Serving:
Calories: 180, Fat: 20g, Carbohydrates: 3g, Sugar: 1.2g, Protein: 21g, Sodium: 686mg

Chicken Wings with Prawn Paste

Prep time: 20 minutes, cook time: 8 minutes; Serves 6

5 Ingredients:
- Corn flour, as required
- 2 pounds mid-joint chicken wings

What you'll need from the store cupboard:
- 2 tablespoons prawn paste
- 4 tablespoons olive oil
- 1½ teaspoons sugar
- 2 teaspoons sesame oil
- 1 teaspoon Shaoxing wine
- 2 teaspoons fresh ginger juice

Instructions:
1. Preheat the Air fryer to 360 ° F and grease an Air fryer basket.
2. Mix all the ingredients in a bowl except wings and corn flour.
3. Rub the chicken wings generously with marinade and refrigerate overnight.
4. Coat the chicken wings evenly with corn flour and keep aside.
5. Set the Air fryer to 390 ° F and arrange the chicken wings in the Air fryer basket.
6. Cook for about 8 minutes and dish out to serve hot.

Nutrition Facts Per Serving:
Calories: 416, Fat: 31.5g, Carbohydrates: 11.2g, Sugar: 1.6g, Protein: 24.4g, Sodium: 661mg

Creamy Chicken Tenders

Prep time: 15 minutes, cook time: 20 minutes; Serves 8

5 Ingredients:
- 2 pounds chicken tenders
- 1 cup feta cheese

What you'll need from the store cupboard:
- 4 tablespoons olive oil
- 1 cup cream
- Salt and black pepper, to taste

Instructions:
1. Preheat the Air fryer to 340 ° F and grease an Air fryer basket.
2. Season the chicken tenders with salt and black pepper.
3. Arrange the chicken tenderloins in the Air fryer basket and drizzle with olive oil.\
4. Cook for about 15 minutes and set the Air fryer to 390 ° F.
5. Cook for about 5 more minutes and dish out to serve warm.
6. Repeat with the remaining mixture and dish out to serve hot.

Nutrition Facts Per Serving:
Calories: 344, Fat: 21.1g, Carbohydrates: 1.7g, Sugar: 1.4g, Protein: 35.7g, Sodium: 317mg

Sweet Sriracha Turkey Legs

Prep time: 10 minutes, cook time: 35 minutes; Serves 2

5 Ingredients:
- 1-pound turkey legs
- 1 tablespoon butter
- 1 tablespoon cilantro
- 1 tablespoon chives
- 1 tablespoon scallions

What you'll need from the store cupboard:
- 4 tablespoons sriracha sauce
- 1½ tablespoons soy sauce
- ½ lime, juiced

Instructions:
1. Preheat the Air fryer on Roasting mode to 360 ° F for 3 minutes and grease an Air fryer basket.
2. Arrange the turkey legs in the Air fryer basket and cook for about 30 minutes, flipping several times in between.
3. Mix butter, scallions, sriracha sauce, soy sauce and lime juice in the saucepan and cook for about for 3 minutes until the sauce thickens.
4. Drizzle this sauce over the turkey legs and garnish with cilantro and chives to serve.

Nutrition Facts Per Serving:
Calories: 361, Fat: 16.3g, Carbohydrates: 9.3g, Sugar: 18.2g, Protein: 33.3g, Sodium: 515mg

Chicken Breasts with Chimichurri

Prep time: 15 minutes, cook time: 35 minutes; Serves 1

5 Ingredients:

- 1 chicken breast, bone-in, skin-on

Chimichurri

- ½ bunch fresh cilantro
- 1/4 bunch fresh parsley
- ½ shallot, peeled, cut in quarters

What you' ll need from the store cupboard:

- ½ tablespoon paprika ground
- ½ tablespoon chili powder
- ½ tablespoon fennel ground
- ½ teaspoon black pepper, ground
- ½ teaspoon onion powder
- 1 teaspoon salt
- ½ teaspoon garlic powder
- ½ teaspoon cumin ground
- ½ tablespoon canola oil

Chimichurri

- 2 tablespoons olive oil

- 4 garlic cloves, peeled
- Zest and juice of 1 lemon
- 1 teaspoon kosher salt

Instructions:

1. Preheat the Air fryer to 300 ° F and grease an Air fryer basket.
2. Combine all the spices in a suitable bowl and season the chicken with it.
3. Sprinkle with canola oil and arrange the chicken in the Air fryer basket.
4. Cook for about 35 minutes and dish out in a platter.
5. Put all the ingredients in the blender and blend until smooth.
6. Serve the chicken with chimichurri sauce.

Nutrition Facts Per Serving:
Calories: 140, Fats: 7.9g, Carbohydrates: 1.8g, Sugar: 7.1g, Proteins: 7.2g, Sodium: 581mg

Gyro Seasoned Chicken

Prep time: 10 minutes, cook time: 30 minutes; Serves 4

5 Ingredients:

- 2 pounds chicken thighs

What you' ll need from the store cupboard:

- 1 tablespoon avocado oil
- 2 tablespoons primal palate super gyro seasoning
- 2 tablespoons primal palate new bae seasoning
- 1 tablespoon Himalayan pink salt

Instructions:

1. Preheat the Air fryer to 350 ° F and grease an Air fryer basket.

2. Rub the chicken with avocado oil and half of the spices.
3. Arrange the chicken thighs in the Air fryer basket and cook for about 25 minutes, flipping once in between.
4. Sprinkle the remaining seasoning and cook for 5 more minutes.
5. Dish out and serve warm.

Nutrition Facts Per Serving:
Calories: 545, Fat: 36.4g, Carbohydrates: 0.7g, Sugar: 0g, Protein: 42.5g, Sodium: 272mg

Special Salsa Chicken Steak

Prep time: 10 minutes, cook time: 30 minutes; Serves 6

5 Ingredients:

- 2 pounds chicken steak
- ½ cup shredded Monterey Jack cheese

What you' ll need from the store cupboard:

- 1 cup tomato sauce
- ½ teaspoon garlic powder
- 2 cups salsa
- ½ teaspoon hot pepper sauce
- Salt and black pepper, to taste

Instructions:

1. Preheat the Air fryer to 450 ° F and grease an Air fryer basket.

2. Season the chicken steak with garlic powder, salt and black pepper and marinate for about 8 hours.
3. Mix salsa, tomato sauce and hot pepper sauce in a bowl.
4. Arrange the steak pieces in the Air fryer basket and drizzle with the salsa mixture.
5. Cook for about 30 minutes and dish out to serve hot.

Nutrition Facts Per Serving:
Calories: 345, Fat: 14.3g, Carbohydrates: 7.6g, Sugar: 4.3g, Protein: 45.1g, Sodium: 828mg

Chapter 5 Vegetarian and Vegetable Recipes

Mushrooms with Peas

Prep time: 15 minutes, cook time: 15 minutes; Serves 4

5 Ingredients:
- 16 ounces cremini mushrooms, halved
- ½ cup frozen peas

What you'll need from the store cupboard:
- ½ cup soy sauce
- 4 tablespoons maple syrup
- 4 tablespoons rice vinegar
- 4 garlic cloves, finely chopped
- 2 teaspoons Chinese five spice powder
- ½ teaspoon ground ginger

Instructions:
1. Preheat the Air fryer to 350 º F and grease an Air fryer pan.
2. Mix soy sauce, maple syrup, vinegar, garlic, five spice powder, and ground ginger in a bowl.
3. Arrange the mushrooms in the Air fryer basket and cook for about 10 minutes.
4. Stir in the soy sauce mixture and peas and cook for about 5 more minutes.
5. Dish out the mushroom mixture in plates and serve hot.

Nutrition Facts Per Serving:
Calories: 132, Fats: 0.3g, Carbohydrates: 25g, Sugar: 15.4g, Proteins: 6.1g, Sodium: 6.1mg

Bell Peppers Cups

Prep time: 10 minutes, cook time: 8 minutes; Serves 4

5 Ingredients:
- 8 mini red bell peppers, tops and seeds removed
- 1 teaspoon fresh parsley, chopped
- ¾ cup feta cheese, crumbled

What you'll need from the store cupboard:
- ½ tablespoon olive oil
- Freshly ground black pepper, to taste

Instructions:
1. Preheat the Air fryer to 390 º F and grease an Air fryer basket.
2. Mix feta cheese, parsley, olive oil and black pepper in a bowl.
3. Stuff the bell peppers with feta cheese mixture and arrange in the Air fryer basket.
4. Cook for about 8 minutes and dish out to serve hot.

Nutrition Facts Per Serving:
Calories: 163, Fat: 8.4g, Carbohydrates: 15.5g, Sugar: 11.2 g, Protein: 6.4g, Sodium: 324mg

Easy Glazed Carrots

Prep time: 10 minutes, cook time: 12 minutes; Serves 4

5 Ingredients:
- 3 cups carrots, peeled and cut into large chunks

What you'll need from the store cupboard:
- 1 tablespoon olive oil
- 1 tablespoon honey
- Salt and black pepper, to taste

Instructions:
1. Preheat the Air fryer to 390 º F and grease an Air fryer basket.
2. Mix all the ingredients in a bowl and toss to coat well.
3. Transfer into the Air fryer basket and cook for about 12 minutes.
4. Dish out and serve hot.

Nutrition Facts Per Serving:
Calories: 80, Fat: 3.5g, Carbohydrates: 12.4g, Sugar: 8.4g, Protein: 0.7g, Sodium: 57mg

Ultra-Crispy Tofu

Prep time: 15 minutes, cook time: 30 minutes; Serves 4

5 Ingredients:

- 1 teaspoon chicken bouillon granules
- 12-ounce extra-firm tofu, drained and cubed into 1-inch size
- 1 teaspoon butter

What you'll need from the store cupboard:

- 2 tablespoons low-sodium soy sauce
- 2 tablespoons fish sauce
- 1 teaspoon sesame oil

Instructions:

1. Preheat the Air fryer to 355 º F and grease an Air fryer basket.
2. Mix soy sauce, fish sauce, sesame oil and chicken granules in a bowl and toss to coat well.
3. Stir in the tofu cubes and mix until well combined.
4. Keep aside to marinate for about 30 minutes and then transfer into Air fryer basket.
5. Cook for about 30 minutes, flipping every 10 minutes and serve hot.

Nutrition Facts Per Serving:
Calories: 102, Fat: 7g, Carbohydrates: 2.5g, Sugar: 1.3g, Protein: 9.4g, Sodium: 1155mg

Garden Fresh Veggie Medley

Prep time: 10 minutes, cook time: 15 minutes; Serves 4

5 Ingredients:

- 2 yellow bell peppers seeded and chopped
- 1 eggplant, chopped
- 1 zucchini, chopped
- 3 tomatoes, chopped
- 2 small onions, chopped

What you'll need from the store cupboard:

- 2 garlic cloves, minced
- 2 tablespoons herbs de Provence
- 1 tablespoon olive oil
- 1 tablespoon balsamic vinegar
- Salt and black pepper, to taste

Instructions:

1. Preheat the Air fryer to 355 º F and grease an Air fryer basket.
2. Mix all the ingredients in a bowl and toss to coat well.
3. Transfer into the Air fryer basket and cook for about 15 minutes.
4. Keep in the Air fryer for about 5 minutes and dish out to serve hot.

Nutrition Facts Per Serving:
Calories: 119, Fat: 4.2g, Carbohydrates: 19.3g, Sugar: 10.7g, Protein: 3.6g, Sodium: 16mg

Family Favorite Potatoes

Prep time: 10 minutes, cook time: 20 minutes; Serves 4

5 Ingredients:

- 1¾ pound waxy potatoes, cubed and boiled
- ½ cup Greek plain yoghurt

What you'll need from the store cupboard:

- 2 tablespoons olive oil, divided
- 1 tablespoon paprika, divided
- Salt and black pepper, to taste

Instructions:

1. Preheat the Air fryer to 355 º F and grease an Air fryer basket.
2. Mix 1 tablespoon olive oil, 1/3 tablespoon of paprika and black pepper in a bowl and toss to coat well.
3. Transfer into the Air fryer basket and cook for about 20 minutes.
4. Mix yogurt, remaining oil, salt and black pepper in a bowl and serve with potatoes.

Nutrition Facts Per Serving:
Calories: 228, Fat: 8.1g, Carbohydrates: 33.5g, Sugar: 3.9g, Protein: 7.1g, Sodium: 24mg

Veggie-filled Pumpkin Basket

Prep time: 15 minutes, cook time: 30 minutes; Serves 6

5 Ingredients:
- 1 sweet potato, peeled and chopped
- 1 parsnip, peeled and chopped
- ½ cup peas, shelled
- 1 onion, chopped
- 1 pumpkin, seeded

What you' ll need from the store cupboard:
- 2 garlic cloves, minced
- 2 teaspoons herb mix

Instructions:
1. Preheat the Air fryer to 355 º F and grease an Air fryer basket.
2. Mix all the ingredients in a bowl except pumpkin and toss to coat well.
3. Stuff the vegetable mixture half way into the pumpkin and transfer into the Air fryer basket.
4. Cook for about 30 minutes and dish out to serve warm.

Nutrition Facts Per Serving:
Calories: 91, Fat: 2.3g, Carbohydrates: 15.2g, Sugar: 5.3g, Protein: 3.5g, Sodium: 33mg

Crispy Bacon-Wrapped Asparagus Bundles

Prep time: 20 minutes, cook time: 8 minutes; Serves 4

5 Ingredients:
- 1 pound asparagus
- 4 bacon slices
- ½ tablespoon sesame seeds, toasted

What you' ll need from the store cupboard:
- 1 garlic clove, minced
- 1½ tablespoons brown sugar
- 1½ tablespoons olive oil
- ½ tablespoon sesame oil, toasted

Instructions:
1. Preheat the Air fryer to 355 º F and grease an Air fryer basket.
2. Mix garlic, brown sugar, olive oil and sesame oil in a bowl till sugar is dissolved.
3. Divide asparagus into 4 equal bunches and wrap a bacon slice around each bunch.
4. Rub the asparagus bunch with garlic mixture and arrange in the Air fryer basket.
5. Sprinkle with sesame seeds and cook for about 8 minutes.
6. Dish out and serve hot.

Nutrition Facts Per Serving:
Calories: 255, Fat: 19.3g, Carbohydrates: 8g, Sugar: 5.4g, Protein: 13.1g, Sodium: 650mg

Perfectly Roasted Mushrooms

Prep time: 10 minutes, cook time: 32 minutes; Serves 4

5 Ingredients:
- 1 tablespoon butter
- 2 pounds mushrooms, quartered
- 2 tablespoons white vermouth

What you' ll need from the store cupboard:
- 2 teaspoons herbs de Provence
- ½ teaspoon garlic powder

Instructions:
1. Preheat the Air fryer to 320 º F and grease an Air fryer pan.
2. Mix herbs de Provence, garlic powder and butter in the Air fryer pan and transfer into the Air fryer basket.
3. Cook for about 2 minutes and stir in the mushrooms.
4. Cook for about 25 minutes and add white vermouth.
5. Cook for 5 more minutes and dish out to serve warm.

Nutrition Facts Per Serving:
Calories: 83, Fat: 3.5g, Carbohydrates: 7.9g, Sugar: 4g, Protein: 7.2g, Sodium: 34mg

Cold Salad with Pasta and Veggies

Prep time: 30 minutes, cook time: 1 hour 35 minutes; Serves 12

5 Ingredients:
- 3 medium zucchinis, sliced into ½-inch thick rounds
- 3 small eggplants, sliced into ½-inch thick rounds
- 4 medium tomatoes, cut in eighths
- 8 cups cooked pasta
- ½ cup Parmesan cheese, grated

What you' ll need from the store cupboard:
- 2 tablespoons olive oil, divided
- ½ cup fat-free Italian dressing
- Salt, to taste

Instructions:
1. Preheat the Air fryer to 355 º F and grease an Air fryer basket.
2. Mix zucchini and 1 tablespoon of olive oil in a bowl and toss to coat well.
3. Arrange the zucchini slices in the Air fryer basket and cook for about 25 minutes.
4. Mix eggplants and 1 tablespoon of olive oil in another bowl and toss to coat well.
5. Arrange the eggplant slices in the Air fryer basket and cook for about 40 minutes.
6. Set the Air fryer to 320 º F and place tomatoes into the prepared basket.
7. Cook for about 30 minutes and combine all the Air fried vegetables.
8. Stir in the remaining ingredients and refrigerate covered for at least 2 hours to serve.

Nutrition Facts Per Serving:
Calories: 319, Fat: 5.7g, Carbohydrates: 55.2g, Sugar: 4.7g, Protein: 12.9g, Sodium: 229mg

Chewy Glazed Parsnips

Prep time: 10 minutes, cook time: 44 minutes; Serves 6

5 Ingredients:
- 2 pounds parsnips, peeled and cut into 1-inch chunks
- 1 tablespoon butter, melted

What you' ll need from the store cupboard:
- 2 tablespoons maple syrup
- 1 tablespoon dried parsley flakes, crushed
- ¼ teaspoon red pepper flakes, crushed

Instructions:
1. Preheat the Air fryer to 355 º F and grease an Air fryer basket.
2. Mix parsnips and butter in a bowl and toss to coat well.
3. Arrange the parsnips in the Air fryer basket and cook for about 40 minutes.
4. Meanwhile, mix remaining ingredients in a large bowl.
5. Transfer this mixture into the Air fryer basket and cook for about 4 more minutes.
6. Dish out and serve warm.

Nutrition Facts Per Serving:
Calories: 148, Fat: 2.4g, Carbohydrates: 31.8g, Sugar: 11.2g, Protein: 1.9g, Sodium: 30mg

Caramelized Brussels Sprout

Prep time: 10 minutes, cook time: 35 minutes; Serves 4

5 Ingredients:
- 1 pound Brussels sprouts, trimmed and halved
- 4 teaspoons butter, melted

What you' ll need from the store cupboard:
- Salt and black pepper, to taste

Instructions:
1. Preheat the Air fryer to 400 º F and grease an Air fryer basket.
2. Mix all the ingredients in a bowl and toss to coat well.
3. Arrange the Brussels sprouts in the Air fryer basket and cook for about 35 minutes.
4. Dish out and serve warm.

Nutrition Facts Per Serving:
Calories: 83, Fats: 4.2g, Carbohydrates: 10.3g, Sugar: 2.5g, Proteins: 3.9g, Sodium: 55mg

Refreshingly Zesty Broccoli

Prep time: 10 minutes, cook time: 15 minutes; Serves 4

5 Ingredients:
- 1 tablespoon butter
- 1 large head broccoli, cut into bite-sized pieces
- 1 tablespoon white sesame seeds
- 2 tablespoons vegetable stock

What you' ll need from the store cupboard:
- 1 tablespoon fresh lemon juice
- 3 garlic cloves, chopped
- ½ teaspoon fresh lemon zest, grated finely
- ½ teaspoon red pepper flakes, crushed

Instructions:
1. Preheat the Air fryer to 355 º F and grease an Air fryer pan.
2. Mix butter, vegetable stock and lemon juice in the Air fryer pan.
3. Transfer into the Air fryer and cook for about 2 minutes.
4. Stir in garlic and broccoli and cook for about 14 minutes.
5. Add sesame seeds, lemon zest and red pepper flakes and cook for 5 minutes.
6. Dish out and serve warm.

Nutrition Facts Per Serving:
Calories: 102, Fat: 4.6g, Carbohydrates: 12.8g, Sugar: 3g, Protein: 5.4g, Sodium: 92mg

Cheesy Mushrooms

Prep time: 10 minutes, cook time: 8 minutes; Serves 4

5 Ingredients:
- 6-ounce button mushrooms, stemmed
- 2 tablespoons mozzarella cheese, grated
- 2 tablespoons cheddar cheese, grated

What you' ll need from the store cupboard:
- 2 tablespoons olive oil
- 2 tablespoons Italian dried mixed herbs
- Salt and freshly ground black pepper, to taste
- 1 teaspoon dried dill

Instructions:
1. Preheat the Air fryer to 355 º F and grease an Air fryer basket.
2. Mix mushrooms, Italian dried mixed herbs, oil, salt and black pepper in a bowl and toss to coat well.
3. Arrange the mushrooms in the Air fryer basket and top with mozzarella cheese and cheddar cheese.
4. Cook for about 8 minutes and sprinkle with dried dill to serve.

Nutrition Facts Per Serving:
Calories: 94, Fat: 8.9g, Carbohydrates: 1.7g, Sugar: 0.8g, Protein: 3.3g, Sodium: 46mg

Radish and Mozzarella Salad with Balsamic Vinaigrette

Prep time: 15 minutes, cook time: 30 minutes; Serves 4

5 Ingredients:
- 1½ pounds radishes, trimmed and halved
- ½ pound fresh mozzarella, sliced

What you' ll need from the store cupboard:
- Salt and freshly ground black pepper, to taste
- 3 tablespoons olive oil
- 1 teaspoon honey
- 1 tablespoon balsamic vinegar

Instructions:
1. Preheat the Air fryer to 350 º F and grease an Air fryer basket.
2. Mix radishes, salt, black pepper and 2 tablespoons of olive oil in a bowl and toss to coat well.
3. Arrange the radishes in the Air fryer basket and cook for about 30 minutes, flipping twice in between.
4. Dish out in a bowl and top with the remaining ingredients to serve.

Nutrition Facts Per Serving:
Calories: 265, Fat: 18.5g, Carbohydrates: 9.3g, Sugar: 4.6g, Protein: 17.4g, Sodium: 411mg

Simply Awesome Vegetables

Prep time: 10 minutes, cook time: 35 minutes; Serves 4

5 Ingredients:
- ½ pound carrots, peeled and sliced
- 1 pound yellow squash, sliced
- 1 pound zucchini, sliced
- 1 tablespoon tarragon leaves, chopped

What you' ll need from the store cupboard:
- 6 teaspoons olive oil, divided
- 1 teaspoon kosher salt
- ½ teaspoon ground white pepper

Instructions:
1. Preheat the Air fryer to 400 ° F and grease an Air fryer basket.
2. Mix 2 teaspoons olive oil and carrots in a bowl until combined.
3. Transfer into the Air fryer basket and cook for about 5 minutes.
4. Meanwhile, mix remaining 4 teaspoons of olive oil, yellow squash, zucchini, salt and white pepper in a large bowl.
5. Transfer this veggie mixture into the Air fryer basket with carrots.
6. Cook for about 30 minutes and dish out in a bowl.
7. Top with tarragon leaves and mix well to serve.

Nutrition Facts Per Serving:
Calories: 122, Fat: 7.4g, Carbohydrates: 13.6g, Sugar: 6.7g, Protein: 3.3g, Sodium: 643mg

Sautéed Bacon with Spinach

Prep time: 10 minutes, cook time: 9 minutes; Serves 2

5 Ingredients:
- 3 meatless bacon slices, chopped
- 1 onion, chopped
- 4-ounce fresh spinach

What you' ll need from the store cupboard:
- 2 tablespoons olive oil
- 1 garlic clove, minced

Instructions:
1. Preheat the Air fryer to 340 ° F and grease an Air fryer pan.
2. Put olive oil and garlic in the Air fryer pan and place in the Air fryer basket.
3. Cook for about 2 minutes and add bacon and onions.
4. Cook for about 3 minutes and stir in the spinach.
5. Cook for about 4 minutes and dish out in a bowl to serve.

Nutrition Facts Per Serving:
Calories: 385, Fat: 31.8g, Carbohydrates: 8.3g, Sugar: 2.6g, Protein: 17.9g, Sodium: 1017mg

Breadcrumbs Stuffed Mushrooms

Prep time: 15 minutes, cook time: 10 minutes; Serves 4

5 Ingredients:
- 1½ spelt bread slices
- 1 tablespoon flat-leaf parsley, finely chopped
- 16 small button mushrooms, stemmed and gills removed

What you' ll need from the store cupboard:
- 1½ tablespoons olive oil
- 1 garlic clove, crushed
- Salt and black pepper, to taste

Instructions:
1. Preheat the Air fryer to 390 ° F and grease an Air fryer basket.
2. Put the bread slices in a food processor and pulse until fine crumbs form.
3. Transfer the crumbs into a bowl and stir in the olive oil, garlic, parsley, salt, and black pepper.
4. Stuff the breadcrumbs mixture in each mushroom cap and arrange the mushrooms in the Air fryer basket.
5. Cook for about 10 minutes and dish out in a bowl to serve warm.

Nutrition Facts Per Serving:
Calories: 64, Fat: 5.5g, Carbohydrates: 3.3g, Sugar: 0.5g, Protein: 1.6g, Sodium: 65mg

Sautéed Spinach

Prep time: 15 minutes, cook time: 9 minutes; Serves 2

5 Ingredients:
- 1 small onion, chopped
- 6 ounces fresh spinach

What you'll need from the store cupboard:
- 2 tablespoons olive oil
- 1 teaspoon ginger, minced
- Salt and black pepper, to taste

Instructions:
1. Preheat the Air fryer to 360 º F and grease an Air fryer pan.
2. Put olive oil, onions and ginger in the Air fryer pan and place in the Air fryer basket.
3. Cook for about 4 minutes and add spinach, salt, and black pepper.
4. Cook for about 4 more minutes and dish out in a bowl to serve.

Nutrition Facts Per Serving:
Calories: 156, Fat: 14.4g, Carbohydrates: 6.9g, Sugar: 1.9g, Protein: 2.9g, Sodium: 146mg

Oatmeal Stuffed Bell Pepper

Prep time: 10 minutes, cook time: 16 minutes; Serves 2

5 Ingredients:
- 1 large red bell pepper, halved and seeded
- 1 cup cooked oatmeal
- 2 tablespoons canned red kidney beans
- 2 tablespoons plain yogurt

What you'll need from the store cupboard:
- 1/8 teaspoon ground cumin
- 1/8 teaspoon smoked paprika
- Salt and black pepper, to taste

Instructions:
1. Preheat the Air fryer to 355 º F and grease an Air fryer pan.
2. Put the bell peppers in the Air fryer pan and cook for about 8 minutes.
3. Meanwhile, mix oatmeal with remaining ingredients in a bowl.
4. Stuff the oatmeal mixture in each pepper half and cook for about 8 minutes.
5. Dish out in a bowl and serve warm.

Nutrition Facts Per Serving:
Calories: 233, Fat: 3.3g, Carbohydrates: 41.3g, Sugar: 5.2g, Protein: 9.8g, Sodium: 18mg

Versatile Stuffed Tomato

Prep time: 15 minutes, cook time: 22 minutes; Serves 4

5 Ingredients:
- 4 tomatoes, tops and seeds removed
- 1 carrot, peeled and chopped
- 1 onion, chopped
- 1 cup frozen peas, thawed
- 2 cups cold cooked rice

What you'll need from the store cupboard:
- 1 teaspoon olive oil
- 1 garlic clove, minced
- 1 tablespoon soy sauce

Instructions:
1. Preheat the Air fryer to 355 º F and grease an Air fryer basket.
2. Heat olive oil in a skillet on low heat and add carrots, onions, peas and garlic.
3. Cook for about 2 minutes and stir in the soy sauce and rice.
4. Stuff the rice mixture into the tomatoes and arrange into the Air fryer basket.
5. Cook for about 20 minutes and dish out to serve warm.

Nutrition Facts Per Serving:
Calories: 421, Fat: 2.2g, Carbohydrates: 89.1g, Sugar: 7.2g, Protein: 10.5g, Sodium: 277mg

Brussel Sprout Salad

Prep time: 20 minutes, cook time: 15 minutes; Serves 4

5 Ingredients:

- 1 pound fresh medium Brussels sprouts, trimmed and halved vertically
- 2 apples, cored and chopped
- 1 red onion, sliced
- 4 cups lettuce, torn

What you'll need from the store cupboard:

- 3 teaspoons olive oil
- Salt and ground black pepper, as required

For Dressing

- 2 tablespoons extra-virgin olive oil
- 2 tablespoons fresh lemon juice
- 1 tablespoon apple cider vinegar
- 1 tablespoon honey
- 1 teaspoon Dijon mustard
- Salt and ground black pepper, as required

Instructions:

1. Preheat the Air fryer to 360 º F and grease an Air fryer basket.
2. Mix Brussels sprout, oil, salt, and black pepper in a bowl and toss to coat well.
3. Arrange the Brussels sprouts in the Air fryer basket and cook for about 15 minutes, flipping once in between.
4. Dish out the Brussel sprouts in a serving bowl and keep aside to cool.
5. Add apples, onion, and lettuce and mix well.
6. Mix all the ingredients for dressing in a bowl and pour over the salad.
7. Toss to coat well and serve immediately.

Nutrition Facts Per Serving:
Calories: 235, Fat: 11.3g, Carbohydrates: 34.5g, Sugar: 20.3g, Protein: 4.9g, Sodium: 88mg

Garden Fresh Green Beans

Prep time: 10 minutes, cook time: 12 minutes; Serves 4

5 Ingredients:

- 1 pound green beans, washed and trimmed
- 1 teaspoon butter, melted

What you'll need from the store cupboard:

- 1 tablespoon fresh lemon juice
- ¼ teaspoon garlic powder
- Salt and freshly ground pepper, to taste

Instructions:

1. Preheat the Air fryer to 400 º F and grease an Air fryer basket.
2. Put all the ingredients in a large bowl and transfer into the Air fryer basket.
3. Cook for about 8 minutes and dish out in a bowl to serve warm.

Nutrition Facts Per Serving:
Calories: 45, Fats: 1.1g, Carbohydrates: 8.3g, Sugar: 1.7g, Proteins: 2.1g, Sodium: 14mg

Eggplant Salad

Prep time: 15 minutes, cook time: 15 minutes; Serves 2

5 Ingredients:

- 1 eggplant, cut into ½-inch-thick slices crosswise
- 1 avocado, peeled, pitted and chopped

What you'll need from the store cupboard:

- 2 tablespoons canola oil
- Salt and ground black pepper, as required
- 1 teaspoon fresh lemon juice

For Dressing

- 1 tablespoon extra-virgin olive oil
- 1 tablespoon red wine vinegar
- 1 tablespoon honey
- 1 tablespoon fresh oregano leaves, chopped
- 1 teaspoon fresh lemon zest, grated
- 1 teaspoon Dijon mustard
- Salt and ground black pepper, as required

Instructions:

1. Preheat the Air fryer to 400 º F and grease an Air fryer basket.
2. Mix eggplant, oil, salt, and black pepper in a bowl and toss to coat well.
3. Arrange the eggplants pieces in the Air fryer basket and cook for about 15 minutes, flipping twice in between.

4. Dish out the Brussel sprouts in a serving bowl and keep aside to cool.
5. Add avocado and lemon juice and mix well.
6. Mix all the ingredients for dressing in a bowl and pour over the salad.
7. Toss to coat well and serve immediately.

Nutrition Facts Per Serving:
Calories: 489, Fat: 41.4g, Carbohydrates: 32.7g, Sugar: 16.2g, Protein: 4.6g, Sodium: 118mg

Potato Salad

Prep time: 10 minutes, cook time: 40 minutes; Serves 6

5 Ingredients:
- 4 Russet potatoes
- 3 hard-boiled eggs, peeled and chopped
- 1 cup celery, chopped
- ½ cup red onion, chopped

What you' ll need from the store cupboard:
- 1 tablespoon olive oil
- Salt, as required
- 1 tablespoon prepared mustard
- ¼ teaspoon celery salt
- ¼ teaspoon garlic salt
- ¼ cup mayonnaise

Instructions:

1. Preheat the Air fryer to 390 º F and grease an Air fryer basket.
2. Prick the potatoes with a fork and rub with olive oil and salt.
3. Arrange the potatoes in the Air fryer basket and cook for about 40 minutes.
4. Dish out the potatoes in a serving bowl and keep aside to cool.
5. Add the remaining ingredients and mix well.
6. Refrigerate for about 2 hours and serve immediately.

Nutrition Facts Per Serving:
Calories: 196, Fat: 8.1g, Carbohydrates: 26.5g, Sugar: 3.1g, Protein: 5.6g, Sodium: 180mg

Cauliflower Salad

Prep time: 20 minutes, cook time: 10 minutes; Serves 4

5 Ingredients:
- ¼ cup golden raisins
- 1 cup boiling water
- 1 head cauliflower, cut into small florets
- ¼ cup pecans, toasted and chopped
- 2 tablespoons fresh mint leaves, chopped

What you' ll need from the store cupboard:
- ¼ cup olive oil
- 1 tablespoon curry powder
- Salt, to taste

For Dressing
- 1 cup mayonnaise
- 2 tablespoons sugar
- 1 tablespoon fresh lemon juice

Instructions:

1. Preheat the Air fryer to 390 º F and grease an Air fryer basket.
2. Mix the cauliflower, curry powder, salt, and olive oil in a bowl and toss to coat well.
3. Arrange the cauliflower florets in the Air fryer basket and cook for about 10 minutes.
4. Dish out the cauliflower florets in a serving bowl and keep aside to cool.
5. Meanwhile, add the raisins in boiling water in a bowl for about 20 minutes.
6. Drain the raisins well and mix with the cauliflower florets.
7. Mix all the ingredients for dressing in a bowl and pour over the salad.
8. Toss to coat well and serve immediately.

Nutrition Facts Per Serving:
Calories: 162, Fat: 3.1g, Carbohydrates: 25.3g, Sugar: 1.6g, Protein: 11.3g, Sodium: 160mg

Radish Salad

Prep time: 15 minutes, cook time: 30 minutes; Serves 4

5 Ingredients:
- 1½ pounds radishes, trimmed and halved
- ½ pound fresh mozzarella, sliced
- 6 cups fresh salad greens

What you'll need from the store cupboard:
- 3 tablespoons olive oil
- 1 teaspoon honey
- 1 tablespoon balsamic vinegar
- Salt and black pepper, to taste

Instructions:
1. Preheat the Air fryer to 350 º F and grease an Air fryer basket.
2. Mix the radishes, salt, black pepper, and olive oil in a bowl and toss to coat well.
3. Arrange the radishes in the Air fryer basket and cook for about 30 minutes, flipping twice in between.
4. Dish out the radishes in a serving bowl and keep aside to cool.
5. Add mozzarella cheese and greens and mix well.
6. Mix honey, oil, vinegar, salt, and black pepper in a bowl and pour over the salad.
7. Toss to coat well and serve immediately.

Nutrition Facts Per Serving:
Calories: 468, Fat: 38.5g, Carbohydrates: 33.1g, Sugar: 17.1g, Protein: 3.3g, Sodium: 127mg

Zucchini Salad

Prep time: 15 minutes, cook time: 30 minutes; Serves 4

5 Ingredients:
- 1 pound zucchini, cut into rounds
- 5 cups fresh spinach, chopped
- ¼ cup feta cheese, crumbled

What you'll need from the store cupboard:
- 2 tablespoons olive oil
- 1 teaspoon garlic powder
- Salt and black pepper, as required
- 2 tablespoons fresh lemon juice

Instructions:
1. Preheat the Air fryer to 400 º F and grease an Air fryer basket.
2. Mix the zucchini, oil, garlic powder, salt, and black pepper in a bowl and toss to coat well.
3. Arrange the zucchini slices in the Air fryer basket and cook for about 30 minutes, flipping thrice in between.
4. Dish out the zucchini slices in a serving bowl and keep aside to cool.
5. Add spinach, feta cheese, lemon juice, a little bit of salt and black pepper and mix well.
6. Toss to coat well and serve immediately.

Nutrition Facts Per Serving:
Calories: 116, Fat: 9.4g, Carbohydrates: 6.2g, Sugar: 2.8g, Protein: 4g, Sodium: 186mg

Caramelized Carrots

Prep time: 10 minutes, cook time: 15 minutes; Serves 3

5 Ingredients:
- 1 small bag baby carrots

What you'll need from the store cupboard:
- ½ cup butter, melted
- ½ cup brown sugar

Instructions:
1. Preheat the Air fryer to 400 º F and grease an Air fryer basket.
2. Mix the butter and brown sugar in a bowl.
3. Add the carrots and toss to coat well.
4. Arrange the carrots in the Air fryer basket and cook for about 15 minutes.
5. Dish out and serve warm.

Nutrition Facts Per Serving:
Calories: 416, Fat: 30.9g, Carbohydrates: 36.2g, Sugar: 30.7g, Protein: 1.3g, Sodium: 343mg

Mixed Veggie Salad

Prep time: 25 minutes, cook time: 1 hour 20 minutes; Serves 8

5 Ingredients:

- 3 medium carrots, cut into ½-inch thick rounds
- 3 small radishes, sliced into ½-inch thick rounds
- 8 cherry tomatoes, cut in eighths
- 2 red bell peppers, seeded and chopped
- ½ cup Parmesan cheese, grated

What you'll need from the store cupboard:

- 2 tablespoons olive oil, divided
- ½ cup Italian dressing
- Salt, as required

Instructions:

1. Preheat the Air fryer to 365 º F and grease an Air fryer basket.
2. Mix carrots and 1 tablespoon of olive oil in a bowl and toss to coat well.
3. Arrange the carrots in the Air fryer basket and cook for about 25 minutes.
4. Mix radishes and 1 tablespoon of olive oil in another bowl and toss to coat well.
5. Arrange the radishes in the Air fryer basket and cook for about 40 minutes.
6. Set the Air fryer to 330 º F and place the cherry tomatoes into the Air fryer basket.
7. Cook for about 15 minutes and combine all the Air fried vegetables.
8. Stir in the remaining ingredients except Parmesan cheese and refrigerate covered for at least 2 hours to serve.
9. Garnish with Parmesan cheese and serve.

Nutrition Facts Per Serving:
Calories: 137, Fat: 9.5g, Carbohydrates: 15.4g, Sugar: 1.8g, Protein: 26.2g, Sodium: 249mg

Rice and Beans Stuffed Bell Peppers

Prep time: 15 minutes, cook time: 15 minutes; Serves 5

5 Ingredients:

- 1 (15-ounces) can diced tomatoes with juice
- 1 (15-ounces) can red kidney beans, rinsed and drained
- 1 cup cooked rice
- 5 large bell peppers, tops removed and seeded
- ½ cup mozzarella cheese, shredded

What you'll need from the store cupboard:

- 1½ teaspoons Italian seasoning

Instructions:

1. Preheat the Air fryer to 360 º F and grease an Air fryer pan.
2. Mix rice, tomatoes with juice, beans, and Italian seasoning in a bowl.
3. Stuff the rice mixture in each bell pepper half and arrange in the Air fryer pan.
4. Cook for about 12 minutes and top with mozzarella cheese.
5. Cook for about 3 more minutes and dish out to serve warm.

Nutrition Facts Per Serving:
Calories: 487, Fat: 2.5g, Carbohydrates: 94.3g, Sugar: 10.2g, Protein: 24.6g, Sodium: 37mg

Sweet and Sour Brussel Sprouts

Prep time: 10 minutes, cook time: 10 minutes; Serves 2

5 Ingredients:

- 2 cups Brussels sprouts, trimmed and halved lengthwise

What you'll need from the store cupboard:

- 1 tablespoon balsamic vinegar
- 1 tablespoon maple syrup
- Salt, as required

Instructions:

1. Preheat the Air fryer to 400 º F and grease an Air fryer basket.
2. Mix all the ingredients in a bowl and toss to coat well.
3. Arrange the Brussel sprouts in the Air fryer basket and cook for about 10 minutes, shaking once halfway through.
4. Dish out in a bowl and serve hot.

Nutrition Facts Per Serving:
Calories: 66, Fat: 0.3g, Carbohydrates: 14.8g, Sugar: 7.9g, Protein: 3g, Sodium: 101mg

Cheesy Brussel Sprouts

Prep time: 15 minutes, cook time: 10 minutes; Serves 3

5 Ingredients:

- 1 pound Brussels sprouts, trimmed and halved
- ¼ cup whole wheat breadcrumbs
- ¼ cup Parmesan cheese, shredded

What you'll need from the store cupboard:

- 1 tablespoon balsamic vinegar
- 1 tablespoon extra-virgin olive oil
- Salt and black pepper, to taste

Instructions:

1. Preheat the Air fryer to 400 º F and grease an Air fryer basket.
2. Mix Brussel sprouts, vinegar, oil, salt, and black pepper in a bowl and toss to coat well.
3. Arrange the Brussel sprouts in the Air fryer basket and cook for about 5 minutes.
4. Sprinkle with breadcrumbs and cheese and cook for about 5 more minutes.
5. Dish out and serve hot.

Nutrition Facts Per Serving:
Calories: 240, Fats: 12.6g, Carbohydrates: 19.4g, Sugar: 3.4g, Proteins: 16.3g, Sodium: 548mg

Spiced Eggplant

Prep time: 15 minutes, cook time: 27 minutes; Serves 3

5 Ingredients:

- 2 medium eggplants, cubed
- 2 tablespoons butter, melted
- 2 tablespoons Parmesan cheese, shredded

What you'll need from the store cupboard:

- 1 tablespoon Maggi seasoning sauce
- 1 teaspoon sumac
- 1 teaspoon garlic powder
- 1 teaspoon onion powder
- Salt and ground black pepper, as required
- 1 tablespoon fresh lemon juice

Instructions:

1. Preheat the Air fryer to 320 º F and grease an Air fryer basket.
2. Mix the eggplant cubes, butter, seasoning sauce and spices in a bowl and toss to coat well.
3. Arrange the eggplant cubes in the Air fryer basket and cook for about 15 minutes.
4. Dish out in a bowl and set the Air fryer to 350 º F.
5. Cook for about 12 minutes, tossing once in between.
6. Dish out in a bowl and sprinkle with lemon juice and Parmesan cheese to serve.

Nutrition Facts Per Serving:
Calories: 173, Fat: 8.9g, Carbohydrates: 23g, Sugar: 11.6g, Protein: 4.6g, Sodium: 276mg

Buttered Broccoli

Prep time: 10 minutes, cook time: 7 minutes; Serves 4

5 Ingredients:

- 4 cups fresh broccoli florets
- 2 tablespoons butter, melted
- ¼ cup water

What you'll need from the store cupboard:

- Salt and black pepper, to taste

Instructions:

1. Preheat the Air fryer to 400 º F and grease an Air fryer basket.
2. Mix broccoli, butter, salt, and black pepper in a bowl and toss to coat well.
3. Place water at the bottom of Air fryer pan and arrange the broccoli florets into the Air fryer basket.
4. Cook for about 7 minutes and dish out in a bowl to serve hot.

Nutrition Facts Per Serving:
Calories: 82, Fat: 6.1g, Carbohydrates: 6g, Sugar: 1.6g, Protein: 2.6g, Sodium: 110mg

Garlic Broccoli

Prep time: 15 minutes, cook time: 20 minutes; Serves 3

5 Ingredients:
- 1 tablespoon butter
- 2 teaspoons vegetable bouillon granules
- 1 large head broccoli, cut into bite-sized pieces

What you' ll need from the store cupboard:
- 1 tablespoon fresh lemon juice
- 3 garlic cloves, sliced
- ½ teaspoon fresh lemon zest, finely grated
- ½ teaspoon red pepper flakes, crushed

Instructions:
1. Preheat the Air fryer to 355 º F and grease an Air fryer pan.
2. Mix the butter, bouillon granules, and lemon juice in the Air fryer pan.
3. Cook for about 1½ minutes and stir in the garlic.
4. Cook for about 30 seconds and add broccoli, lemon zest, and red pepper flakes.
5. Cook for about 18 minutes and dish out in a bowl to serve hot.

Nutrition Facts Per Serving:
Calories: 80, Fat: 4.3g, Carbohydrates: 8.9g, Sugar: 2.1g, Protein: 3.5g, Sodium: 85mg

Parmesan Broccoli

Prep time: 10 minutes, cook time: 20 minutes; Serves 2

5 Ingredients:
- 10 ounces frozen broccoli
- 2 tablespoons Parmesan cheese, grated

What you' ll need from the store cupboard:
- 3 tablespoons balsamic vinegar
- 1 tablespoon olive oil
- 1/8 teaspoon cayenne pepper
- Salt and black pepper, as required

Instructions:
1. Preheat the Air fryer to 400 º F and grease an Air fryer basket.
2. Mix broccoli, vinegar, oil, cayenne, salt, and black pepper in a bowl and toss to coat well.
3. Arrange broccoli into the Air fryer basket and cook for about 20 minutes.
4. Dish out in a bowl and top with Parmesan cheese to serve.

Nutrition Facts Per Serving:
Calories: 173, Fat: 11.5g, Carbohydrates: 10.7g, Sugar: 2.5g, Protein: 10g, Sodium: 505mg

Broccoli with Olives

Prep time: 15 minutes, cook time: 19 minutes; Serves 4

5 Ingredients:
- 2 pounds broccoli, stemmed and cut into 1-inch florets
- 1/3 cup Kalamata olives, halved and pitted
- ¼ cup Parmesan cheese, grated

What you' ll need from the store cupboard:
- 2 tablespoons olive oil
- Salt and ground black pepper, as required
- 2 teaspoons fresh lemon zest, grated

Instructions:
1. Preheat the Air fryer to 400 º F and grease an Air fryer basket.
2. Boil the broccoli for about 4 minutes and drain well.
3. Mix broccoli, oil, salt, and black pepper in a bowl and toss to coat well.
4. Arrange broccoli into the Air fryer basket and cook for about 15 minutes.
5. Stir in the olives, lemon zest and cheese and dish out to serve.

Nutrition Facts Per Serving:
Calories: 169, Fat: 10.2g, Carbohydrates: 16g, Sugar: 3.9g, Protein: 8.5g, Sodium: 254mg

Almond Asparagus

Prep time: 15 minutes, cook time: 6 minutes; Serves 3

5 Ingredients:
- 1 pound asparagus
- 1/3 cup almonds, sliced

What you'll need from the store cupboard:
- 2 tablespoons olive oil
- 2 tablespoons balsamic vinegar
- Salt and black pepper, to taste

Instructions:
1. Preheat the Air fryer to 400 º F and grease an Air fryer basket.
2. Mix asparagus, oil, vinegar, salt, and black pepper in a bowl and toss to coat well.
3. Arrange asparagus into the Air fryer basket and sprinkle with the almond slices.
4. Cook for about 6 minutes and dish out to serve hot.

Nutrition Facts Per Serving:
Calories: 173, Fat: 14.8g, Carbohydrates: 8.2g, Sugar: 3.3g, Protein: 5.6g, Sodium: 54mg

Veggies Stuffed Eggplants

Prep time: 20 minutes, cook time: 14 minutes; Serves 5

5 Ingredients:
- 10 small eggplants, halved lengthwise
- 1 onion, chopped
- 1 tomato, chopped
- ¼ cup cottage cheese, chopped
- ½ green bell pepper, seeded and chopped

What you'll need from the store cupboard:
- 1 tablespoon fresh lime juice
- 1 tablespoon vegetable oil
- ½ teaspoon garlic, chopped
- Salt and ground black pepper, as required
- 2 tablespoons tomato paste

Instructions:
1. Preheat the Air fryer to 320 º F and grease an Air fryer basket.
2. Cut a slice from one side of each eggplant lengthwise and scoop out the flesh in a bowl.
3. Drizzle the eggplants with lime juice and arrange in the Air fryer basket.
4. Cook for about 4 minutes and remove from the Air fryer.
5. Heat vegetable oil in a skillet over medium heat and add garlic and onion.
6. Sauté for about 2 minutes and stir in the eggplant flesh, tomato, salt, and black pepper.
7. Sauté for about 3 minutes and add cheese, bell pepper, tomato paste, and cilantro.
8. Cook for about 1 minute and stuff this mixture into the eggplants.
9. Close each eggplant with its cut part and set the Air fryer to 360 º F.
10. Arrange in the Air fryer basket and cook for about 5 minutes.
11. Dish out in a serving plate and serve hot.

Nutrition Facts Per Serving:
Calories: 83, Fat: 3.2g, Carbohydrates: 11.9g, Sugar: 6.1g, Protein: 3.4g, Sodium: 87mg

Sautéed Green Beans

Prep time: 10 minutes, cook time: 10 minutes; Serves 2

5 Ingredients:
- 8 ounces fresh green beans, trimmed and cut in half

What you'll need from the store cupboard:
- 1 teaspoon sesame oil
- 1 tablespoon soy sauce

Instructions:
1. Preheat the Air fryer to 390 º F and grease an Air fryer basket.
2. Mix green beans, soy sauce, and sesame oil in a bowl and toss to coat well.
3. Arrange green beans into the Air fryer basket and cook for about 10 minutes, tossing once in between.
4. Dish out onto serving plates and serve hot.

Nutrition Facts Per Serving:
Calories: 59, Fats: 2.4g, Carbohydrates: 59g, Sugar: 1.7g, Proteins: 2.6g, Sodium: 458mg

Stuffed Potatoes

Prep time: 15 minutes, cook time: 31 minutes; Serves 4

5 Ingredients:

- 4 potatoes, peeled
- 1 tablespoon butter
- ½ of brown onion, chopped
- 2 tablespoons chives, chopped
- ½ cup Parmesan cheese, grated

What you' ll need from the store cupboard:

- 3 tablespoons canola oil

Instructions:

1. Preheat the Air fryer to 390 º F and grease an Air fryer basket.
2. Coat the potatoes with canola oil and arrange into the Air fryer basket.
3. Cook for about 20 minutes and transfer into a platter.
4. Cut each potato in half and scoop out the flesh from each half.
5. Heat butter in a frying pan over medium heat and add onions.
6. Sauté for about 5 minutes and dish out in a bowl.
7. Mix the onions with the potato flesh, chives, and half of cheese.
8. Stir well and stuff the potato halves evenly with the onion potato mixture.
9. Top with the remaining cheese and arrange the potato halves into the Air fryer basket.
10. Cook for about 6 minutes and dish out to serve warm.

Nutrition Facts Per Serving:
Calories: 328, Fat: 11.3g, Carbohydrates: 34.8g, Sugar: 3.1g, Protein: 5.8g, Sodium: 77mg

Hasselback Potatoes

Prep time: 20 minutes, cook time: 30 minutes; Serves 4

5 Ingredients:

- 4 potatoes
- 2 tablespoons Parmesan cheese, shredded
- 1 tablespoon fresh chives, chopped

What you' ll need from the store cupboard:

- 2 tablespoons olive oil

Instructions:

1. Preheat the Air fryer to 355 º F and grease an Air fryer basket.
2. Cut slits along each potato about ¼-inch apart with a sharp knife, making sure slices should stay connected at the bottom.
3. Coat the potatoes with olive oil and arrange into the Air fryer basket.
4. Cook for about 30 minutes and dish out in a platter.
5. Top with chives and Parmesan cheese to serve.

Nutrition Facts Per Serving:
Calories: 218, Fat: 7.9g, Carbohydrates: 33.6g, Sugar: 2.5g, Protein: 4.6g, Sodium: 55mg

Red Wine Infused Mushrooms

Prep time: 15 minutes, cook time: 30 minutes; Serves 6

5 Ingredients:

- 1 tablespoon butter
- 2 pounds fresh mushrooms, quartered

What you' ll need from the store cupboard:

- 2 teaspoons Herbs de Provence
- ½ teaspoon garlic powder
- 2 tablespoons red wine

Instructions:

1. Preheat the Air fryer to 325 º F and grease an Air fryer pan.
2. Mix the butter, Herbs de Provence, and garlic powder in the Air fryer pan and toss to coat well.
3. Cook for about 2 minutes and stir in the mushrooms and red wine.
4. Cook for about 28 minutes and dish out in a platter to serve hot.

Nutrition Facts Per Serving:
Calories: 54, Fat: 2.4g, Carbohydrates: 5.3g, Sugar: 2.7g, Protein: 4.8g, Sodium: 23mg

Green Beans and Mushroom Casserole

Prep time: 15 minutes, cook time: 12 minutes; Serves 6

5 Ingredients:
- 24 ounces fresh green beans, trimmed
- 2 cups fresh button mushrooms, sliced
- 1/3 cup French fried onions

What you' ll need from the store cupboard:
- 3 tablespoons olive oil
- 2 tablespoons fresh lemon juice
- 1 teaspoon ground sage
- 1 teaspoon garlic powder
- 1 teaspoon onion powder
- Salt and black pepper, to taste

Instructions:

1. Preheat the Air fryer to 400 º F and grease an Air fryer basket.
2. Mix the green beans, mushrooms, oil, lemon juice, sage, and spices in a bowl and toss to coat well.
3. Arrange the green beans mixture into the Air fryer basket and cook for about 12 minutes.
4. Dish out in a serving dish and top with fried onions to serve.

Nutrition Facts Per Serving:
Calories: 65, Fat: 1.6g, Carbohydrates: 11g, Sugar: 2.4g, Protein: 3g, Sodium: 52mg

Okra with Green Beans

Prep time: 10 minutes, cook time: 20 minutes; Serves 2

5 Ingredients:
- ½ (10-ounces) bag frozen cut okra
- ½ (10-ounces) bag frozen cut green beans

What you' ll need from the store cupboard:
- ¼ cup nutritional yeast
- 3 tablespoons balsamic vinegar
- Salt and black pepper, to taste

Instructions:
1. Preheat the Air fryer to 400 º F and grease an Air fryer basket.
2. Mix the okra, green beans, nutritional yeast, vinegar, salt, and black pepper in a bowl and toss to coat well.
3. Arrange the okra mixture into the Air fryer basket and cook for about 20 minutes.
4. Dish out in a serving dish and serve hot.

Nutrition Facts Per Serving:
Calories: 126, Fat: 1.3g, Carbohydrates: 19.7g, Sugar: 2.1g, Protein: 11.9g, Sodium: 100mg

Stuffed Okra

Prep time: 15 minutes, cook time: 12 minutes; Serves 2

5 Ingredients:
- 8 ounces large okra
- ¼ cup chickpea flour
- ¼ of onion, chopped
- 2 tablespoons coconut, grated freshly

What you' ll need from the store cupboard:
- 1 teaspoon garam masala powder
- ½ teaspoon ground turmeric
- ½ teaspoon red chili powder
- ½ teaspoon ground cumin
- Salt, to taste

Instructions:

1. Preheat the Air fryer to 390 º F and grease an Air fryer basket.
2. Mix the flour, onion, grated coconut, and spices in a bowl and toss to coat well.
3. Stuff the flour mixture into okra and arrange into the Air fryer basket.
4. Cook for about 12 minutes and dish out in a serving plate.

Nutrition Facts Per Serving:
Calories: 166, Fat: 3.7g, Carbohydrates: 26.6g, Sugar: 5.3g, Protein: 7.6g, Sodium: 103mg

Parmesan Asparagus

Prep time: 15 minutes, cook time: 10 minutes; Serves 3

5 Ingredients:
- 1 pound fresh asparagus, trimmed
- 1 tablespoon Parmesan cheese, grated
- 1 tablespoon butter, melted

What you'll need from the store cupboard:
- 1 teaspoon garlic powder
- Salt and black pepper, to taste

Instructions:
1. Preheat the Air fryer to 400 º F and grease an Air fryer basket.
2. Mix the asparagus, cheese, butter, garlic powder, salt, and black pepper in a bowl and toss to coat well.
3. Arrange the asparagus into the Air fryer basket and cook for about 10 minutes.
4. Dish out in a serving plate and serve hot.

Nutrition Facts Per Serving:
Calories: 73, Fat: 2.7g, Carbohydrates: 6.6g, Sugar: 3.1g, Protein: 4.2g, Sodium: 95mg

Lemony Green Beans

Prep time: 15 minutes, cook time: 12 minutes; Serves 3

5 Ingredients:
- 1 pound green beans, trimmed and halved
- 1 teaspoon butter, melted

What you'll need from the store cupboard:
- 1 tablespoon fresh lemon juice
- ¼ teaspoon garlic powder

Instructions:
1. Preheat the Air fryer to 400 º F and grease an Air fryer basket.
2. Mix all the ingredients in a bowl and toss to coat well.
3. Arrange the green beans into the Air fryer basket and cook for about 12 minutes.
4. Dish out in a serving plate and serve hot.

Nutrition Facts Per Serving:
Calories: 60, Fat: 1.5g, Carbohydrates: 11.1g, Sugar: 2.3g, Protein: 2.8g, Sodium: 70mg

Glazed Veggies

Prep time: 20 minutes, cook time: 20 minutes; Serves 4

5 Ingredients:
- 2 ounces cherry tomatoes
- 1 large parsnip, peeled and chopped
- 1 large carrot, peeled and chopped
- 1 large zucchini, chopped
- 1 green bell pepper, seeded and chopped

What you'll need from the store cupboard:
- 6 tablespoons olive oil, divided
- 3 tablespoons honey
- 1 teaspoon Dijon mustard
- 1 teaspoon mixed dried herbs
- 1 teaspoon garlic paste
- Salt and black pepper, to taste

Instructions:
1. Preheat the Air fryer to 350 º F and grease an Air fryer pan.
2. Arrange cherry tomatoes, parsnip, carrot, zucchini and bell pepper in the Air fryer pan and drizzle with 3 tablespoons of olive oil.
3. Cook for about 15 minutes and remove from the Air fryer.
4. Mix remaining olive oil, honey, mustard, herbs, garlic, salt, and black pepper in a bowl.
5. Pour this mixture over the vegetables in the Air fryer pan and set the Air fryer to 390 º F.
6. Cook for about 5 minutes and dish out to serve hot.

Nutrition Facts Per Serving:
Calories: 288, Fat: 21.4g, Carbohydrates: 26.7g, Sugar: 18.7g, Protein: 2.1g, Sodium: 79mg

Veggie Stuffed Bell Peppers

Prep time: 20 minutes, cook time: 25 minutes; Serves 6

5 Ingredients:

- 6 large bell peppers, tops and seeds removed
- 1 carrot, peeled and finely chopped
- 1 potato, peeled and finely chopped
- ½ cup fresh peas, shelled
- 1/3 cup cheddar cheese, grated

What you' ll need from the store cupboard:

- 2 garlic cloves, minced
- Salt and black pepper, to taste

Instructions:

1. Preheat the Air fryer to 350 º F and grease an Air fryer basket.
2. Mix vegetables, garlic, salt and black pepper in a bowl.
3. Stuff the vegetable mixture in each bell pepper and arrange in the Air fryer pan.
4. Cook for about 20 minutes and top with cheddar cheese.
5. Cook for about 5 more minutes and dish out to serve warm.

Nutrition Facts Per Serving:
Calories: 101, Fat: 2.5g, Carbohydrates: 17.1g, Sugar: 7.4g, Protein: 4.1g, Sodium: 51mg

Spices Stuffed Eggplants

Prep time: 15 minutes, cook time: 12 minutes; Serves 4

5 Ingredients:

- 8 baby eggplants

What you' ll need from the store cupboard:

- 4 teaspoons olive oil, divided
- ¾ tablespoon dry mango powder
- ¾ tablespoon ground coriander
- ½ teaspoon ground cumin
- ½ teaspoon ground turmeric
- ½ teaspoon garlic powder
- Salt, to taste

Instructions:

1. Preheat the Air fryer to 370 º F and grease an Air fryer basket.
2. Make 2 slits from the bottom of each eggplant leaving the stems intact.
3. Mix one teaspoon of oil and spices in a bowl and fill each slit of eggplants with this mixture.
4. Brush the outer side of each eggplant with remaining oil and arrange in the Air fryer basket.
5. Cook for about 12 minutes and dish out in a serving plate to serve hot.

Nutrition Facts Per Serving:
Calories: 317, Fats: 6.7g, Carbohydrates: 65g, Sugar: 33g, Proteins: 10.9g, Sodium: 61mg

Stuffed Pumpkin

Prep time: 20 minutes, cook time: 35 minutes; Serves 4

5 Ingredients:

- 2 tomatoes, chopped
- 1 bell pepper, chopped
- 1 beetroot, chopped
- ½ cup green beans, shelled
- ½ of butternut pumpkin, seeded

What you' ll need from the store cupboard:

- 2 garlic cloves, minced
- 2 teaspoons mixed dried herbs
- Salt and black pepper, to taste

Instructions:

1. Preheat the Air fryer to 360 º F and grease an Air fryer basket.
2. Mix all the ingredients in a bowl except pumpkin and toss to coat well.
3. Stuff the vegetable mixture into the pumpkin and place into the Air fryer basket.
4. Cook for about 35 minutes and keep aside to slightly cool.
5. Dish out and serve warm.

Nutrition Facts Per Serving:
Calories: 48, Fats: 0.4g, Carbohydrates: 11.1g, Sugar: 5.7g, Proteins: 1.8g, Sodium: 25mg

Tofu with Capers Sauce

Prep time: 10 minutes, cook time: 27 minutes; Serves 4

5 Ingredients:
- 4 tablespoons fresh parsley, divided
- 1 (14-ounces) block extra-firm tofu, pressed and cut into 8 rectangular cutlets
- 1 cup panko breadcrumbs
- 2 teaspoons cornstarch
- 2 tablespoons capers

What you' ll need from the store cupboard:
- 1 cup vegetable broth
- ½ cup lemon juice
- 2 garlic cloves, peeled
- ½ cup mayonnaise
- Salt and black pepper, to taste

Instructions:
1. Preheat the Air fryer to 375 º F and grease an Air fryer basket.
2. Put half of lemon juice, 2 tablespoons parsley, 2 garlic cloves, salt and black pepper in a food processor and pulse until smooth.
3. Transfer the mixture into a bowl and marinate tofu in it.
4. Place the mayonnaise in a shallow bowl and put the panko breadcrumbs in another bowl.
5. Coat the tofu pieces with mayonnaise and then, roll into the breadcrumbs.
6. Arrange the tofu pieces in the Air fryer pan and cook for about 20 minutes.
7. Mix broth, remaining lemon juice, remaining garlic, remaining parsley, cornstarch, salt and black pepper in a food processor and pulse until smooth.
8. Transfer the sauce into a small pan and stir in the capers.
9. Boil the sauce over medium heat and allow to simmer for about 7 minutes.
10. Dish out the tofu onto serving plates and drizzle with the caper sauce to serve.

Nutrition Facts Per Serving:
Calories: 307, Fat: 15.6g, Carbohydrates: 15.6g, Sugar: 3.4g, Protein: 10.8g, Sodium: 586mg

Tofu with Orange Sauce

Prep time: 20 minutes, cook time: 20 minutes; Serves 4

5 Ingredients:
- 1 pound extra-firm tofu, pressed and cubed
- ½ cup water
- 4 teaspoons cornstarch, divided
- 2 scallions (green part), chopped

What you' ll need from the store cupboard:
- 1 tablespoon tamari
- 1/3 cup fresh orange juice
- 1 tablespoon honey
- 1 teaspoon orange zest, grated
- 1 teaspoon garlic, minced
- 1 teaspoon fresh ginger, minced
- ¼ teaspoon red pepper flakes, crushed

Instructions:
1. Preheat the Air fryer to 390 º F and grease an Air fryer basket.
2. Mix the tofu, cornstarch, and tamari in a bowl and toss to coat well.
3. Arrange half of the tofu pieces in the Air fryer pan and cook for about 10 minutes.
4. Repeat with the remaining tofu and dish out in a bowl.
5. Put all the ingredients except scallions in a small pan over medium-high heat and bring to a boil.
6. Pour this sauce over the tofu and garnish with scallions to serve.

Nutrition Facts Per Serving:
Calories: 148, Fat: 6.7g, Carbohydrates: 13g, Sugar: 6.9g, Protein: 12.1g, Sodium: 263mg

Broccoli with Cauliflower

Prep time: 15 minutes, cook time: 20 minutes; Serves 4

5 Ingredients:
- 1½ cups broccoli, cut into 1-inch pieces
- 1½ cups cauliflower, cut into 1-inch pieces

What you' ll need from the store cupboard:
- 1 tablespoon olive oil
- Salt, as required

Instructions:
1. Preheat the Air fryer to 375 º F and grease an Air fryer basket.
2. Mix the vegetables, olive oil, and salt in a bowl and toss to coat well.
3. Arrange the veggie mixture in the Air fryer basket and cook for about 20 minutes, tossing once in between.
4. Dish out in a bowl and serve hot.

Nutrition Facts Per Serving:
Calories: 51, Fat: 3.7g, Carbohydrates: 4.3g, Sugar: 1.5g, Protein: 1.7g, Sodium: 61mg

Herbed Veggies Combo

Prep time: 15 minutes, cook time: 35 minutes; Serves 4

5 Ingredients:
- ½ pound carrots, peeled and sliced
- 1 pound yellow squash, sliced
- 1 pound zucchini, sliced
- ½ tablespoon fresh basil, chopped
- ½ tablespoon tarragon leaves, chopped

What you' ll need from the store cupboard:
- 6 teaspoons olive oil, divided
- Salt and ground white pepper, to taste

Instructions:
1. Preheat the Air fryer to 400 º F and grease an Air fryer basket.
2. Mix two teaspoons of oil and carrot slices in a bowl.
3. Arrange the carrot slices in the Air fryer basket and cook for about 5 minutes.
4. Mix the remaining oil, yellow squash, zucchini, salt, and white pepper in a large bowl and toss to coat well.
5. Transfer the zucchini mixture into air fryer basket with carrots and cook for about 30 minutes, tossing twice in between.
6. Dish out in a bowl and sprinkle with the herbs to serve.

Nutrition Facts Per Serving:
Calories: 120, Fat: 7.4g, Carbohydrates: 13.3g, Sugar: 6.7g, Protein: 3.3g, Sodium: 101mg

Spicy Tofu

Prep time: 10 minutes, cook time: 13 minutes; Serves 3

5 Ingredients:
- 1 (14-ounces) block extra-firm tofu, pressed and cut into ¾-inch cubes
- 3 teaspoons cornstarch

What you' ll need from the store cupboard:
- 1½ tablespoons avocado oil
- 1½ teaspoons paprika
- 1 teaspoon onion powder
- 1 teaspoon garlic powder
- Salt and black pepper, to taste

Instructions:
1. Preheat the Air fryer to 390 º F and grease an Air fryer basket.
2. Mix the tofu, oil, cornstarch, and spices in a bowl and toss to coat well.
3. Arrange the tofu pieces in the Air fryer basket and cook for about 13 minutes, tossing twice in between.
4. Dish out the tofu onto serving plates and serve hot.

Nutrition Facts Per Serving:
Calories: 121, Fat: 6.6g, Carbohydrates: 7g, Sugar: 1.4g, Protein: 11.3g, Sodium: 68mg

Sweet and Spicy Parsnips

Prep time: 15 minutes, cook time: 44 minutes; Serves 6

5 Ingredients:
- 2 pounds parsnip, peeled and cut into 1-inch chunks
- 1 tablespoon butter, melted

What you'll need from the store cupboard:
- 2 tablespoons honey
- 1 tablespoon dried parsley flakes, crushed
- ¼ teaspoon red pepper flakes, crushed
- Salt and ground black pepper, to taste

Instructions:
1. Preheat the Air fryer to 355 ° F and grease an Air fryer basket.
2. Mix the parsnips and butter in a bowl and toss to coat well.
3. Arrange the parsnip chunks in the Air fryer basket and cook for about 40 minutes.
4. Mix the remaining ingredients in another large bowl and stir in the parsnip chunks.
5. Transfer the parsnip chunks in the Air fryer basket and cook for about 4 minutes.
6. Dish out the parsnip chunks onto serving plates and serve hot.

Nutrition Facts Per Serving:
Calories: 155, Fat: 2.4g, Carbohydrates: 33.1g, Sugar: 13g, Protein: 1.9g, Sodium: 57mg

Herbed Carrots

Prep time: 15 minutes, cook time: 14 minutes; Serves 8

5 Ingredients:
- 6 large carrots, peeled and sliced lengthwise
- 2 tablespoons olive oil
- ½ tablespoon fresh oregano, chopped
- ½ tablespoon fresh parsley, chopped
- Salt and black pepper, to taste

What you'll need from the store cupboard:
- 2 tablespoons olive oil, divided
- ½ cup fat-free Italian dressing
- Salt, to taste

Instructions:
1. Preheat the Air fryer to 360 ° F and grease an Air fryer basket.
2. Mix the carrot slices and olive oil in a bowl and toss to coat well.
3. Arrange the carrot slices in the Air fryer basket and cook for about 12 minutes.
4. Dish out the carrot slices onto serving plates and sprinkle with herbs, salt and black pepper.
5. Transfer into the Air fryer basket and cook for 2 more minutes.
6. Dish out and serve hot.

Nutrition Facts Per Serving:
Calories: 93, Fat: 7.2g, Carbohydrates: 7.3g, Sugar: 3.8g, Protein: 0.7g, Sodium: 252mg

Curried Eggplant

Prep time: 15 minutes, cook time: 10 minutes; Serves 2

5 Ingredients:
- 1 large eggplant, cut into ½-inch thick slices

What you'll need from the store cupboard:
- 1 garlic clove, minced
- ½ fresh red chili, chopped
- 1 tablespoon vegetable oil
- ¼ teaspoon curry powder
- Salt, to taste

Instructions:
1. Preheat the Air fryer to 300 ° F and grease an Air fryer basket.
2. Mix all the ingredients in a bowl and toss to coat well.
3. Arrange the eggplant slices in the Air fryer basket and cook for about 10 minutes, tossing once in between.
4. Dish out onto serving plates and serve hot.

Nutrition Facts Per Serving:
Calories: 121, Fat: 7.3g, Carbohydrates: 14.2g, Sugar: 7g, Protein: 2.4g, Sodium: 83mg

Herbed Eggplant

Prep time: 15 minutes, cook time: 15 minutes; Serves 2

5 Ingredients:
- 1 large eggplant, cubed

What you'll need from the store cupboard:
- ½ teaspoon dried marjoram, crushed
- ½ teaspoon dried oregano, crushed
- ½ teaspoon dried thyme, crushed
- ½ teaspoon garlic powder
- Salt and black pepper, to taste
- Olive oil cooking spray

Instructions:
1. Preheat the Air fryer to 390 º F and grease an Air fryer basket.
2. Mix herbs, garlic powder, salt, and black pepper in a bowl.
3. Spray the eggplant cubes with cooking spray and rub with the herb mixture.
4. Arrange the eggplant cubes in the Air fryer basket and cook for about 15 minutes, flipping twice in between.
5. Dish out onto serving plates and serve hot.

Nutrition Facts Per Serving:
Calories: 62, Fat: 0.5g, Carbohydrates: 14.5g, Sugar: 7.1g, Protein: 2.4g, Sodium: 83mg

Salsa Stuffed Eggplants

Prep time: 15 minutes, cook time: 25 minutes; Serves 2

5 Ingredients:
- 1 large eggplant
- 8 cherry tomatoes, quartered
- ½ tablespoon fresh parsley

What you'll need from the store cupboard:
- 2 teaspoons olive oil, divided
- 2 teaspoons fresh lemon juice, divided
- 2 tablespoons tomato salsa
- Salt and black pepper, as required

Instructions:
1. Preheat the Air fryer to 390 º F and grease an Air fryer basket.
2. Arrange the eggplant into the Air fryer basket and cook for about 15 minutes.
3. Cut the eggplant in half lengthwise and drizzle evenly with one teaspoon of oil.
4. Set the Air fryer to 355 º F and arrange the eggplant into the Air fryer basket, cut-side up.
5. Cook for another 10 minutes and dish out in a bowl.
6. Scoop out the flesh from the eggplant and transfer into a bowl.
7. Stir in the tomatoes, salsa, parsley, salt, black pepper, remaining oil, and lemon juice.
8. Squeeze lemon juice on the eggplant halves and stuff with the salsa mixture to serve.

Nutrition Facts Per Serving:
Calories: 192, Fat: 6.1g, Carbohydrates: 33.8g, Sugar: 20.4g, Protein: 6.9g, Sodium: 204mg

Sesame Seeds Bok Choy

Prep time: 10 minutes, cook time: 6 minutes; Serves 4

5 Ingredients:
- 4 bunches baby bok choy, bottoms removed and leaves separated
- 1 teaspoon sesame seeds

What you'll need from the store cupboard:
- Olive oil cooking spray
- 1 teaspoon garlic powder

Instructions:
1. Preheat the Air fryer to 325 º F and grease an Air fryer basket.
2. Arrange the bok choy leaves into the Air fryer basket and spray with the cooking spray.
3. Sprinkle with garlic powder and cook for about 6 minutes, shaking twice in between.
4. Dish out in the bok choy onto serving plates and serve garnished with sesame seeds.

Nutrition Facts Per Serving:
Calories: 26, Fat: 0.7g, Carbohydrates: 4g, Sugar: 1.9g, Protein: 2.5g, Sodium: 98mg

Basil Tomatoes

Prep time: 10 minutes, cook time: 10 minutes; Serves 2

5 Ingredients:
- 2 tomatoes, halved
- 1 tablespoon fresh basil, chopped

What you'll need from the store cupboard:
- Olive oil cooking spray
- Salt and black pepper, as required

Instructions:
1. Preheat the Air fryer to 320 º F and grease an Air fryer basket.
2. Spray the tomato halves evenly with olive oil cooking spray and season with salt, black pepper and basil.
3. Arrange the tomato halves into the Air fryer basket, cut sides up.
4. Cook for about 10 minutes and dish out onto serving plates.

Nutrition Facts Per Serving:
Calories: 22, Fat: 4.8g, Carbohydrates: 4.8g, Sugar: 3.2g, Protein: 1.1g, Sodium: 84mg

Couscous Stuffed Tomatoes

Prep time: 10 minutes, cook time: 25 minutes; Serves 4

5 Ingredients:
- 4 tomatoes, tops and seeds removed
- 1 parsnip, peeled and finely chopped
- 1 cup mushrooms, chopped
- 1½ cups couscous

What you'll need from the store cupboard:
- 1 teaspoon olive oil
- 1 garlic clove, minced
- 1 tablespoon mirin sauce

Instructions:
1. Preheat the Air fryer to 355 º F and grease an Air fryer basket.
2. Heat olive oil in a skillet on low heat and add parsnips, mushrooms and garlic.
3. Cook for about 5 minutes and stir in the mirin sauce and couscous.
4. Stuff the couscous mixture into the tomatoes and arrange into the Air fryer basket.
5. Cook for about 20 minutes and dish out to serve warm.

Nutrition Facts Per Serving:
Calories: 361, Fat: 2g, Carbohydrates: 75.5g, Sugar: 5.1g, Protein: 10.4g, Sodium: 37mg

Sweet and Spicy Cauliflower

Prep time: 15 minutes, cook time: 25 minutes; Serves 4

5 Ingredients:
- 1 head cauliflower, cut into florets
- ¾ cup onion, thinly sliced
- 2 scallions, chopped

What you'll need from the store cupboard:
- 5 garlic cloves, finely sliced
- 1½ tablespoons soy sauce
- 1 tablespoon hot sauce
- 1 tablespoon rice vinegar
- 1 teaspoon coconut sugar
- Pinch of red pepper flakes
- Ground black pepper, as required

Instructions:
1. Preheat the Air fryer to 350 º F and grease an Air fryer basket.
2. Arrange the cauliflower florets into the Air fryer basket and cook for about 10 minutes.
3. Add the onions and garlic and cook for 10 more minutes.
4. Meanwhile, mix soy sauce, hot sauce, vinegar, coconut sugar, red pepper flakes, and black pepper in a bowl.
5. Pour the soy sauce mixture into the cauliflower mixture.
6. Cook for about 5 minutes and dish out onto serving plates.
7. Garnish with scallions and serve warm.

Nutrition Facts Per Serving:
Calories: 72, Fat: 0.2g, Carbohydrates: 13.8g, Sugar: 3.1g, Protein: 3.6g, Sodium: 1300mg

Spiced Butternut Squash

Prep time: 15 minutes, cook time: 20 minutes; Serves 4

5 Ingredients:
- 1 medium butternut squash, peeled, seeded and cut into chunk
- 2 teaspoons cumin seeds
- 2 tablespoons pine nuts
- 2 tablespoons fresh cilantro, chopped

What you' ll need from the store cupboard:
- 1/8 teaspoon garlic powder
- 1/8 teaspoon chili flakes, crushed
- Salt and ground black pepper, as required
- 1 tablespoon olive oil

Instructions:

1. Preheat the Air fryer to 375 º F and grease an Air fryer basket.
2. Mix the squash, spices and olive oil in a bowl.
3. Arrange the butternut squash chunks into the Air fryer basket and cook for about 20 minutes.
4. Dish out the butternut squash chunks onto serving plates and serve garnished with pine nuts and cilantro.

Nutrition Facts Per Serving:
Calories: 165, Fat: 6.9g, Carbohydrates: 27.6g, Sugar: 5.2g, Protein: 3.1g, Sodium: 50mg

Herbed Potatoes

Prep time: 20 minutes, cook time: 15 minutes; Serves 4

5 Ingredients:
- 6 small potatoes, chopped
- 2 tablespoons fresh parsley, chopped

What you' ll need from the store cupboard:
- 3 tablespoons olive oil
- 2 teaspoons mixed dried herbs
- Salt and black pepper, to taste

Instructions:
1. Preheat the Air fryer to 360 º F and grease an Air fryer basket.
2. Mix the potatoes, oil, herbs, salt and black pepper in a bowl.
3. Arrange the chopped potatoes into the Air fryer basket and cook for about 15 minutes, tossing once in between.
4. Dish out the potatoes onto serving plates and serve garnished with parsley.

Nutrition Facts Per Serving:
Calories: 268, Fat: 10.8g, Carbohydrates: 40.4g, Sugar: 3g, Protein: 4.4g, Sodium: 55mg

Spicy Potatoes

Prep time: 10 minutes, cook time: 20 minutes; Serves 6

5 Ingredients:
- 1¾ pounds waxy potatoes, peeled and cubed

What you' ll need from the store cupboard:
- 1 tablespoon olive oil
- ½ teaspoon ground cumin
- ½ teaspoon ground coriander
- ½ teaspoon paprika
- Salt and black pepper, to taste

Instructions:
1. Preheat the Air fryer to 355 º F and grease an Air fryer basket.
2. Mix the potatoes, olive oil, and spices in a bowl and toss to coat well.
3. Transfer into the Air fryer basket and cook for about 20 minutes.
4. Dish out the potato cubes onto serving plates and serve hot.

Nutrition Facts Per Serving:
Calories: 113, Fat: 2.5g, Carbohydrates: 21g, Sugar: 1.5g, Protein: 2.3g, Sodium: 35mg

Tofu with Peanut Butter Sauce

Prep time: 20 minutes, cook time: 15 minutes; Serves 3

5 Ingredients:

For Tofu
- 1 (14-ounces) block tofu, pressed and cut into strips
- 6 bamboo skewers, presoaked and halved

What you' ll need from the store cupboard:

For Tofu
- 2 tablespoons fresh lime juice
- 2 tablespoons soy sauce
- 1 tablespoon maple syrup
- 1 teaspoon Sriracha sauce
- 2 teaspoons fresh ginger, peeled
- 2 garlic cloves, peeled

For Sauce
- 1 (2-inches) piece fresh ginger, peeled
- 2 garlic cloves, peeled
- ½ cup creamy peanut butter
- 1 tablespoon soy sauce
- 1 tablespoon fresh lime juice
- 1-2 teaspoons Sriracha sauce
- 6 tablespoons of water

Instructions:
1. Preheat the Air fryer to 370 º F and grease an Air fryer basket.
2. Put all the ingredients except tofu in a food processor and pulse until smooth.
3. Transfer the mixture into a bowl and marinate tofu in it.
4. Thread one tofu strip onto each little bamboo stick and arrange them in the Air fryer basket.
5. Cook for about 15 minutes and dish out onto serving plates.
6. Mix all the ingredients for the sauce in a food processor and pulse until smooth.
7. Drizzle the sauce over tofu and serve warm.

Nutrition Facts Per Serving:
Calories: 385, Fats: 27.3g, Carbohydrates: 9.3g, Sugar: 9.1g, Proteins: 23g, Sodium: 1141mg

Veggie Rice

Prep time: 20 minutes, cook time: 18 minutes; Serves 2

5 Ingredients:
- 2 cups cooked white rice
- 1 large egg, lightly beaten
- ½ cup frozen peas, thawed
- ½ cup frozen carrots, thawed
- ½ teaspoon sesame seeds, toasted

What you' ll need from the store cupboard:
- 1 tablespoon vegetable oil
- 2 teaspoons sesame oil, toasted and divided
- 1 tablespoon water
- Salt and ground white pepper, as required
- 1 teaspoon soy sauce
- 1 teaspoon Sriracha sauce

Instructions:
1. Preheat the Air fryer to 380 º F and grease an Air fryer pan.
2. Mix the rice, vegetable oil, 1 teaspoon of sesame oil, water, salt, and white pepper in a bowl.
3. Transfer the rice mixture into the Air fryer basket and cook for about 12 minutes.
4. Pour the beaten egg over rice and cook for about 4 minutes.
5. Stir in the peas and carrots and cook for 2 more minutes.
6. Meanwhile, mix soy sauce, Sriracha sauce, sesame seeds and the remaining sesame oil in a bowl.
7. Dish out the potato cubes onto serving plates and drizzle with sauce to serve.

Nutrition Facts Per Serving:
Calories: 163, Fat: 8.4g, Carbohydrates: 15.5g, Sugar: 11.2g, Protein: 6.4g, Sodium: 324mg

Tofu with Veggies

Prep time: 25 minutes, cook time: 22 minutes; Serves 3

5 Ingredients:

- ½ (14-ounces) block firm tofu, pressed and crumbled
- 1 cup carrot, peeled and chopped
- 3 cups cauliflower rice
- ½ cup broccoli, finely chopped
- ½ cup frozen peas

What you' ll need from the store cupboard:

- 4 tablespoons low-sodium soy sauce, divided
- 1 teaspoon ground turmeric
- 1 tablespoon fresh ginger, minced
- 2 garlic cloves, minced
- 1 tablespoon rice vinegar
- 1½ teaspoons sesame oil, toasted

Instructions:

1. Preheat the Air fryer to 370 º F and grease an Air fryer pan.
2. Mix the tofu, carrot, onion, 2 tablespoons of soy sauce, and turmeric in a bowl.
3. Transfer the tofu mixture into the Air fryer basket and cook for about 10 minutes.
4. Meanwhile, mix the cauliflower rice, broccoli, peas, ginger, garlic, vinegar, sesame oil, and remaining soy sauce in a bowl.
5. Stir in the cauliflower rice into the Air fryer pan and cook for about 12 minutes.
6. Dish out the tofu mixture onto serving plates and serve hot.

Nutrition Facts Per Serving:
Calories: 162, Fat: 5.5g, Carbohydrates: 20.4g, Sugar: 8.3g, Protein: 11.4g, Sodium: 1263mg

Delightful Mushrooms

Prep time: 20 minutes, cook time: 22 minutes; Serves 4

5 Ingredients:

- 2 cups mushrooms, sliced
- 2 tablespoons cheddar cheese, shredded
- 1 tablespoon fresh chives, chopped

What you' ll need from the store cupboard:

- 2 tablespoons olive oil

Instructions:

1. Preheat the Air fryer to 355 º F and grease an Air fryer basket.
2. Coat the mushrooms with olive oil and arrange into the Air fryer basket.
3. Cook for about 20 minutes and dish out in a platter.
4. Top with chives and cheddar cheese and cook for 2 more minutes.
5. Dish out and serve warm.

Nutrition Facts Per Serving:
Calories: 218, Fat: 7.9g, Carbohydrates: 33.6g, Sugar: 2.5g, Protein: 4.6g, Sodium: 55mg

Sesame Seeds Bok Choy

Prep time: 10 minutes, cook time: 6 minutes; Serves 4

5 Ingredients:

- 4 bunches spinach leaves
- 2 teaspoons sesame seeds

What you' ll need from the store cupboard:

- 1 teaspoon garlic powder
- 1 teaspoon ginger powder
- Salt, to taste

Instructions:

1. Preheat the Air fryer to 325 º F and grease an Air fryer basket.
2. Arrange the spinach leaves into the Air fryer basket and season with salt, garlic powder and ginger powder.
3. Cook for about 6 minutes, shaking once in between and dish out onto serving plates.
4. Top with sesame seeds and serve hot.

Nutrition Facts Per Serving:
Calories: 26, Fat: 0.7g, Carbohydrates: 4g, Sugar: 1.9g, Protein: 2.5g, Sodium: 98mg

Chapter 6 Beef, Lamb and Pork Recipes

Sweet and Sour Pork Chops

Prep time: 10 minutes, cook time: 16 minutes; Serves 4

5 Ingredients:
- 6 pork loin chops

What you'll need from the store cupboard:
- Salt and black pepper, to taste
- 2 garlic cloves, minced
- 2 tablespoons honey
- 2 tablespoons soy sauce
- 1 tablespoon balsamic vinegar
- ¼ teaspoon ground ginger

Instructions:
1. Preheat the Air fryer to 355 º F and grease a baking tray.
2. Season the chops with a little salt and black pepper.
3. Mix rest of the ingredients in a large bowl and add chops.
4. Coat with marinade generously and cover to refrigerate for about 8 hours.
5. Arrange the chops in a baking tray and transfer into the Air fryer.
6. Cook for about 16 minutes, flipping once in between and dish out to serve hot.

Nutrition Facts Per Serving:
Calories: 282, Fats: 19.9g, Carbohydrates: 6.6g, Sugar: 5.9g, Proteins: 18.4g, Sodium: 357mg

Perfect Skirt Steak

Prep time: 15 minutes, cook time: 30 minutes; Serves 4

5 Ingredients:
- 1 cup fresh parsley leaves, chopped finely
- 3 tablespoons fresh oregano, chopped finely
- 3 tablespoons fresh mint leaves, chopped finely
- 2 (8-ounce) skirt steaks

What you'll need from the store cupboard:
- 3 garlic cloves, minced
- 1 tablespoon ground cumin
- 2 teaspoons smoked paprika
- 1 teaspoon cayenne pepper
- 1 teaspoon red pepper flakes, crushed
- Salt and freshly ground black pepper, to taste
- ¾ cup olive oil
- 3 tablespoons red wine vinegar

Instructions:
1. Preheat the Air fryer to 390 º F and grease an Air fryer basket.
2. Season the steaks with a little salt and black pepper.
3. Mix all the ingredients in a large bowl except the steaks.
4. Put ¼ cup of the herb mixture and steaks in a resealable bag and shake well.
5. Refrigerate for about 24 hours and reserve the remaining herb mixture.
6. Keep the steaks at room temperature for about 30 minutes and transfer into the Air fryer basket.
7. Cook for about 10 minutes and sprinkle with remaining herb mixture to serve.

Nutrition Facts Per Serving:
Calories: 561, Fat: 50.3g, Carbohydrates: 6.1g, Sugar: 0.6g, Protein: 31.9g, Sodium: 297mg

Super Simple Steaks

Prep time: 5 minutes, cook time: 14 minutes; Serves 2

5 Ingredients:
- ½ pound quality cuts steak

What you'll need from the store cupboard:
- Salt and black pepper, to taste

Instructions:
1. Preheat the Air fryer to 390 º F and grease an Air fryer basket.
2. Season the steaks evenly with salt and black pepper and transfer into the Air fryer basket.
3. Cook for about 14 minutes and dish out to serve.

Nutrition Facts Per Serving:
Calories: 211, Fat: 7.1g, Carbohydrates: 0g, Sugar: 0g, Protein: 34.4g, Sodium: 75mg

Filling Pork Chops

Prep time: 20 minutes, cook time: 12 minutes; Serves 2

5 Ingredients:

- 2 (1-inch thick) pork chops
- ½ tablespoon fresh cilantro, chopped
- ½ tablespoon fresh rosemary, chopped
- ½ tablespoon fresh parsley, chopped

What you' ll need from the store cupboard:

- 2 garlic cloves, minced
- 2 tablespoons olive oil
- ¾ tablespoon Dijon mustard
- 1 tablespoon ground coriander
- 1 teaspoon sugar
- Salt, to taste

Instructions:

1. Preheat the Air fryer to 390 º F and grease an Air fryer basket.
2. Mix all the ingredients in a large bowl except the chops.
3. Coat the pork chops with marinade generously and cover to refrigerate for about 3 hours.
4. Keep the pork chops at room temperature for about 30 minutes and transfer into the Air fryer basket.
5. Cook for about 12 minutes, flipping once in between and dish out to serve hot.

Nutrition Facts Per Serving:
Calories: 276, Fat: 19.1g, Carbohydrates: 3.9g, Sugar: 2.1g, Protein: 22.6g, Sodium: 185mg

Garlicky Lamb Chops

Prep time: 20 minutes, cook time: 22 minutes; Serves 4

5 Ingredients:

- 1 tablespoon fresh oregano, chopped
- 1 tablespoon fresh thyme, chopped
- 8 (4-ounce) lamb chops

What you' ll need from the store cupboard:

- ¼ cup olive oil, divided
- 1 bulb garlic
- Salt and black pepper, to taste

Instructions:

1. Preheat the Air fryer to 390 º F and grease an Air fryer basket.
2. Rub the garlic bulb with about 2 tablespoons of the olive oil.
3. Arrange the garlic bulb in the Air fryer basket and cook for about 12 minutes.
4. Mix remaining oil, herbs, salt and black pepper in a large bowl.
5. Coat the pork chops with about 1 tablespoon of the herb mixture.
6. Place half of the chops in the Air fryer basket with garlic bulb and cook for about 5 minutes.
7. Repeat with the remaining lamb chops and serve with herb mixture.

Nutrition Facts Per Serving:
Calories: 551, Fat: 29.4g, Carbohydrates: 4.7g, Sugar: 0.9g, Protein: 64.5g, Sodium: 175mg

Caramelized Pork

Prep time: 10 minutes, cook time: 17 minutes; Serves 6

5 Ingredients:

- 2 pounds pork shoulder, cut into 1½-inch thick slices

What you' ll need from the store cupboard:

- 1/3 cup soy sauce
- 2 tablespoons sugar
- 1 tablespoon honey

Instructions:

1. Preheat the Air fryer to 335 º F and grease an Air fryer basket.
2. Mix all the ingredients in a large bowl and coat chops well.
3. Cover and refrigerate for about 8 hours.
4. Arrange the chops in the Air fryer basket and cook for about 10 minutes, flipping once in between.
5. Set the Air fryer to 390 º F and cook for 7 more minutes.
6. Dish out in a platter and serve hot.

Nutrition Facts Per Serving:
Calories: 475, Fat: 32.4g, Carbohydrates: 8g, Sugar: 7.1g, Protein: 36.1g, Sodium: 902mg

114

Nut Crusted Rack of Lamb

Prep time: 15 minutes, cook time: 35 minutes; Serves 6

5 Ingredients:
- 1¾ pound rack of lamb
- 1 egg
- 1 tablespoon breadcrumbs
- 3-ounce almonds, chopped finely
- 1 tablespoon fresh rosemary, chopped

What you' ll need from the store cupboard:
- 1 tablespoon olive oil
- 1 garlic clove, minced
- Salt and black pepper, to taste

Instructions:
1. Preheat the Air fryer to 220 º F and grease an Air fryer basket.
2. Mix garlic, olive oil, salt and black pepper in a bowl.
3. Whisk the egg in a shallow dish and mix breadcrumbs, almonds and rosemary in another shallow dish.
4. Coat the rack of lamb with garlic mixture evenly, dip into the egg and dredge into the breadcrumb mixture.
5. Arrange the rack of lamb in the Air fryer basket and cook for about 30 minutes.
6. Set the Air fryer to 390 º F and cook for about 5 more minutes.
7. Dish out and serve warm.

Nutrition Facts Per Serving:
Calories: 366, Fat: 20g, Carbohydrates: 4.4g, Sugar: 0.7g, Protein: 41.3g, Sodium: 120mg

Flavorsome Pork Chops with Peanut Sauce

Prep time: 15 minutes, cook time: 12 minutes; Serves 4

5 Ingredients:
- 1 pound pork chops, cubed into 1-inch size
- 1 shallot, chopped finely
- ¾ cup ground peanuts
- ¾ cup coconut milk

What you' ll need from the store cupboard:

For Pork:
- 1 teaspoon fresh ginger, minced
- 1 garlic clove, minced
- 2 tablespoon soy sauce
- 1 tablespoon olive oil
- 1 teaspoon hot pepper sauce

For Peanut Sauce:
- 1 tablespoon olive oil
- 1 garlic clove, minced
- 1 teaspoon ground coriander
- 1 tablespoon olive oil
- 1 teaspoon hot pepper sauce

Instructions:
1. Preheat the Air fryer to 390 º F and grease an Air fryer basket.

For Pork:
2. Mix all the ingredients in a bowl and keep aside for about 30 minutes.
3. Arrange the chops in the Air fryer basket and cook for about 12 minutes, flipping once in between.

For Peanut Sauce:
4. Heat olive oil in a pan on medium heat and add shallot and garlic.
5. Sauté for about 3 minutes and stir in coriander.
6. Sauté for about 1 minute and add rest of the ingredients.
7. Cook for about 5 minutes and pour over the pork chops to serve.

Nutrition Facts Per Serving:
Calories: 725, Fat: 62.9g, Carbohydrates: 9.5g, Sugar: 2.8g, Protein: 34.4g, Sodium: 543mg

Comforting Sausage Casserole

Prep time: 15 minutes, cook time: 30 minutes; Serves 4

5 Ingredients:
- 6-ounce flour
- 2 eggs
- 1 red onion, sliced thinly
- ¾ cup milk
- 8 small sausages

What you' ll need from the store cupboard:
- 1 tablespoon olive oil
- 1 garlic clove, minced
- Salt and black pepper, to taste

Instructions:
1. Preheat the Air fryer to 320 º F and grease a casserole dish.
2. Sift the flour in a bowl and whisk in the eggs.
3. Combine well and add onion, garlic, milk, 2/3 cup cold water salt and black pepper.
4. Pierce 1 rosemary sprig in each sausage and transfer into the casserole dish.
5. Top evenly with the flour mixture and cook for about 30 minutes.
6. Dish out and serve warm.

Nutrition Facts Per Serving:
Calories: 339, Fat: 14.5g, Carbohydrates: 37.7g, Sugar: 3.5g, Protein: 14.1g, Sodium: 249mg

Classic Skirt Steak Strips with Veggies

Prep time: 10 minutes, cook time: 17 minutes; Serves 4

5 Ingredients:
- 1 (12-ounce) skirt steak, cut into thin strips
- ½ pound fresh mushrooms, quartered
- 6-ounce snow peas
- 1 onion, cut into half rings

What you' ll need from the store cupboard:
- ¼ cup olive oil, divided
- 2 tablespoons soy sauce
- 2 tablespoons honey
- Salt and black pepper, to taste

Instructions:
1. Preheat the Air fryer to 390 º F and grease an Air fryer basket.
2. Mix 2 tablespoons of oil, soy sauce and honey in a bowl and coat steak strips with this marinade.
3. Put vegetables, remaining oil, salt and black pepper in another bowl and toss well.
4. Transfer the steak strips and vegetables in the Air fryer basket and cook for about 17 minutes.
5. Dish out and serve warm.

Nutrition Facts Per Serving:
Calories: 360, Fat: 21.5g, Carbohydrates: 16.7g, Sugar: 12.6g, Protein: 26.7g, Sodium: 522mg

Smoky Flavored Pork Ribs

Prep time: 10 minutes, cook time: 13 minutes; Serves 6

5 Ingredients:
- 1¾ pound pork ribs

What you' ll need from the store cupboard:
- ¼ cup honey, divided
- ¾ cup BBQ sauce
- 2 tablespoons tomato ketchup
- 1 tablespoon Worcestershire sauce
- 1 tablespoon soy sauce
- ½ teaspoon garlic powder
- Freshly ground white pepper, to taste

Instructions:
1. Preheat the Air fryer to 355 º F and grease an Air fryer basket.
2. Mix 3 tablespoons of honey and remaining ingredients in a large bowl except the ribs.
3. Coat the pork ribs with marinade generously and cover to refrigerate for about 30 minutes.
4. Transfer the ribs into the Air fryer basket and cook for about 13 minutes.
5. Coat with remaining honey and serve hot.

Nutrition Facts Per Serving:
Calories: 461, Fat: 23.5g, Carbohydrates: 25.1g, Sugar: 21.5g, Protein: 35.4g, Sodium: 661mg

Moist Stuffed Pork Roll

Prep time: 20 minutes, cook time: 15 minutes; Serves 4

5 Ingredients:

- 1 scallion, chopped
- ¼ cup sun-dried tomatoes, chopped finely
- 2 tablespoons fresh parsley, chopped
- 4 (6-ounce) pork cutlets, pounded slightly

What you' ll need from the store cupboard:

- Salt and black pepper, to taste
- 2 teaspoons paprika
- ½ tablespoon olive oil

Instructions:

1. Preheat the Air fryer to 390 º F and grease an Air fryer basket.
2. Mix scallion, tomatoes, parsley, salt and black pepper in a large bowl.
3. Coat the cutlets with tomato mixture and roll each cutlet.
4. Secure the cutlets with cocktail sticks and rub with paprika, salt and black pepper.
5. Coat evenly with oil and transfer into the Air fryer basket.
6. Cook for about 15 minutes, flipping once in between and dish out to serve hot.

Nutrition Facts Per Serving:
Calories: 265, Fats: 7.9g, Carbohydrates: 1.4g, Sugar: 0.5g, Proteins: 44.9g, Sodium: 100mg

Veal Rolls

Prep time: 15 minutes, cook time: 15 minutes; Serves 4

5 Ingredients:

- 4 (6-ounce) veal cutlets
- 2 tablespoons fresh sage leaves
- 4 cured ham slices
- 1 tablespoon unsalted butter, melted

What you' ll need from the store cupboard:

- Salt and black pepper, to taste

Instructions:

1. Preheat the Air fryer to 390 º F and grease an Air fryer basket.
2. Season the veal cutlets with salt and roll them up tightly.
3. Wrap 1 ham slice around each roll and coat with 1 tablespoon of the butter.
4. Top rolls with the sage leaves and transfer into the Air fryer basket.
5. Cook for about 10 minutes, flipping once in between and set the Air fryer to 300 º F.
6. Cook for about 5 more minutes and dish out to serve hot.

Nutrition Facts Per Serving:
Calories: 467, Fat: 24.8g, Carbohydrates: 1.7g, Sugar: 0g, Protein: 56g, Sodium: 534mg

Gourmet Meatloaf

Prep time: 15 minutes, cook time: 25 minutes; Serves 4

5 Ingredients:

- 14-ounce lean ground beef
- 1 chorizo sausage, chopped finely
- 1 small onion, chopped
- 3 tablespoons breadcrumbs
- 2 tablespoons fresh mushrooms, sliced thinly

What you' ll need from the store cupboard:

- 1 garlic clove, minced
- Salt and black pepper, to taste
- 2 tablespoons olive oil

Instructions:

1. Preheat the Air fryer to 390 º F and grease an Air fryer basket.
2. Mix all the ingredients in a large bowl except mushrooms.
3. Place the beef mixture in the pan and smooth the surface with the back of spatula.
4. Top with mushroom slices and press into the meatloaf gently.
5. Drizzle evenly with oil and arrange in the Air fryer basket.
6. Cook for about 25 minutes and cut into desires size wedges to serve.

Nutrition Facts Per Serving:
Calories: 284, Fat: 14.4g, Carbohydrates: 5.6g, Sugar: 1.1g, Protein: 31.7g, Sodium: 128mg

Scrumptious Lamb Chops

Prep time: 20 minutes, cook time: 8 minutes; Serves 4

5 Ingredients:
- 2 tablespoons fresh mint leaves, minced
- 4 (6-ounce) lamb chops
- 2 carrots, peeled and cubed
- 1 parsnip, peeled and cubed
- 1 fennel bulb, cubed

What you' ll need from the store cupboard:
- 1 garlic clove, minced
- 2 tablespoons dried rosemary
- 3 tablespoons olive oil
- Salt and black pepper, to taste

Instructions:
1. Preheat the Air fryer to 390 º F and grease an Air fryer basket.
2. Mix herbs, garlic and oil in a large bowl and coat chops generously with this mixture.
3. Marinate in the refrigerator for about 3 hours.
4. Soak the vegetables in a large pan of water for about 15 minutes.
5. Arrange the chops in the Air fryer basket and cook for about 2 minutes.
6. Remove the chops and place the vegetables in the Air fryer basket.
7. Top with the chops and cook for about 6 minutes.
8. Dish out and serve warm.

Nutrition Facts Per Serving:
Calories: 470, Fat: 23.5g, Carbohydrates: 14.8g, Sugar: 3.1g, Protein: 49.4g, Sodium: 186mg

Fantastic Leg of Lamb

Prep time: 10 minutes, cook time: 1 hour 15 minutes; Serves 4

5 Ingredients:
- 2 pounds (3 ounce) leg of lamb
- 2 fresh rosemary sprigs
- 2 fresh thyme sprigs

What you' ll need from the store cupboard:
- 2 tablespoons olive oil
- Salt and black pepper, to taste

Instructions:
1. Preheat the Air fryer to 300 º F and grease an Air fryer basket.
2. Sprinkle the leg of lamb with oil, salt and black pepper and wrap with herb sprigs.
3. Arrange the leg of lamb in the Air fryer basket and cook for about 75 minutes.
4. Dish out and serve warm.

Nutrition Facts Per Serving:
Calories: 534, Fat: 25.8g, Carbohydrates: 2.4g, Sugar: 0g, Protein: 69.8g, Sodium: 190mg

Easy Rib Eye Steak

Prep time: 10 minutes, cook time: 14 minutes; Serves 4

5 Ingredients:
- 2 lbs. rib eye steak

What you' ll need from the store cupboard:
- 1 tablespoon olive oil
- 1 tablespoon steak rubº

Instructions:
1. Preheat the Air fryer to 400 º F and grease an Air fryer basket.
2. Rub the steak generously with steak rub and coat with olive oil.
3. Transfer the steak in the Air fryer basket and cook for about 14 minutes, flipping once in between.
4. Dish out the steak and cut into desired size slices to serve.

Nutrition Facts Per Serving:
Calories: 438, Fat: 35.8g, Carbohydrates: 0g, Sugar: 0g, Protein: 26.8g, Sodium: 157mg
(Note: To prepare the Steak Rub - 2 tablespoons fresh cracked black pepper, 2 tablespoons kosher salt, 2 tablespoons paprika, 1 tablespoon crushed red pepper flakes, 1 tablespoon crushed coriander seeds (not ground), 1 tablespoon garlic powder, 1 tablespoon onion powder, 2 teaspoons cayenne pepper. Mix all ingredients in a medium bowl and stir well to combine.)

Buttered Striploin Steak

Prep time: 10 minutes, cook time: 12 minutes; Serves 2

5 Ingredients:
- 2 (7-ounces) striploin steak
- 1½ tablespoons butter, softened

What you'll need from the store cupboard:
- Salt and black pepper, to taste

Instructions:
1. Preheat the Air fryer to 390 º F and grease an Air fryer basket.
2. Rub the steak generously with salt and black pepper and coat with butter.
3. Transfer the steak in the Air fryer basket and cook for about 12 minutes, flipping once in between.
4. Dish out the steak and cut into desired size slices to serve.

Nutrition Facts Per Serving:
Calories: 595, Fat: 37.6g, Carbohydrates: 0g, Sugar: 0g, Protein: 58.1g, Sodium: 452mg

Simple New York Strip Steak

Prep time: 10 minutes, cook time: 10 minutes; Serves 2

5 Ingredients:
- 1 (9½-ounces) New York strip steak

What you'll need from the store cupboard:
- 1 teaspoon olive oil
- Crushed red pepper flakes, to taste
- Salt and black pepper, to taste

Instructions:
1. Preheat the Air fryer to 400 º F and grease an Air fryer basket.
2. Rub the steak generously with red pepper flakes, salt and black pepper and coat with olive oil.
3. Transfer the steak in the Air fryer basket and cook for about 10 minutes, flipping once in between.
4. Dish out the steak and cut into desired size slices to serve.

Nutrition Facts Per Serving:
Calories: 186, Fat: 7g, Carbohydrates: 0g, Sugar: 0g, Protein: 30.2g, Sodium: 177mg

Crispy Sirloin Steak

Prep time: 15 minutes, cook time: 10 minutes; Serves 2

5 Ingredients:
- 1 cup white flour
- 2 eggs
- 1 cup panko breadcrumbs
- 2 (6-ounces) sirloin steaks, pounded

What you'll need from the store cupboard:
- 1 teaspoon garlic powder
- 1 teaspoon onion powder
- Salt and black pepper, to taste

Instructions:
1. Preheat the Air fryer to 360 º F and grease an Air fryer basket.
2. Place the flour in a shallow bowl and whisk eggs in a second dish.
3. Mix the panko breadcrumbs and spices in a third bowl.
4. Rub the steak with flour, dip into the eggs and coat with breadcrumb mixture.
5. Transfer the steak in the Air fryer basket and cook for about 10 minutes, flipping once in between.
6. Dish out the steak and cut into desired size slices to serve.

Nutrition Facts Per Serving:
Calories: 561, Fat: 50.3g, Carbohydrates: 6.1g, Sugar: 0.6g, Protein: 31.9g, Sodium: 100mg

Steak with Bell Peppers

Prep time: 20 minutes, cook time: 22 minutes; Serves 4

5 Ingredients:
- 1¼ pounds beef steak, cut into thin strips
- 2 green bell peppers, seeded and cubed
- 1 red bell pepper, seeded and cubed
- 1 red onion, sliced

What you' ll need from the store cupboard:
- 1 teaspoon dried oregano, crushed
- 1 teaspoon onion powder
- 1 teaspoon garlic powder
- 1 teaspoon red chili powder
- 1 teaspoon paprika
- Salt, to taste
- 2 tablespoons olive oil

Instructions:

1. Preheat the Air fryer to 390 $^\circ$ F and grease an Air fryer basket.
2. Mix the oregano and spices in a bowl.
3. Add bell peppers, onion, oil, and beef strips and mix until well combined.
4. Transfer half of the steak strips in the Air fryer basket and cook for about 11 minutes, flipping once in between.
5. Repeat with the remaining mixture and dish out to serve hot.

Nutrition Facts Per Serving:
Calories: 372, Fats: 16.3g, Carbohydrates: 11.2g, Sugar: 6.2g, Proteins: 44.6g, Sodium: 143mg

Beef Roast

Prep time: 10 minutes, cook time: 50 minutes; Serves 6

5 Ingredients:
- 2½ pounds beef eye of round roast, trimmed

What you' ll need from the store cupboard:
- 2 tablespoons olive oil
- ½ teaspoon onion powder
- ½ teaspoon garlic powder
- ½ teaspoon cayenne pepper
- ½ teaspoon ground black pepper
- Salt, to taste

Instructions:

1. Preheat the Air fryer to 360 $^\circ$ F and grease an Air fryer basket.
2. Rub the roast generously with all the spices and coat with olive oil.
3. Arrange the roast in the Air fryer basket and cook for about 50 minutes.
4. Dish out the roast and cover with foil.
5. Cut into desired size slices and serve.

Nutrition Facts Per Serving:
Calories: 397, Fat: 12.4g, Carbohydrates: 0.5g, Sugar: 0.2g, Protein: 55.5g, Sodium: 99mg

Buttered Filet Mignon

Prep time: 10 minutes, cook time: 14 minutes; Serves 4

5 Ingredients:
- 2 (6-ounces) filet mignon steaks
- 1 tablespoon butter, softened

What you' ll need from the store cupboard:
- Salt and black pepper, to taste

Instructions:

1. Preheat the Air fryer to 390 $^\circ$ F and grease an Air fryer basket.
2. Rub the steak generously with salt and black pepper and coat with butter.
3. Arrange the steaks in the Air fryer basket and cook for about 14 minutes.
4. Dish out the steaks and cut into desired size slices to serve.

Nutrition Facts Per Serving:
Calories: 403, Fat: 22g, Carbohydrates: 0g, Sugar: 0g, Protein: 48.7g, Sodium: 228mg

Bacon Wrapped Filet Mignon

Prep time: 15 minutes, cook time: 15 minutes; Serves 2

5 Ingredients:
- 2 bacon slices
- 2 (6-ounces) filet mignon steaks

What you' ll need from the store cupboard:
- Salt and black pepper, to taste
- 1 teaspoon avocado oil

Instructions:
1. Preheat the Air fryer to 375 º F and grease an Air fryer basket.
2. Wrap each mignon steak with 1 bacon slice and secure with a toothpick.
3. Season the steak generously with salt and black pepper and coat with avocado oil.
4. Arrange the steaks in the Air fryer basket and cook for about 15 minutes, flipping once in between.
5. Dish out the steaks and cut into desired size slices to serve.

Nutrition Facts Per Serving:
Calories: 512, Fat: 28.6g, Carbohydrates: 0.5g, Sugar: 0g, Protein: 59.4g, Sodium: 857mg

Beef Short Ribs

Prep time: 15 minutes, cook time: 16 minutes; Serves 8

5 Ingredients:
- 4 pounds bone-in beef short ribs
- 1/3 cup scallions, chopped

What you' ll need from the store cupboard:
- 1 tablespoon fresh ginger, finely grated
- 1 cup low-sodium soy sauce
- ½ cup rice vinegar
- 1 tablespoon Sriracha
- 2 tablespoons brown sugar
- 1 teaspoon ground black pepper

Instructions:
1. Preheat the Air fryer to 385 º F and grease an Air fryer basket.
2. Put the ribs with all other ingredients in a resealable bag and seal the bag.
3. Shake to coat well and refrigerate overnight.
4. Remove the short ribs from resealable bag and arrange in the Air fryer basket in 2 batches.
5. Cook for about 8 minutes, flipping once in between and dish out onto a serving platter.
6. Repeat with the remaining ribs and serve hot.

Nutrition Facts Per Serving:
Calories: 507, Fat: 20.5g, Carbohydrates: 6.3g, Sugar: 2.8g, Protein: 67.3g, Sodium: 1200mg

Herbed Beef Roast

Prep time: 10 minutes, cook time: 45 minutes; Serves 5

5 Ingredients:
- 2 pounds beef roast

What you' ll need from the store cupboard:
- 1 tablespoon olive oil
- 1 teaspoon dried rosemary, crushed
- 1 teaspoon dried thyme, crushed
- Salt, to taste

Instructions:
1. Preheat the Air fryer to 360 º F and grease an Air fryer basket.
2. Rub the roast generously with herb mixture and coat with olive oil.
3. Arrange the roast in the Air fryer basket and cook for about 45 minutes.
4. Dish out the roast and cover with foil for about 10 minutes.
5. Cut into desired size slices and serve.

Nutrition Facts Per Serving:
Calories: 362, Fat: 14.2g, Carbohydrates: 0.3g, Sugar: 0g, Protein: 55.1g, Sodium: 151mg

Beef Tips with Onion

Prep time: 15 minutes, cook time: 10 minutes; Serves 2

5 Ingredients:
- 1 pound top round beef, cut into 1½-inch cubes
- ½ yellow onion, chopped

What you'll need from the store cupboard:
- 2 tablespoons Worcestershire sauce
- 1 tablespoon avocado oil
- 1 teaspoon onion powder
- 1 teaspoon garlic powder
- Salt and black pepper, to taste

Instructions:

1. Preheat the Air fryer to 360 º F and grease an Air fryer basket.
2. Mix the beef tips, onion, Worcestershire sauce, oil, and spices in a bowl.
3. Arrange the beef mixture in the Air fryer basket and cook for about 10 minutes.
4. Dish out the steak mixture onto serving plates and cut into desired size slices to serve.

Nutrition Facts Per Serving:
Calories: 266, Fat: 10.5g, Carbohydrates: 4g, Sugar: 2.5g, Protein: 36.3g, Sodium: 192mg

Buttered Rib Eye Steak

Prep time: 20 minutes, cook time: 14 minutes; Serves 2

5 Ingredients:
- ½ cup unsalted butter, softened
- 2 tablespoons fresh parsley, chopped
- 2 (8-ounces) rib eye steaks

What you'll need from the store cupboard:
- 2 teaspoons garlic, minced
- 1 teaspoon Worcestershire sauce
- 1 tablespoon olive oil
- Salt and black pepper, to taste

Instructions:

1. Preheat the Air fryer to 400 º F and grease an Air fryer basket.
2. Mix the butter, parsley, garlic, Worcestershire sauce, and salt in a bowl.
3. Place the butter mixture onto a parchment paper, roll into a log and refrigerate for about 3 hours.
4. Rub the steak generously with olive oil, salt and black pepper.
5. Arrange the steaks in the Air fryer basket and cook for about 14 minutes, flipping once in between.
6. Dish out the steak onto serving plates and cut into desired size slices.
7. Cut the butter log into slices and top over the steak to serve.

Nutrition Facts Per Serving:
Calories: 731, Fat: 68.8g, Carbohydrates: 1.2g, Sugar: 0.4g, Protein: 27.3g, Sodium: 375mg

Beef Cheeseburgers

Prep time: 15 minutes, cook time: 12 minutes; Serves 2

5 Ingredients:
- ½ pound ground beef
- 2 tablespoons fresh cilantro, minced
- 2 slices cheddar cheese
- 2 salad leaves
- 2 dinner rolls, cut into half

What you'll need from the store cupboard:
- 1 garlic clove, minced
- Salt and black pepper, to taste

Instructions:

1. Preheat the Air fryer to 390 º F and grease an Air fryer basket.
2. Mix the beef, garlic, cilantro, salt, and black pepper in a bowl.
3. Make 2 equal-sized patties from the beef mixture and arrange in the Air fryer basket.
4. Cook for about 11 minutes and top each patty with 1 cheese slice.
5. Cook for about 1 more minute and dish out in a platter.
6. Place dinner rolls in a serving platter and arrange salad leaf between each dinner roll.
7. Top with 1 patty and immediately serve.

Nutrition Facts Per Serving:
Calories: 773, Fat: 42.9g, Carbohydrates: 45g, Sugar: 4.9g, Protein: 50.8g, Sodium: 710mg

Beef Jerky

Prep time: 20 minutes, cook time: 1 hour; Serves 3

5 Ingredients:
- 1 pound bottom round beef, cut into thin strips

What you' ll need from the store cupboard:
- ½ cup dark brown sugar
- ½ cup soy sauce
- ¼ cup Worcestershire sauce
- 1 tablespoon chili pepper sauce
- 1 tablespoon hickory liquid smoke
- 1 teaspoon garlic powder
- 1 teaspoon onion powder
- 1 teaspoon cayenne pepper
- ½ teaspoon smoked paprika
- ½ teaspoon ground black pepper

Instructions:

1. Preheat the Air fryer to 180 º F and grease an Air fryer basket.
2. Mix the brown sugar, all sauces, liquid smoke, and spices in a bowl.
3. Coat the beef strips with this marinade generously and marinate overnight.
4. Place half of the beef strips in the Air fryer basket in a single layer.
5. Arrange a cooking rack over the strips and layer with the remaining beef strips.
6. Cook for about 1 hour and dish out to serve.

Nutrition Facts Per Serving:
Calories: 471, Fat: 14.8g, Carbohydrates: 33.1g, Sugar: 28.8g, Protein: 48.7g, Sodium: 2000mg

Beef and Veggie Kebabs

Prep time: 20 minutes, cook time: 12 minutes; Serves 4

5 Ingredients:
- 1 pound sirloin steak, cut into-inch chunks
- 8 ounces baby Bella mushrooms, stems removed
- 1 large bell pepper, seeded and cut into 1-inch pieces
- 1 red onion, cut into 1-inch pieces

What you' ll need from the store cupboard:
- ¼ cup soy sauce
- ¼ cup olive oil
- 1 tablespoon garlic, minced
- 1 teaspoon brown sugar
- ½ teaspoon ground cumin
- Salt and black pepper, to taste

Instructions:

1. Preheat the Air fryer to 390 º F and grease an Air fryer basket.
2. Mix soy sauce, oil, garlic, brown sugar, cumin, salt, and black pepper in a large bowl.
3. Coat the steak cubes generously with marinade and refrigerate to marinate for about 30 minutes.
4. Thread the steak cubes, mushrooms, bell pepper, and onion onto metal skewers.
5. Place the skewers in the Air fryer basket and cook for about 12 minutes, flipping once in between.
6. Dish out in a platter and serve hot.

Nutrition Facts Per Serving:
Calories: 369, Fat: 20g, Carbohydrates: 10.5g, Sugar: 4.7g, Protein: 37.6g, Sodium: 1018mg

Beef Stuffed Bell Peppers

Prep time: 20 minutes, cook time: 26 minutes; Serves 4

5 Ingredients:
- ½ medium onion, chopped
- 1 pound lean ground beef
- ½ cup jasmine rice, cooked
- 2/3 cup light Mexican cheese, shredded and divided
- 4 bell peppers, tops and seeds removed

What you' ll need from the store cupboard:
- 1 teaspoon olive oil

- 2 garlic cloves, minced
- 1 teaspoon dried basil, crushed
- 1 teaspoon garlic salt
- ½ teaspoon red chili powder
- Ground black pepper, as required
- 8 ounces tomato sauce, divided
- 2 teaspoons Worcestershire sauce

Instructions:

1. Preheat the Air fryer to 400 ° F and grease an Air fryer basket.
2. Heat olive oil in a medium skillet over medium heat and add onion and garlic.
3. Sauté for about 5 minutes and add the ground beef, basil, and spices.
4. Cook for about 10 minutes and drain off the excess grease from skillet.
5. Stir in the rice, half of the cheese, 2/3 of the tomato sauce and Worcestershire sauce and mix well.
6. Stuff the beef mixture in each bell pepper and arrange the bell peppers in the Air fryer basket.
7. Cook for about 7 minutes and top with the remaining tomato sauce and cheese.
8. Cook for 4 more minutes and dish out in a bowl to serve warm.

Nutrition Facts Per Serving:
Calories: 439, Fat: 3.1g, Carbohydrates: 34.4g, Sugar: 1.6g, Protein: 11.3g, Sodium: 160mg

Smoky Beef Burgers

Prep time: 20 minutes, cook time: 10 minutes; Serves 4

5 Ingredients:
- 1 pound ground beef
- 4 whole-wheat hamburger buns, split and toasted

What you' ll need from the store cupboard:
- 1 tablespoon Worcestershire sauce
- 1 teaspoon Maggi seasoning sauceo
- 3-4 drops liquid smoke
- 1 teaspoon dried parsley
- ½ teaspoon garlic powder
- ½ teaspoon onion powder
- Salt and ground black pepper, as required

Instructions:
1. Preheat the Air fryer to 350 ° F and grease an Air fryer basket.
2. Mix the beef, sauces, liquid smoke, parsley, and spices in a bowl.
3. Make 4 equal-sized patties from the beef mixture and arrange in the Air fryer basket.
4. Cook for about 10 minutes and dish out to serve on a bun.

Nutrition Facts Per Serving:
Calories: 316, Fats: 8.8g, Carbohydrates: 20.4g, Sugar: 4.4g, Proteins: 37.8g, Sodium: 384mg

Cheesy Beef Meatballs

Prep time: 20 minutes, cook time: 34 minutes; Serves 8

5 Ingredients:
- 2 pounds ground beef
- 1¼ cups breadcrumbs
- ¼ cup Parmigiana-Reggiano cheese, grated
- 2 large eggs
- ¼ cup fresh parsley, chopped

What you' ll need from the store cupboard:
- 1 small garlic clove, chopped
- 1 teaspoon dried oregano, crushed
- Salt and black pepper, to taste

Instructions:
1. Preheat the Air fryer to 350 ° F and grease an Air fryer basket.
2. Mix all the ingredients in a bowl until well combined.
3. Shape the mixture into 2-inches balls gently and arrange half of the meatballs in the Air fryer basket.
4. Cook for about 12 minutes and flip the side.
5. Cook for about 5 minutes and dish out to serve warm.

Nutrition Facts Per Serving:
Calories: 307, Fat: 10.4g, Carbohydrates: 12.4g, Sugar: 1.2g, Protein: 39.3g, Sodium: 251mg

Beef and Mushroom Meatloaf

Prep time: 15 minutes, cook time: 25 minutes; Serves 4

5 Ingredients:
- 1 pound lean ground beef
- 1 small onion, finely chopped
- 3 tablespoons dry breadcrumbs
- 1 egg, lightly beaten
- 2 mushrooms, thickly sliced

What you' ll need from the store cupboard:
- Salt and ground black pepper, as required
- 1 tablespoon olive oil

Instructions:
1. Preheat the Air fryer to 390 º F and grease an Air fryer basket.
2. Mix the beef, onion, olive oil, breadcrumbs, egg, salt, and black pepper in a bowl until well combined.
3. Shape the mixture into loaves and top with mushroom slices.
4. Arrange the loaves in the Air fryer basket and cook for about 25 minutes.
5. Cut into desired size wedges and serve warm.

Nutrition Facts Per Serving:
Calories: 267, Fat: 12g, Carbohydrates: 6.1g, Sugar: 1.3g, Protein: 37g, Sodium: 167mg

Breaded Pork Chops

Prep time: 15 minutes, cook time: 15 minutes; Serves 2

5 Ingredients:
- 2 (6-ounces) pork chops
- ¼ cup plain flour
- 1 egg
- 4 ounces breadcrumbs

What you' ll need from the store cupboard:
- Salt and black pepper, to taste
- 1 tablespoon vegetable oil

Instructions:
1. Preheat the Air fryer to 400 º F and grease an Air fryer basket.
2. Season the chops with salt and black pepper.
3. Place the flour in a shallow bowl and whisk an egg in a second bowl.
4. Mix the breadcrumbs and vegetable oil in a third bowl.
5. Coat the pork chops with flour, dip into egg and dredge into the breadcrumb mixture.
6. Arrange the chops in the Air fryer basket and cook for about 15 minutes, flipping once in between.
7. Dish out and serve hot.

Nutrition Facts Per Serving:
Calories: 621, Fat: 26.1g, Carbohydrates: 53.3g, Sugar: 3.7g, Protein: 43.9g, Sodium: 963mg

Pork Spare Ribs

Prep time: 15 minutes, cook time: 20 minutes; Serves 6

5 Ingredients:
- 12 (1-inch) pork spare ribs
- ½ cup cornstarch

What you' ll need from the store cupboard:
- 5-6 garlic cloves, minced
- ½ cup rice vinegar
- 2 tablespoons soy sauce
- 2 tablespoons olive oil
- Salt and black pepper, to taste

Instructions:
1. Preheat the Air fryer to 390 º F and grease an Air fryer basket.
2. Mix the garlic, vinegar, soy sauce, salt, and black pepper in a large bowl.
3. Coat the ribs generously with this mixture and refrigerate to marinate overnight.
4. Place the cornstarch in a shallow bowl and dredge the ribs in it.
5. Drizzle with olive oil and arrange the ribs in the Air fryer basket.
6. Cook for about 20 minutes, flipping once in between.
7. Dish out and serve hot.

Nutrition Facts Per Serving:
Calories: 557, Fat: 51.3g, Carbohydrates: 11g, Sugar: 0.1g, Protein: 35g, Sodium: 997mg

Bacon Wrapped Pork Tenderloin

Prep time: 15 minutes, cook time: 30 minutes; Serves 4

5 Ingredients:
- 1 (1½ pound) pork tenderloins
- 4 bacon strips

What you'll need from the store cupboard:
- 2 tablespoons Dijon mustard

Instructions:
1. Preheat the Air fryer to 360 ° F and grease an Air fryer basket.
2. Rub the tenderloin evenly with mustard and wrap the tenderloin with bacon strips.
3. Arrange the pork tenderloin in the Air fryer basket and cook for about 30 minutes, flipping once in between.
4. Dish out the steaks and cut into desired size slices to serve.

Nutrition Facts Per Serving:
Calories: 504, Fat: 26.2g, Carbohydrates: 0.8g, Sugar: 9.1g, Protein: 61.9g, Sodium: 867mg

Pork Tenderloin with Bell Peppers

Prep time: 20 minutes, cook time: 15 minutes; Serves 3

5 Ingredients:
- 1 large red bell pepper, seeded and cut into thin strips
- 1 red onion, thinly sliced
- 10½-ounces pork tenderloin, cut into 4 pieces

What you'll need from the store cupboard:
- 2 teaspoons Herbs de Provence
- Salt and ground black pepper, as required
- 1 tablespoon olive oil
- ½ tablespoon Dijon mustard

Instructions:
1. Preheat the Air fryer to 390 ° F and grease an Air fryer pan.
2. Mix the bell pepper, onion, Herbs de Provence, salt, black pepper, and ½ tablespoon of oil in a bowl.
3. Rub the tenderloins evenly with mustard, salt, and black pepper and drizzle with the remaining oil.
4. Place bell pepper mixture in the Air fryer basket and top with the pork tenderloin.
5. Cook for about 15 minutes, flipping once in between.
6. Dish out the steaks and cut into desired size slices to serve.

Nutrition Facts Per Serving:
Calories: 218, Fat: 8.8g, Carbohydrates: 7.1g, Sugar: 3.7g, Protein: 27.7g, Sodium: 110mg

Pork Tenderloin with Bacon and Veggies

Prep time: 20 minutes, cook time: 28 minutes; Serves 3

5 Ingredients:
- 3 potatoes
- ¾ pound frozen green beans
- 6 bacon slices
- 3 (6-ounces) pork tenderloins

What you'll need from the store cupboard:
- 2 tablespoons olive oil

Instructions:
1. Preheat the Air fryer to 390 ° F and grease an Air fryer basket.
2. Wrap 4-6 green beans with one bacon slice and coat the pork tenderloins with olive oil.
3. Pierce the potatoes with a fork and arrange in the Air fryer basket.
4. Cook for about 15 minutes and add the pork tenderloins.
5. Cook for about 6 minutes and dish out in a bowl.
6. Arrange the bean rolls into the Air fryer basket and top with the pork tenderloins.
7. Cook for about 7 minutes and dish out in a platter.
8. Cut each tenderloin into desired size slices to serve alongside the potatoes and green beans rolls.

Nutrition Facts Per Serving:
Calories: 918, Fat: 47.7g, Carbohydrates: 42.4g, Sugar: 4g, Protein: 77.9g, Sodium: 1400mg

Pork Loin with Potatoes

Prep time: 15 minutes, cook time: 25 minutes; Serves 5

5 Ingredients:
- 2 pounds pork loin
- 1 teaspoon fresh parsley, chopped
- 3 large red potatoes, chopped

What you'll need from the store cupboard:
- 3 tablespoons olive oil, divided
- Salt and ground black pepper, as required
- ½ teaspoon garlic powder
- ½ teaspoon red pepper flakes, crushed

Instructions:
1. Preheat the Air fryer to 325 º F and grease an Air fryer pan.
2. Rub the pork loin evenly with 1½ tablespoons olive oil, parsley, salt, and black pepper.
3. Mix the potatoes, remaining oil, garlic powder, red pepper flakes, salt, and black pepper in a bowl.
4. Arrange the pork loin in the Air fryer basket and place potato pieces on sides.
5. Cook for about 25 minutes and dish out in a bowl.
6. Cut into desired size slices and serve alongside potatoes.

Nutrition Facts Per Serving:
Calories: 556, Fats: 28.3g, Carbohydrates: 29.6g, Sugar: 1.9g, Proteins: 44.9g, Sodium: 132mg

Pork Rolls

Prep time: 20 minutes, cook time: 15 minutes; Serves 4

5 Ingredients:
- 1 scallion, chopped
- ¼ cup sun-dried tomatoes, finely chopped
- 2 tablespoons fresh parsley, chopped
- 4 (6-ounces) pork cutlets, pounded slightly

What you'll need from the store cupboard:
- Salt and black pepper, as required
- 2 teaspoons paprika
- ½ tablespoon olive oil

Instructions:
1. Preheat the Air fryer to 390 º F and grease an Air fryer basket.
2. Mix the scallion, tomatoes, parsley, salt, and black pepper in a bowl.
3. Spread the tomato mixture over each pork cutlet and roll each cutlet, securing with cocktail sticks
4. Coat the outer part of rolls with paprika, salt and black pepper and drizzle with olive oil.
5. Arrange the pork rolls in the Air fryer basket and cook for about 15 minutes.
6. Dish out onto serving plates and serve hot.

Nutrition Facts Per Serving:
Calories: 244, Fat: 8.2g, Carbohydrates: 14.5g, Sugar: 1.7g, Protein: 20.1g, Sodium: 708mg

Glazed Ham

Prep time: 10 minutes, cook time: 40 minutes; Serves 4

5 Ingredients:
- 1 pound (10½ ounce) ham joint

What you'll need from the store cupboard:
- ¾ cup whiskey
- 2 tablespoons French mustard
- 2 tablespoons honey

Instructions:
1. Preheat the Air fryer to 320 º F and grease an Air fryer pan.
2. Mix all the ingredients in a bowl except ham.
3. Keep ham joint for about 30 minutes at room temperature and place in the Air fryer pan.
4. Top with half of the whiskey mixture and transfer into the Air fryer.
5. Cook for about 15 minutes and flip the side.
6. Coat with the remaining whiskey mixture and cook for about 25 minutes.
7. Dish out in a platter and serve warm.

Nutrition Facts Per Serving:
Calories: 558, Fat: 22.2g, Carbohydrates: 18.6g, Sugar: 8.7g, Protein: 43g, Sodium: 3456mg

Pork Neck Salad

Prep time: 20 minutes, cook time: 12 minutes; Serves 2

5 Ingredients:
- ½ pound pork neck
- 1 ripe tomato, thickly sliced
- 1 red onion, sliced
- 1 scallion, chopped
- 1 bunch fresh basil leaves

What you' ll need from the store cupboard:
- 1 tablespoon soy sauce
- 1 tablespoon fish sauce
- ½ tablespoon oyster sauce

Instructions:
1. Preheat the Air fryer to 340 º F and grease an Air fryer basket.
2. Mix all the sauces in a bowl and coat the pork neck in it.
3. Refrigerate for about 3 hours and then transfer into the Air fryer basket.
4. Cook for about 12 minutes and dish out in a platter.
5. Cut into desired size slices and keep aside.
6. Mix rest of the ingredients in a bowl and top with the pork slices to serve.

Nutrition Facts Per Serving:
Calories: 448, Fat: 39.7g, Carbohydrates: 15.2g, Sugar: 8.5g, Protein: 20.5g, Sodium: 2000mg

Simple Lamb Chops

Prep time: 10 minutes, cook time: 6 minutes; Serves 2

5 Ingredients:
- 4 (4-ounces) lamb chops

What you' ll need from the store cupboard:
- Salt and black pepper, to taste
- 1 tablespoon olive oil

Instructions:
1. Preheat the Air fryer to 390 º F and grease an Air fryer basket.
2. Mix the olive oil, salt, and black pepper in a large bowl and add chops.
3. Arrange the chops in the Air fryer basket and cook for about 6 minutes.
4. Dish out the lamb chops and serve hot.

Nutrition Facts Per Serving:
Calories: 486, Fat: 31.7g, Carbohydrates: 0.8g, Sugar: 0g, Protein: 63.8g, Sodium: 250mg

Pesto Coated Rack of Lamb

Prep time: 15 minutes, cook time: 15 minutes; Serves 4

5 Ingredients:
- ½ bunch fresh mint
- 1 (1½-pounds) rack of lamb

What you' ll need from the store cupboard:
- 1 garlic clove
- ¼ cup extra-virgin olive oil
- ½ tablespoon honey
- Salt and black pepper, to taste

Instructions:
1. Preheat the Air fryer to 200 º F and grease an Air fryer basket.
2. Put the mint, garlic, oil, honey, salt, and black pepper in a blender and pulse until smooth to make pesto.
3. Coat the rack of lamb with this pesto on both sides and arrange in the Air fryer basket.
4. Cook for about 15 minutes and cut the rack into individual chops to serve.

Nutrition Facts Per Serving:
Calories: 406, Fat: 27.7g, Carbohydrates: 2.9g, Sugar: 2.2g, Protein: 34.9g, Sodium: 161mg

Herbed Lamb Chops

Prep time: 10 minutes, cook time: 7 minutes; Serves 2

5 Ingredients:
- 4 (4-ounces) lamb chops

What you'll need from the store cupboard:
- 1 tablespoon fresh lemon juice
- 1 tablespoon olive oil
- 1 teaspoon dried rosemary
- 1 teaspoon dried thyme
- 1 teaspoon dried oregano
- ½ teaspoon ground cumin
- ½ teaspoon ground coriander
- Salt and black pepper, to taste

Instructions:
1. Preheat the Air fryer to 390 º F and grease an Air fryer basket.
2. Mix the lemon juice, oil, herbs, and spices in a large bowl.
3. Coat the chops generously with the herb mixture and refrigerate to marinate for about 1 hour.
4. Arrange the chops in the Air fryer basket and cook for about 7 minutes, flipping once in between.
5. Dish out the lamb chops in a platter and serve hot.

Nutrition Facts Per Serving:
Calories: 491, Fat: 24g, Carbohydrates: 1.6g, Sugar: 0.2g, Protein: 64g, Sodium: 253mg

Za'atar Lamb Loin Chops

Prep time: 10 minutes, cook time: 30 minutes; Serves 4

5 Ingredients:
- 8 (3½-ounces) bone-in lamb loin chops, trimmed

What you'll need from the store cupboard:
- 3 garlic cloves, crushed
- 1 tablespoon fresh lemon juice
- 1 teaspoon olive oil
- 1 tablespoon Za'ataro
- Salt and black pepper, to taste

Instructions:
1. Preheat the Air fryer to 400 º F and grease an Air fryer basket.
2. Mix the garlic, lemon juice, oil, Za'atar, salt, and black pepper in a large bowl.
3. Coat the chops generously with the herb mixture and arrange the chops in the Air fryer basket.
4. Cook for about 15 minutes, flipping twice in between and dish out the lamb chops to serve hot.

Nutrition Facts Per Serving:
Calories: 433, Fat: 17.6g, Carbohydrates: 0.6g, Sugar: 0.2g, Protein: 64.1g, Sodium: 201mg
(Note: Za'atar - Za'atar is generally made with ground dried thyme, oregano, marjoram, or some combination thereof, mixed with toasted sesame seeds, and salt, though other spices such as sumac might also be added. Some commercial varieties also include roasted flour.)

Mustard Lamb Loin Chops

Prep time: 15 minutes, cook time: 30 minutes; Serves 4

5 Ingredients:
- 8 (4-ounces) lamb loin chops

What you'll need from the store cupboard:
- 2 tablespoons Dijon mustard
- 1 tablespoon fresh lemon juice
- ½ teaspoon olive oil
- 1 teaspoon dried tarragon
- Salt and black pepper, to taste

Instructions:
1. Preheat the Air fryer to 390 º F and grease an Air fryer basket.
2. Mix the mustard, lemon juice, oil, tarragon, salt, and black pepper in a large bowl.
3. Coat the chops generously with the mustard mixture and arrange in the Air fryer basket.
4. Cook for about 15 minutes, flipping once in between and dish out to serve hot.

Nutrition Facts Per Serving:
Calories: 433, Fat: 17.6g, Carbohydrates: 0.6g, Sugar: 0.2g, Protein: 64.1g, Sodium: 201mg

Spiced Lamb Steaks

Prep time: 15 minutes, cook time: 15 minutes; Serves 3

5 Ingredients:
- ½ onion, roughly chopped
- 1½ pounds boneless lamb sirloin steaks

What you'll need from the store cupboard:
- 5 garlic cloves, peeled
- 1 tablespoon fresh ginger, peeled
- 1 teaspoon garam masala
- 1 teaspoon ground fennel
- ½ teaspoon ground cumin
- ½ teaspoon ground cinnamon
- ½ teaspoon cayenne pepper
- Salt and black pepper, to taste

Instructions:
1. Preheat the Air fryer to 330 º F and grease an Air fryer basket.
2. Put the onion, garlic, ginger, and spices in a blender and pulse until smooth.
3. Coat the lamb steaks with this mixture on both sides and refrigerate to marinate for about 24 hours.
4. Arrange the lamb steaks in the Air fryer basket and cook for about 15 minutes, flipping once in between.
5. Dish out the steaks in a platter and serve warm.

Nutrition Facts Per Serving:
Calories: 252, Fat: 16.7g, Carbohydrates: 4.2g, Sugar: 0.7g, Protein: 21.7g, Sodium: 42mg

Leg of Lamb with Brussels Sprout

Prep time: 20 minutes, cook time: 1 hour 30 minutes; Serves 6

5 Ingredients:
- 2¼ pounds leg of lamb
- 1 tablespoon fresh rosemary, minced
- 1 tablespoon fresh lemon thyme
- 1½ pounds Brussels sprouts, trimmed

What you'll need from the store cupboard:
- 3 tablespoons olive oil, divided
- 1 garlic clove, minced
- Salt and ground black pepper, as required
- 2 tablespoons honey

Instructions:
1. Preheat the Air fryer to 300 º F and grease an Air fryer basket.
2. Make slits in the leg of lamb with a sharp knife.
3. Mix 2 tablespoons of oil, herbs, garlic, salt, and black pepper in a bowl.
4. Coat the leg of lamb with oil mixture generously and arrange in the Air fryer basket.
5. Cook for about 75 minutes and set the Air fryer to 390 º F.
6. Coat the Brussels sprout evenly with the remaining oil and honey and arrange them in the Air fryer basket with leg of lamb.
7. Cook for about 15 minutes and dish out to serve warm.

Nutrition Facts Per Serving:
Calories: 449, Fats: 19.9g, Carbohydrates: 16.6g, Sugar: 8.2g, Proteins: 51.7g, Sodium: 185mg

Sausage Meatballs

Prep time: 15 minutes, cook time: 15 minutes; Serves 4

5 Ingredients:
- 3½-ounce sausage, casing removed
- ½ medium onion, minced finely
- 1 teaspoon fresh sage, chopped finely
- 3 tablespoons Italian breadcrumbs

What you'll need from the store cupboard:
- ½ teaspoon garlic, minced
- Salt and black pepper, to taste

Instructions:
1. Preheat the Air fryer to 355 º F and grease an Air fryer basket.
2. Mix all the ingredients in a bowl until well combined.
3. Shape the mixture into equal-sized balls and arrange the balls in the Air fryer basket.
4. Cook for about 15 minutes and dish out to serve warm.

Nutrition Facts Per Serving:
Calories: 111, Fat: 7.3g, Carbohydrates: 5.2g, Sugar: 0.9g, Protein: 5.7g, Sodium: 224mg

Honey Mustard Cheesy Meatballs

Prep time: 15 minutes, cook time: 15 minutes; Serves 8

5 Ingredients:
- 2 onions, chopped
- 1 pound ground beef
- 4 tablespoons fresh basil, chopped
- 2 tablespoons cheddar cheese, grated

What you' ll need from the store cupboard:
- 2 teaspoons garlic paste
- 2 teaspoons honey
- Salt and black pepper, to taste
- 2 teaspoons mustard

Instructions:

1. Preheat the Air fryer to 385 ° F and grease an Air fryer basket.
2. Mix all the ingredients in a bowl until well combined.
3. Shape the mixture into equal-sized balls gently and arrange the meatballs in the Air fryer basket.
4. Cook for about 15 minutes and dish out to serve warm.

Nutrition Facts Per Serving:
Calories: 134, Fat: 4.4g, Carbohydrates: 4.6g, Sugar: 2.7g, Protein: 18.2g, Sodium: 50mg

Italian Beef Meatballs

Prep time: 10 minutes, cook time: 15 minutes; Serves 6

5 Ingredients:
- 2 large eggs
- 2 pounds ground beef
- ¼ cup fresh parsley, chopped
- 1¼ cups panko breadcrumbs
- ¼ cup Parmigiano Reggiano, grated

What you' ll need from the store cupboard:
- 1 teaspoon dried oregano
- 1 small garlic clove, chopped
- Salt and black pepper, to taste
- 1 teaspoon vegetable oil

Instructions:

1. Preheat the Air fryer to 350 ° F and grease an Air fryer basket.
2. Mix beef with all other ingredients in a bowl until well combined.
3. Make equal-sized balls from the mixture and arrange the balls in the Air fryer basket.
4. Cook for about 13 minutes and dish out to serve warm.

Nutrition Facts Per Serving:
Calories: 398, Fat: 13.8g, Carbohydrates: 3.6g, Sugar: 1.3g, Protein: 51.8g, Sodium: 272mg

Simple Beef Burgers

Prep time: 20 minutes, cook time: 12 minutes; Serves 6

5 Ingredients:
- 2 pounds ground beef
- 12 cheddar cheese slices
- 12 dinner rolls

What you' ll need from the store cupboard:
- 6 tablespoons tomato ketchup
- Salt and black pepper, to taste

Instructions:

1. Preheat the Air fryer to 390 ° F and grease an Air fryer basket.
2. Mix the beef, salt and black pepper in a bowl.
3. Make small equal-sized patties from the beef mixture and arrange half of patties in the Air fryer basket.
4. Cook for about 12 minutes and top each patty with 1 cheese slice.
5. Arrange the patties between rolls and drizzle with ketchup.
6. Repeat with the remaining batch and dish out to serve hot.

Nutrition Facts Per Serving:
Calories: 537, Fat: 28.3g, Carbohydrates: 7.6g, Sugar: 4.2g, Protein: 60.6g, Sodium: 636mg

Lamb with Potatoes

Prep time: 20 minutes, cook time: 15 minutes; Serves 2

5 Ingredients:
- ½ pound lamb meat
- 2 small potatoes, peeled and halved
- ½ small onion, peeled and halved
- ¼ cup frozen sweet potato fries

What you' ll need from the store cupboard:
- 1 garlic clove, crushed
- ½ tablespoon dried rosemary, crushed
- 1 teaspoon olive oil

Instructions:
1. Preheat the Air fryer to 355 º F and arrange a divider in the Air fryer.
2. Rub the lamb evenly with garlic and rosemary and place on one side of Air fryer divider.
3. Cook for about 20 minutes and meanwhile, microwave the potatoes for about 4 minutes.
4. Dish out the potatoes in a large bowl and stir in the olive oil and onions.
5. Transfer into the Air fryer divider and change the side of lamb ramp.
6. Cook for about 15 minutes, flipping once in between and dish out in a bowl.

Nutrition Facts Per Serving:
Calories: 399, Fat: 18.5g, Carbohydrates: 32.3g, Sugar: 3.8g, Protein: 24.5g, Sodium: 104mg

Herbed Pork Burgers

Prep time: 15 minutes, cook time: 45 minutes; Serves 8

5 Ingredients:
- 2 small onions, chopped
- 21-ounce ground pork
- 2 teaspoons fresh basil, chopped
- 8 burger buns
- ½ cup cheddar cheese, grated

What you' ll need from the store cupboard:
- 2 teaspoons mustard
- 2 teaspoons garlic puree
- 2 teaspoons tomato puree
- Salt and freshly ground black pepper, to taste
- 2 teaspoons dried mixed herbs, crushed

Instructions:
1. Preheat the Air fryer to 395 º F and grease an Air fryer basket.
2. Mix all the ingredients in a bowl except cheese and buns.
3. Make 8 equal-sized patties from the pork mixture and arrange thee patties in the Air fryer basket.
4. Cook for about 45 minutes, flipping once in between and arrange the patties in buns with cheese to serve.

Nutrition Facts Per Serving:
Calories: 289, Fat: 6.5g, Carbohydrates: 29.2g, Sugar: 4.9g, Protein: 28.7g, Sodium: 384mg

Veggie Stuffed Beef Rolls

Prep time: 20 minutes, cook time: 14 minutes; Serves 6

5 Ingredients:
- 2 pounds beef flank steak, pounded to 1/8-inch thickness
- 6 Provolone cheese slices
- 3-ounce roasted red bell peppers
- ¾ cup fresh baby spinach

What you' ll need from the store cupboard:
- 3 tablespoons prepared pesto
- Salt and black pepper, to taste

Instructions:
1. Preheat the Air fryer to 400 º F and grease an Air fryer basket.
2. Place the steak onto a smooth surface and spread evenly with pesto.
3. Top with the cheese slices, red peppers and spinach.
4. Roll up the steak tightly around the filling and secure with the toothpicks.
5. Arrange the roll in the Air fryer basket and cook for about 14 minutes, flipping once in between.
6. Dish out in a platter and serve warm.

Nutrition Facts Per Serving:
Calories: 447, Fats: 23.4g, Carbohydrates: 1.8g, Sugar: 0.6g, Proteins: 53.2g, Sodium: 472mg

Chinese Style Pork Meatballs

Prep time: 15 minutes, cook time: 20 minutes; Serves 3

5 Ingredients:

- 1 egg, beaten
- 6-ounce ground pork
- ¼ cup cornstarch

What you'll need from the store cupboard:

- 1 teaspoon oyster sauce
- ½ tablespoon light soy sauce
- ½ teaspoon sesame oil
- ¼ teaspoon five spice powder
- ½ tablespoon olive oil
- ¼ teaspoon brown sugar

Instructions:

1. Preheat the Air fryer to 390 º F and grease an Air fryer basket.
2. Mix all the ingredients in a bowl except cornstarch and oil until well combined.
3. Shape the mixture into equal-sized balls and place the cornstarch in a shallow dish.
4. Roll the meatballs evenly into cornstarch mixture and arrange in the Air fryer basket.
5. Cook for about 10 minutes and dish out to serve warm.

Nutrition Facts Per Serving:
Calories: 171, Fat: 6.6g, Carbohydrates: 10.8g, Sugar: 0.7g, Protein: 16.9g, Sodium: 254mg

Spicy Lamb Kebabs

Prep time: 20 minutes, cook time: 8 minutes; Serves 6

5 Ingredients:

- 4 eggs, beaten
- 1 cup pistachios, chopped
- 1 pound ground lamb
- 4 tablespoons plain flour
- 4 tablespoons flat-leaf parsley, chopped

What you'll need from the store cupboard:

- 2 teaspoons chili flakes
- 4 garlic cloves, minced
- 2 tablespoons fresh lemon juice
- 2 teaspoons cumin seeds
- 1 teaspoon fennel seeds
- 2 teaspoons dried mint
- 2 teaspoons salt
- Olive oil
- 1 teaspoon coriander seeds
- 1 teaspoon freshly ground black pepper

Instructions:

1. Preheat the Air fryer to 355 º F and grease an Air fryer basket.
2. Mix lamb, pistachios, eggs, lemon juice, chili flakes, flour, cumin seeds, fennel seeds, coriander seeds, mint, parsley, salt and black pepper in a large bowl.
3. Thread the lamb mixture onto metal skewers to form sausages and coat with olive oil.
4. Place the skewers in the Air fryer basket and cook for about 8 minutes.
5. Dish out in a platter and serve hot.

Nutrition Facts Per Serving:
Calories: 284, Fat: 15.8g, Carbohydrates: 8.4g, Sugar: 1.1g, Protein: 27.9g, Sodium: 932mg

Beef and Veggie Spring Rolls

Prep time: 10 minutes, cook time: 14 minutes; Serves 8

5 Ingredients:
- 2-ounce Asian rice noodles, soaked in warm water, drained and cut into small lengths
- 7-ounce ground beef
- 1 small onion, chopped
- 1 cup fresh mixed vegetables
- 1 packet spring roll skins

What you'll need from the store cupboard:
- 2 tablespoons olive oil
- Salt and black pepper, to taste

Instructions:
1. Preheat the Air fryer to 350 º F and grease an Air fryer basket.
2. Heat olive oil in a pan and add the onion and garlic.
3. Sauté for about 5 minutes and stir in the beef.
4. Cook for about 5 minutes and add vegetables and soy sauce.
5. Cook for about 7 minutes and stir in the noodles.
6. Place the spring rolls skin onto a smooth surface and put the filling mixture diagonally in it.
7. Fold in both sides to seal properly and brush with oil.
8. Arrange the rolls in batches in the Air fryer basket and cook for about 14 minutes, tossing in between.
9. Cook for about 15 minutes, flipping once in between and dish out in a platter.

Nutrition Facts Per Serving:
Calories: 147, Fat: 5.4g, Carbohydrates: 15.9g, Sugar: 0.6g, Protein: 8.7g, Sodium: 302mg

Beef Pot Pie

Prep time: 10 minutes, cook time: 1 hour 27 minutes; Serves 3

5 Ingredients:
- 1 pound beef stewing steak, cubed
- 1 can ale mixed into 1 cup water
- 2 beef bouillon cubes
- 1 tablespoon plain flour
- 1 prepared short crust pastry

What you'll need from the store cupboard:
- 1 tablespoon olive oil
- 1 tablespoon tomato puree
- 2 tablespoons onion paste
- Salt and black pepper, to taste

Instructions:
1. Preheat the Air fryer to 390 º F and grease 2 ramekins lightly.
2. Heat olive oil in a pan and add steak cubes.
3. Cook for about 5 minutes and stir in the onion paste and tomato puree.
4. Cook for about 6 minutes and add the ale mixture, bouillon cubes, salt and black pepper.
5. Bring to a boil and reduce the heat to simmer for about 1 hour.
6. Mix flour and 3 tablespoons of warm water in a bowl and slowly add this mixture into the beef mixture.
7. Roll out the short crust pastry and line 2 ramekins with pastry.
8. Divide the beef mixture evenly in the ramekins and top with extra pastry.
9. Transfer into the Air fryer and cook for about 10 minutes.
10. Set the Air fryer to 335 º F and cook for about 6 more minutes.
11. Dish out and serve warm.

Nutrition Facts Per Serving:
Calories: 442, Fat: 14.2g, Carbohydrates: 19g, Sugar: 1.2g, Protein: 50.6g, Sodium: 583mg

Tomato Stuffed Pork Roll

Prep time: 20 minutes, cook time: 15 minutes; Serves 4

5 Ingredients:
- 1 scallion, chopped
- ¼ cup sun-dried tomatoes, chopped finely
- 2 tablespoons fresh parsley, chopped
- 4 (6-ounce) pork cutlets, pounded slightly

What you'll need from the store cupboard:
- Salt and freshly ground black pepper, to taste
- 2 teaspoons paprika
- ½ tablespoon olive oil

Instructions:
1. Preheat the Air fryer to 390 ° F and grease an Air fryer basket.
2. Mix scallion, tomatoes, parsley, salt and black pepper in a bowl.
3. Coat each cutlet with tomato mixture and roll up the cutlet, securing with cocktail sticks.
4. Coat the rolls with oil and rub with paprika, salt and black pepper.
5. Arrange the rolls in the Air fryer basket and cook for about 15 minutes, flipping once in between.
6. Dish out in a platter and serve warm.

Nutrition Facts Per Serving:
Calories: 244, Fat: 14.5g, Carbohydrates: 20.1g, Sugar: 1.7g, Protein: 8.2g, Sodium: 670mg

Ham Rolls

Prep time: 15 minutes, cook time: 15 minutes; Serves 4

5 Ingredients:
- 12-ounce refrigerated pizza crust, rolled into ¼ inch thickness
- 1/3 pound cooked ham, sliced
- ¾ cup Mozzarella cheese, shredded
- 3 cups Colby cheese, shredded
- 3-ounce roasted red bell peppers

What you'll need from the store cupboard:
- 1 tablespoon olive oil

Instructions:
1. Preheat the Air fryer to 360 ° F and grease an Air fryer basket.
2. Arrange the ham, cheeses and roasted peppers over one side of dough and fold to seal.
3. Brush the dough evenly with olive oil and cook for about 15 minutes, flipping twice in between.
4. Dish out in a platter and serve warm.

Nutrition Facts Per Serving:
Calories: 594, Fat: 35.8g, Carbohydrates: 35.4g, Sugar: 2.8g, Protein: 33g, Sodium: 1545mg

Ham Pinwheels

Prep time: 15 minutes, cook time: 11 minutes; Serves 4

5 Ingredients:
- 1 puff pastry sheet
- 10 ham slices
- 1 cup Gruyere cheese, shredded plus more for sprinkling

What you'll need from the store cupboard:
- 4 teaspoons Dijon mustard

Instructions:
1. Preheat the Air fryer to 375 ° F and grease an Air fryer basket.
2. Place the puff pastry onto a smooth surface and spread evenly with the mustard.
3. Top with the ham and ¾ cup cheese and roll the puff pastry.
4. Wrap the roll in plastic wrap and freeze for about 30 minutes.
5. Remove from the freezer and slice into ½-inch rounds.
6. Arrange the pinwheels in the Air fryer basket and cook for about 8 minutes.
7. Top with remaining cheese and cook for 3 more minutes.
8. Dish out in a platter and serve warm.

Nutrition Facts Per Serving:
Calories: 294, Fat: 19.4g, Carbohydrates: 8.4g, Sugar: 0.2g, Protein: 20.8g, Sodium: 1090mg

Flank Steak Beef

Prep time: 10 minutes, cook time: 20 minutes; Serves 4

5 Ingredients:
- 1 pound flank steaks, sliced
- ¼ cup xanthum gum

What you'll need from the store cupboard:
- 2 teaspoon vegetable oil
- ½ teaspoon ginger
- ½ cup soy sauce
- 1 tablespoon garlic, minced
- ½ cup water
- ¾ cup swerve, packed

Instructions:
1. Preheat the Air fryer to 390 ° F and grease an Air fryer basket.
2. Coat the steaks with xanthum gum on both the sides and transfer into the Air fryer basket.
3. Cook for about 10 minutes and dish out in a platter.
4. Meanwhile, cook rest of the ingredients for the sauce in a saucepan.
5. Bring to a boil and pour over the steak slices to serve.

Nutrition Facts Per Serving:
Calories: 372, Fat: 11.8g, Carbohydrates: 1.8g, Sugar: 27.3g, Protein: 34g, Sodium: 871mg

Pepper Pork Chops

Prep time: 15 minutes, cook time: 6 minutes; Serves 2

5 Ingredients:
- 2 pork chops
- 1 egg white
- ¾ cup xanthum gum

What you'll need from the store cupboard:
- ½ teaspoon sea salt
- ¼ teaspoon freshly ground black pepper
- 1 oil mister

Instructions:
1. Preheat the Air fryer to 400 ° F and grease an Air fryer basket.
2. Whisk egg white with salt and black pepper in a bowl and dip the pork chops in it.
3. Cover the bowl and marinate for about 20 minutes.
4. Pour the xanthum gum over both sides of the chops and spray with oil mister.
5. Arrange the chops in the Air fryer basket and cook for about 6 minutes.
6. Dish out in a bowl and serve warm.

Nutrition Facts Per Serving:
Calories: 541, Fat: 34g, Carbohydrates: 3.4g, Sugar: 1g, Protein: 20.3g, Sodium: 547mg

Garlic Butter Pork Chops

Prep time: 10 minutes, cook time: 8 minutes; Serves 4

5 Ingredients:
- 4 pork chops
- 1 tablespoon coconut butter
- 2 teaspoons parsley

What you'll need from the store cupboard:
- 1 tablespoon coconut oil
- 2 teaspoons garlic, grated
- Salt and black pepper, to taste

Instructions:
1. Preheat the Air fryer to 350 ° F and grease an Air fryer basket.
2. Mix all the seasonings, coconut oil, garlic, butter, and parsley in a bowl and coat the pork chops with it.
3. Cover the chops with foil and refrigerate to marinate for about 1 hour.
4. Remove the foil and arrange the chops in the Air fryer basket.
5. Cook for about 8 minutes and dish out in a bowl to serve warm.

Nutrition Facts Per Serving:
Calories: 311, Fat: 25.5g, Carbohydrates: 1.4g, Sugar: 0.3g, Protein: 18.4g, Sodium: 58mg

Five Spice Pork

Prep time: 15 minutes, cook time: 20 minutes; Serves 4

5 Ingredients:

- 1-pound pork belly

What you' ll need from the store cupboard:

- 2 tablespoons swerve
- 2 tablespoons dark soy sauce
- 1 tablespoon Shaoxing (cooking wine)
- 2 teaspoons garlic, minced
- 2 teaspoons ginger, minced
- 1 tablespoon hoisin sauce
- 1 teaspoon Chinese Five Spice

Instructions:

1. Preheat the Air fryer to 390 º F and grease an Air fryer basket.
2. Mix all the ingredients in a bowl and place in the Ziplock bag.
3. Seal the bag, shake it well and refrigerate to marinate for about 1 hour.
4. Remove the pork from the bag and arrange it in the Air fryer basket.
5. Cook for about 15 minutes and dish out in a bowl to serve warm.

Nutrition Facts Per Serving:

Calories: 604, Fat: 30.6g, Carbohydrates: 1.4g, Sugar: 20.3g, Protein: 19.8g, Sodium: 834mg

Roasted Lamb

Prep time: 15 minutes, cook time: 1 hour 30 minutes; Serves 4

5 Ingredients:

- 2½ pounds half lamb leg roast, slits carved
- 2 garlic cloves, sliced into smaller slithers

What you' ll need from the store cupboard:

- 1 tablespoon dried rosemary
- 1 tablespoon olive oil
- Cracked Himalayan rock salt and cracked peppercorns, to taste

Instructions:

1. Preheat the Air fryer to 400 º F and grease an Air fryer basket.
2. Insert the garlic slithers in the slits and brush with rosemary, oil, salt, and black pepper.
3. Arrange the lamb in the Air fryer basket and cook for about 15 minutes.
4. Set the Air fryer to 350 º F on the Roast mode and cook for 1 hour and 15 minutes.
5. Dish out the lamb chops and serve hot.

Nutrition Facts Per Serving:

Calories: 246, Fat: 7.4g, Carbohydrates: 9.4g, Sugar: 6.5g, Protein: 37.2g, Sodium: 353mg

Chapter 7 Snacks Recipes

Old-Fashioned Onion Rings

Prep time: 10 minutes, cook time: 10 minutes; Serves 4

5 Ingredients:
- 1 large onion, cut into rings
- 1¼ cups all-purpose flour
- 1 cup milk
- 1 egg
- ¾ cup dry bread crumbs

What you' ll need from the store cupboard:
- Salt, to taste

Instructions:
1. Preheat the Air fryer to 360 º F and grease the Air fryer basket.
2. Mix together flour and salt in a dish.
3. Whisk egg with milk in a second dish until well mixed.
4. Place the breadcrumbs in a third dish.
5. Coat the onion rings with the flour mixture and dip into the egg mixture.
6. Lastly dredge in the breadcrumbs and transfer the onion rings in the Air fryer basket.
7. Cook for about 10 minutes and dish out to serve warm.

Nutrition Facts Per Serving:
Calories: 285, Fats: 3.8g, Carbohydrates: 51.6g, Sugar: 5.8g, Proteins: 10.5g, Sodium: 235mg

Party Time Mixed Nuts

Prep time: 15 minutes, cook time: 14 minutes; Serves 3

5 Ingredients:
- ½ cup raw peanuts
- ½ cup raw almonds
- ½ cup raw cashew nuts
- ½ cup raisins
- ½ cup pecans

What you' ll need from the store cupboard:
- 1 tablespoon olive oil
- Salt, to taste

Instructions:
1. Preheat the Air fryer to 320 º F and grease an Air fryer basket.
2. Place the nuts in the Air fryer basket and cook for about 9 minutes, tossing twice in between.
3. Remove the nuts from the Air fryer basket and transfer into a bowl.
4. Drizzle with olive oil and salt and toss to coat well.
5. Return the nuts mixture into the Air fryer basket and cook for about 5 minutes.
6. Dish out and serve warm.

Nutrition Facts Per Serving:
Calories: 489, Fat: 36.9g, Carbohydrates: 34.2g, Sugar: 17.2g, Protein: 14.1g, Sodium: 11mg

Simple Banana Chips

Prep time: 10 minutes, cook time: 10 minutes; Serves 8

5 Ingredients:
- 2 raw bananas, peeled and sliced

What you' ll need from the store cupboard:
- 2 tablespoons olive oil
- Salt and black pepper, to taste

Instructions:
1. Preheat the Air fryer to 355 º F and grease an Air fryer basket.
2. Drizzle banana slices evenly with olive oil and arrange in the Air fryer basket.
3. Cook for about 10 minutes and season with salt and black pepper.
4. Dish out and serve warm.

Nutrition Facts Per Serving:
Calories: 56, Fat: 3.6g, Carbohydrates: 6.7g, Sugar: 3.6g, Protein: 0.3g, Sodium: 0mg

Pineapple Bites with Yogurt Dip

Prep time: 15 minutes, cook time: 10 minutes; Serves 4

5 Ingredients:

- ½ of pineapple, cut into long 1-2 inch thick sticks
- ¼ cup desiccated coconut
- 1 tablespoon fresh mint leaves, minced
- 1 green chili, chopped
- 1 cup vanilla yogurt

What you'll need from the store cupboard:

- 1 tablespoon honey

Instructions:

1. Preheat the Air fryer to 390 º F and grease an Air fryer basket.
2. Place the coconut in a shallow dish.
3. Dip pineapple sticks in the honey and then dredge in the coconut.
4. Transfer the pineapple sticks in the Air fryer basket and cook for about 10 minutes.

For yogurt dip:

5. Mix together mint, chili and vanilla yogurt in a bowl.
6. Serve these pineapple sticks with yogurt dip.

Nutrition Facts Per Serving:
Calories: 518, Fat: 34.9g, Carbohydrates: 20g, Sugar: 0.6g, Protein: 29.9g, Sodium: 1475mg

Warm Spiced Apple Chips

Prep time: 10 minutes, cook time: 16 minutes; Serves 2

5 Ingredients:

- 1 apple, peeled, cored and thinly sliced

What you'll need from the store cupboard:

- 1 tablespoon sugar
- ½ teaspoon ground cinnamon
- Pinch of ground cardamom
- Pinch of ground ginger
- Pinch of salt

Instructions:

1. Preheat the Air fryer to 390 º F and grease an Air fryer basket.
2. Mix together all the ingredients in a bowl until well combined.
3. Arrange the apple slices in the Air fryer basket.
4. Cook for about 8 minutes, flipping in between.
5. Dish out and serve warm.

Nutrition Facts Per Serving:
Calories: 72, Fat: 0.2g, Carbohydrates: 19.2g, Sugar: 15.5g, Protein: 0.3g, Sodium: 78mg

Chicken Nuggets

Prep time: 15 minutes, cook time: 10 minutes; Serves 4

5 Ingredients:

- 20-ounce chicken breast, cut into chunks
- 1 cup all-purpose flour
- 2 tablespoons milk
- 1 egg
- 1 cup panko breadcrumbs

What you'll need from the store cupboard:

- ½ tablespoon mustard powder
- 1 tablespoon garlic powder
- 1 tablespoon onion powder
- Salt and black pepper, to taste

Instructions:

1. Preheat the Air fryer to 390 º F and grease an Air fryer basket.
2. Put chicken along with mustard powder, garlic powder, onion powder, salt and black pepper in a food processor and pulse until combined.
3. Place flour in a shallow dish and whisk the eggs with milk in a second dish.
4. Place breadcrumbs in a third shallow dish.
5. Coat the nuggets evenly in flour and dip in the egg mixture.
6. Roll into the breadcrumbs evenly and arrange the nuggets in an Air fryer basket.
7. Cook for about 10 minutes and dish out to serve warm.

Nutrition Facts Per Serving:
Calories: 220, Fat: 17.1g, Carbohydrates: 6g, Sugar: 3.5g, Protein: 12.8g, Sodium: 332mg

Old-Fashioned Eggplant Slices

Prep time: 10 minutes, cook time: 26 minutes; Serves 2

5 Ingredients:
- 1 medium eggplant, peeled and cut into ½-inch round slices
- ½ cup all-purpose flour
- 1 cup Italian-style breadcrumbs
- 2 eggs, beaten
- 2 tablespoons milk

What you'll need from the store cupboard:
- Salt, to taste
- ¼ cup olive oil

Instructions:
1. Preheat the Air fryer to 390 º F and grease in an Air fryer basket.
2. Season the eggplant slices with salt and keep aside for 1 hour.
3. Place flour in a shallow dish.
4. Whisk the eggs with milk in a second dish.
5. Mix together oil and breadcrumbs in a third shallow dish.
6. Coat the eggplant slices evenly with flour, then dip in the egg mixture and finally coat with breadcrumb mixture.
7. Transfer the eggplant slices in the Air fryer basket and cook for about 8 minutes.
8. Dish out and serve warm.

Nutrition Facts Per Serving:
Calories: 685, Fat: 36.9g, Carbohydrates: 49.1g, Sugar: 5.3g, Protein: 42.1g, Sodium: 2391mg

Basic Salmon Croquettes

Prep time: 15 minutes, cook time: 14 minutes; Serves 16

5 Ingredients:
- 1 large can red salmon, drained
- 2 eggs, lightly beaten
- 2 tablespoons fresh parsley, chopped
- 1 cup breadcrumbs
- 2 tablespoons milk

What you'll need from the store cupboard:
- Salt and black pepper, to taste
- 1/3 cup vegetable oil

Instructions:
1. Preheat the Air fryer to 390 º F and grease an Air fryer basket.
2. Mash the salmon completely in a bowl and stir in eggs, parsley, breadcrumbs, milk, salt and black pepper.
3. Mix until well combined and make 16 equal-sized croquettes from the mixture.
4. Mix together oil and breadcrumbs in a shallow dish and coat the croquettes in this mixture.
5. Place half of the croquettes in the Air fryer basket and cook for about 7 minutes.
6. Repeat with the remaining croquettes and serve warm.

Nutrition Facts Per Serving:
Calories: 110, Fat: 7.1g, Carbohydrates: 5g, Sugar: 0g, Protein: 3.8g, Sodium: 69mg

Bacon-Wrapped Cheese Croquettes

Prep time: 15 minutes, cook time: 8 minutes; Serves 6

5 Ingredients:
- 1 pound thin bacon slices
- 1 pound sharp cheddar cheese block, cut into 1-inch rectangular pieces
- 1 cup all-purpose flour
- 3 eggs
- 1 cup breadcrumbs

What you'll need from the store cupboard:
- 1 tablespoon olive oil
- Salt, to taste

Instructions:
1. Preheat the Air fryer to 390 º F and grease an Air fryer basket.
2. Wrap 1 piece of cheddar cheese with 2 bacon slices, covering completely.
3. Repeat with the remaining cheese and bacon slices.

4. Arrange the croquettes in a baking dish and freeze for about 10 minutes.
5. Place flour in a shallow dish.
6. Whisk the eggs in a second dish.
7. Mix together oil, breadcrumbs and salt in a third shallow dish.
8. Coat the croquettes evenly in flour and dip in the eggs.
9. Dredge in the breadcrumbs mixture and place the croquettes in an Air fryer basket.
10. Cook for about 8 minutes and dish out to serve warm.

Nutrition Facts Per Serving:
Calories: 964, Fat: 68.4g, Carbohydrates: 31.1g, Sugar: 1.7g, Protein: 54.1g, Sodium: 2406mg

Instant Potato Croquettes

Prep time: 20 minutes, cook time: 8 minutes; Serves 4

5 Ingredients:
- 2 medium Russet potatoes, boiled, peeled and mashed
- 2 tablespoons all-purpose flour
- ½ cup Parmesan cheese, grated
- 3 eggs
- ½ cup breadcrumbs

What you' ll need from the store cupboard:
- 2 tablespoons vegetable oil
- Pinch of ground nutmeg
- Salt and black pepper, to taste

Instructions:
1. Mix together potatoes with egg yolk, Parmesan, nutmeg, salt and black pepper.
2. Make equal sized small balls from this mixture and keep aside.
3. Whisk the eggs in a shallow dish.
4. Mix together oil and breadcrumbs in another shallow dish.
5. Dip the croquettes evenly in the eggs and dredge in the breadcrumb mixture.
6. Place the croquettes in an Air fryer basket and cook for about 8 minutes and dish out to serve warm.

Nutrition Facts Per Serving:
Calories: 291, Fat: 14g, Carbohydrates: 30.3g, Sugar: 2.3g, Protein: 11.9g, Sodium: 266mg

Vegetable Nuggets

Prep time: 15 minutes, cook time: 10 minutes; Serves 4

5 Ingredients:
- 1 zucchini, chopped roughly
- ½ of carrot, chopped roughly
- 1 cup all-purpose flour
- 1 egg
- 1 cup panko breadcrumbs

What you' ll need from the store cupboard:
- 1 tablespoon garlic powder
- ½ tablespoon mustard powder
- 1 tablespoon onion powder
- Salt and black pepper, to taste

Instructions:
1. Preheat the Air fryer to 380 º F and grease an Air fryer basket.
2. Put zucchini, carrot, mustard powder, garlic powder, onion powder, salt and black pepper in a food processor and pulse until combined.
3. Place flour in a shallow dish and whisk the eggs with milk in a second dish.
4. Place breadcrumbs in a third shallow dish.
5. Coat the vegetable nuggets evenly in flour and dip in the egg mixture.
6. Roll into the breadcrumbs evenly and arrange the nuggets in an Air fryer basket.
7. Cook for about 10 minutes and dish out to serve warm.

Nutrition Facts Per Serving:
Calories: 281, Fat: 13g, Carbohydrates: 15.4g, Sugar: 1.8g, Protein: 26.2g, Sodium: 249mg

Crispy Kale Chips

Prep time: 10 minutes, cook time: 3 minutes; Serves 4

5 Ingredients:
- 1 head fresh kale, stems and ribs removed and cut into 1½ inch pieces

What you'll need from the store cupboard:
- 1 tablespoon olive oil
- 1 teaspoon soy sauce

Instructions:
1. Preheat the Air fryer to 380 ° F and grease an Air fryer basket.
2. Mix together all the ingredients in a bowl until well combined.
3. Arrange the kale in the Air fryer basket and cook for about 3 minutes, flipping in between.
4. Dish out and serve warm.

Nutrition Facts Per Serving:
Calories: 143, Fats: 3.5g, Carbohydrates: 23.8g, Sugar: 0g, Proteins: 6.9g, Sodium: 173mg

"Light on Fat" French Fries

Prep time: 10 minutes, cook time: 30 minutes; Serves 4

5 Ingredients:
- 1¾ pound potatoes, peeled and cut into thin strips

What you'll need from the store cupboard:
- ¼ cup olive oil
- 1 teaspoon onion powder
- 1 teaspoon garlic powder
- 2 teaspoons paprika

Instructions:
1. Preheat the Air fryer to 375 ° F and grease an Air fryer basket
2. Soak potato strips for about 1 hour in cold water and drain well.
3. Mix together potato strips with the remaining ingredients in a bowl.
4. Arrange the potato strips in the Air fryer basket and cook for about 30 minutes.
5. Dish out and serve warm.

Nutrition Facts Per Serving:
Calories: 24, Fat: 7.4g, Carbohydrates: 32.8, Sugar: 2.8g, Protein: 3.7g, Sodium: 13mg

Crispy Zucchini Fries

Prep time: 10 minutes, cook time: 10 minutes; Serves 4

5 Ingredients:
- 1 pound zucchini, sliced into 2 ½-inch sticks
- ¾ cup panko breadcrumbs

What you'll need from the store cupboard:
- Salt, to taste
- 2 tablespoons olive oil

Instructions:
1. Preheat the Air fryer to 425 ° F and grease an Air fryer basket
2. Season zucchini with salt and keep aside for about 10 minutes.
3. Place breadcrumbs in a shallow dish and coat zucchini fries in it.
4. Arrange the zucchini fries in the Air fryer basket and cook for about 10 minutes.
5. Dish out and serve warm.

Nutrition Facts Per Serving:
Calories: 158, Fat: 8.3g, Carbohydrates: 18.4g, Sugar: 3.2g, Protein: 4.1g, Sodium: 198mg

Sweet and Spicy Carrot Sticks

Prep time: 10 minutes, cook time: 12 minutes; Serves 2

5 Ingredients:
- 1 large carrot, peeled and cut into sticks
- 1 tablespoon fresh rosemary, chopped finely

What you'll need from the store cupboard:
- 1 tablespoon olive oil
- 2 teaspoons sugar
- ¼ teaspoon cayenne pepper
- Salt and black pepper, to taste

Instructions:

1. Preheat the Air fryer to 390 º F and grease an Air fryer basket
2. Mix carrot with all other ingredients in a bowl until well combined.
3. Arrange the carrot sticks in the Air fryer basket and cook for about 12 minutes.
4. Dish out and serve warm.

Nutrition Facts Per Serving:
Calories: 96, Fat: 7.3g, Carbohydrates: 8.7g, Sugar: 5.8g, Protein: 0.4g, Sodium: 26mg

Butternut Squash Fries

Prep time: 15 minutes, cook time: 40 minutes; Serves 2

5 Ingredients:
- 2 pounds butternut squash, peeled and cut into ½ inch strips

What you'll need from the store cupboard:
- 1 teaspoon chili powder
- ½ teaspoon ground cinnamon
- ¼ teaspoon garlic salt

Instructions:
1. Preheat the Air fryer to 390 º F and grease an Air fryer basket
2. Season butternut squash with all other ingredients in a bowl until well combined.
3. Arrange half of the squash fries in the Air fryer basket and cook for about 20 minutes.
4. Repeat with the remaining fries and dish out to serve warm.

Nutrition Facts Per Serving:
Calories: 110, Fat: 7.1g, Carbohydrates: 5g, Sugar: 0g, Protein: 3.8g, Sodium: 69mg

Cheesy Polenta Sticks

Prep time: 10 minutes, cook time: 6 minutes; Serves 4

5 Ingredients:
- 2½ cups cooked polenta
- ¼ cup Parmesan cheese

What you'll need from the store cupboard:
- 1 tablespoon olive oil
- Salt, to taste

Instructions:
1. Preheat the Air fryer to 350 º F and grease a baking dish with olive oil.
2. Place polenta in the baking dish and refrigerate, covered for about 1 hour.
3. Remove from the refrigerator and cut into desired sized slices.
4. Place polenta sticks into the Air fryer and season with salt.
5. Top with Parmesan cheese and cook for about 6 minutes.
6. Dish out and serve warm.

Nutrition Facts Per Serving:
Calories: 398, Fat: 5.7g, Carbohydrates: 76.3g, Sugar: 0.9g, Protein: 9.4g, Sodium: 105mg

Crunchy Spicy Chickpeas

Prep time: 5 minutes, cook time: 20 minutes; Serves 4

5 Ingredients:
- 1 (15-ounce) can chickpeas, rinsed and drained

What you' ll need from the store cupboard:
- 1 tablespoon olive oil
- ½ teaspoon ground cumin
- ½ teaspoon cayenne pepper
- ½ teaspoon smoked paprika
- Salt, taste

Instructions:

1. Preheat the Air fryer to 390 º F and grease an Air fryer basket.
2. Mix together all the ingredients in a bowl and toss to coat well.
3. Place half of the chickpeas in the Air fryer basket and cook for about 10 minutes.
4. Repeat with the remaining chickpeas and dish out to serve warm.

Nutrition Facts Per Serving:
Calories: 419, Fat: 10g, Carbohydrates: 64.9g, Sugar: 11.4g, Protein: 20.6g, Sodium: 65mg

Buttered Corn on the Cob

Prep time: 10 minutes, cook time: 20 minutes; Serves 2

5 Ingredients:
- 2 corn on the cob
- 2 tablespoons butter, softened and divided

What you' ll need from the store cupboard:
- Salt and black pepper, to taste

Instructions:

1. Preheat the Air fryer to 320 º F and grease an Air fryer basket.
2. Season the cobs evenly with salt and black pepper and rub with 1 tablespoon butter.
3. Wrap the cobs in foil paper and arrange in the Air fryer basket.
4. Cook for about 20 minutes and top with remaining butter.
5. Dish out and serve warm.

Nutrition Facts Per Serving:
Calories: 160, Fat: 12g, Carbohydrates: 14.1g, Sugar: 2.3g, Protein: 2.1g, Sodium: 84mg

Easy Crispy Prawns

Prep time: 15 minutes, cook time: 10 minutes; Serves 4

5 Ingredients:
- 1 egg
- ½ pound nacho chips, crushed
- 18 prawns, peeled and deveined

What you' ll need from the store cupboard:
- Salt and black pepper, to taste

Instructions:

1. Preheat the Air fryer to 355 º F and grease an Air fryer basket.
2. Crack egg in a shallow dish and beat well.
3. Place the crushed nacho chips in another shallow dish.
4. Coat prawns into egg and then roll into nacho chips.
5. Place the coated prawns into the Air fryer basket and cook for about 10 minutes.
6. Dish out and serve warm.

Nutrition Facts Per Serving:
Calories: 425, Fat: 17.6g, Carbohydrates: 36.6g, Sugar: 2.2g, Protein: 28.6g, Sodium: 606mg

Bacon-Wrapped Shrimp

Prep time: 15 minutes, cook time: 7 minutes; Serves 6

5 Ingredients:
- 1 pound bacon, sliced thinly
- 1 pound shrimp, peeled and deveined

What you' ll need from the store cupboard:
- Salt, to taste

Instructions:
1. Preheat the Air fryer to 390 º F and grease an Air fryer basket.
2. Wrap 1 shrimp with a bacon slices, covering completely.
3. Repeat with the remaining shrimp and bacon slices.
4. Arrange the bacon wrapped shrimps in a baking dish and freeze for about 15 minutes.
5. Place the shrimps in an Air fryer basket and cook for about 7 minutes.
6. Dish out and serve warm.

Nutrition Facts Per Serving:
Calories: 499, Fats: 32.6g, Carbohydrates: 2.2g, Sugar: 0g, Proteins: 45.2g, Sodium: 1931mg

Nutty Cauliflower Poppers

Prep time: 10 minutes, cook time: 12 minutes; Serves 4

5 Ingredients:
- ¼ cup golden raisins
- 1 cup boiling water
- ¼ cup toasted pine nuts
- 1 head of cauliflower, cut into small florets

What you' ll need from the store cupboard:
- ½ cup olive oil, divided
- 1 tablespoon curry powder
- ¼ teaspoon salt

Instructions:
1. Preheat the Air fryer to 390 º F and grease an Air fryer basket.
2. Put raisins in boiling water in a bowl and keep aside.
3. Drizzle 1 teaspoon olive oil on the pine nuts in another bowl.
4. Place the pine nuts in an Air fryer basket and cook for about 2 minutes.
5. Remove the pine nuts from the Air fryer and keep aside.
6. Mix together cauliflower, salt, curry powder and remaining olive oil in a large bowl.
7. Transfer this mixture into the Air fryer basket and cook for about 12 minutes
8. Dish out the cauliflower in a serving bowl and stir in the pine nuts.
9. Drain raisins and add to the serving bowl.

Nutrition Facts Per Serving:
Calories: 322, Fat: 31.3g, Carbohydrates: 12.7g, Sugar: 7.3g, Protein: 3g, Sodium: 171mg

Seasoned Crab Sticks

Prep time: 10 minutes, cook time: 12 minutes; Serves 4

5 Ingredients:
- 1 packet crab sticks, shred into small pieces

What you' ll need from the store cupboard:
- 2 teaspoon sesame oil
- Cajun seasoning, to taste

Instructions:
1. Preheat the Air fryer to 320 º F and grease an Air fryer basket.
2. Drizzle crab stick pieces with sesame oil and arrange in the Air fryer basket.
3. Cook for about 12 minutes and serve, sprinkled with Cajun seasoning.

Nutrition Facts Per Serving:
Calories: 91.9, Fat: 2.41g, Carbohydrates: 8.8g, Sugar: 2.4g, Protein: 5.6g, Sodium: 2mg

Delightful Fish Nuggets

Prep time: 15 minutes, cook time: 10 minutes; Serves 4

5 Ingredients:
- 1 cup all-purpose flour
- 2 eggs
- ¾ cup breadcrumbs
- 1 pound cod, cut into 1x2½-inch strips

What you' ll need from the store cupboard:
- Pinch of salt
- 2 tablespoons olive oil

Instructions:
1. Preheat the Air fryer to 380 º F and grease an Air fryer basket.
2. Place flour in a shallow dish and whisk the eggs in a second dish.
3. Mix breadcrumbs, salt and oil in a third shallow dish.
4. Coat the fish strips evenly in flour and dip in the egg.
5. Roll into the breadcrumbs evenly and arrange the nuggets in an Air fryer basket.
6. Cook for about 10 minutes and dish out to serve warm.

Nutrition Facts Per Serving:
Calories: 404, Fat: 11.6g, Carbohydrates: 36.8g, Sugar: 1.5g, Protein: 34.6g, Sodium: 307mg

Broccoli Bites

Prep time: 15 minutes, cook time: 12 minutes; Serves 10

5 Ingredients:
- 2 cups broccoli florets
- 2 eggs, beaten
- 1¼ cups cheddar cheese, grated
- ¼ cup Parmesan cheese, grated
- 1¼ cups panko breadcrumbs

What you' ll need from the store cupboard:
- Salt and black pepper, to taste

Instructions:
1. Preheat the Air fryer to 350 º F and grease an Air fryer basket.
2. Mix broccoli with rest of the ingredients and mix until well combined.
3. Make small equal-sized balls from mixture and arrange these balls on a baking sheet.
4. Refrigerate for about half an hour and then transfer into the Air fryer basket.
5. Cook for about 12 minutes and dish out to serve warm.

Nutrition Facts Per Serving:
Calories: 136, Fat: 6.8g, Carbohydrates: 11.3g, Sugar: 1.1g, Protein: 7.3g, Sodium: 226mg

"Good as Gold" Veggie Bites

Prep time: 15 minutes, cook time: 10 minutes; Serves 10

5 Ingredients:
- 1½ pound fresh spinach, blanched, drained and chopped
- ½ of onion, chopped
- 1 carrot, peeled and chopped
- 2 American cheese slices, cut into tiny pieces
- 2 bread slices, toasted and processed into breadcrumbs

What you' ll need from the store cupboard:
- 1 garlic clove, minced
- 1 teaspoon red chili flakes
- Salt, to taste

Instructions:
1. Preheat the Air fryer to 395 º F and grease an Air fryer basket.
2. Mix all the ingredients in a bowl except breadcrumbs until well combined.
3. Make small equal-sized balls from mixture and arrange these balls on a baking sheet.
4. Refrigerate for about half an hour.
5. Place the bread crumbs in a shallow dish and coat the balls evenly in bread crumbs.
6. Transfer the balls into the Air fryer basket and cook for about 10 minutes.
7. Dish out and serve warm.

Nutrition Facts Per Serving:
Calories: 43, Fat: 1.5g, Carbohydrates: 5.6g, Sugar: 1.2g, Protein: 3.1g, Sodium: 139mg

Lava Rice Bites

Prep time: 15 minutes, cook time: 20 minutes; Serves 4

5 Ingredients:
- 3 cups cooked risotto
- 1/3 cup Parmesan cheese, grated
- 1 egg, beaten
- 3-ounce mozzarella cheese, cubed
- ¾ cup bread crumbs

What you' ll need from the store cupboard:
- 1 tablespoon olive oil

Instructions:
1. Preheat the Air fryer to 390 º F and grease an Air fryer basket.
2. Mix risotto, olive oil, Parmesan cheese and egg in a bowl until well combined.
3. Make small equal-sized balls from mixture and put a mozzarella cube in the center of each ball.
4. Smooth the risotto mixture with your finger to cover the cheese.
5. Place the bread crumbs in a shallow dish and coat the balls evenly in bread crumbs.
6. Transfer the balls into the Air fryer basket and cook for about 10 minutes.
7. Dish out and serve warm.

Nutrition Facts Per Serving:
Calories: 279, Fat: 3.7g, Carbohydrates: 50.7g, Sugar: 0.6g, Protein: 9.4g, Sodium: 159mg

Feta and Parsley Filo Triangles

Prep time: 15 minutes, cook time: 5 minutes; Serves 6

5 Ingredients:
- 1 egg yolk
- 4-ounce feta cheese, crumbled
- 1 scallion, chopped finely
- 2 tablespoons fresh parsley, chopped finely
- 2 frozen filo pastry sheets, thawed and cut into three strips

What you' ll need from the store cupboard:
- 2 tablespoons olive oil
- Salt and black pepper, to taste

Instructions:
1. Preheat the Air fryer to 390 º F and grease an Air fryer basket.
2. Whisk egg yolk in a large bowl and beat well.
3. Stir in feta cheese, scallion, parsley, salt and black pepper.
4. Brush pastry with olive oil and put a tablespoon of feta mixture over one corner of filo strip.
5. Fold diagonally to create a triangle and keep folding until filling is completely wrapped.
6. Repeat with the remaining strips and filling and coat the triangles with olive oil.
7. Place the triangles in the Air fryer basket and cook for about 3 minutes.
8. Now, set the Air fryer to 360 degrees F and cook for another 2 minutes.
9. Dish out and serve warm.

Nutrition Facts Per Serving:
Calories: 141, Fat: 9.8g, Carbohydrates: 9.2g, Sugar: 1g, Protein: 4.3g, Sodium: 213mg

Potato Chips

Prep time: 15 minutes, cook time: 30 minutes; Serves 6

5 Ingredients:
- 4 small russet potatoes, thinly sliced
- 2 tablespoons fresh rosemary, finely chopped

What you' ll need from the store cupboard:
- 1 tablespoon olive oil
- ¼ teaspoon salt

Instructions:
1. Preheat the Air fryer to 350 º F and grease an Air fryer basket.
2. Mix together the potato slices, olive oil, rosemary and salt in a bowl.
3. Arrange the potato chips in the Air fryer basket and cook for about 30 minutes.
4. Dish out and serve warm.

Nutrition Facts Per Serving:
Calories: 87, Fat: 0.4g, Carbohydrates: 15.9g, Sugar: 1.1g, Protein: 1.7g, Sodium: 88mg

Vegetable Pastries

Prep time: 15 minutes, cook time: 10 minutes; Serves 8

5 Ingredients:
- 2 large potatoes, boiled and mashed
- ½ cup carrot, peeled and chopped
- ½ cup onion, chopped
- ½ cup green peas, shelled
- 3 puff pastry sheets, each cut into 4 round pieces

What you' ll need from the store cupboard:
- 1 tablespoon olive oil
- Salt and black pepper, to taste
- 2 garlic cloves, minced
- 1 tablespoon curry powder
- 2 tablespoons fresh ginger, minced

Instructions:
1. Preheat the Air fryer to 390 º F and grease an Air fryer basket.
2. Heat olive oil on medium heat in a skillet and add carrot, onion, ginger and garlic.
3. Sauté for about 5 minutes and stir in the mashed potatoes, peas, curry powder, salt and black pepper.
4. Cook for about 2 minutes and dish out in a bowl.
5. Put about 2 tablespoons of vegetable filling mixture over each pastry round.
6. Fold each pastry round into half-circle and press the edges firmly with a fork.
7. Place half of the pastries in the Air fryer basket and cook for about 5 minutes.
8. Dish out in a platter and serve warm.

Nutrition Facts Per Serving:
Calories: 197, Fat: 8.8g, Carbohydrates: 26.8g, Sugar: 2.4g, Protein: 3.7g, Sodium: 56mg

Grilled Cheese Sandwiches

Prep time: 10 minutes, cook time: 5 minutes; Serves 2

5 Ingredients:
- 4 white bread slices
- ½ cup melted butter, softened
- ½ cup sharp cheddar cheese, grated

What you' ll need from the store cupboard:
- 1 tablespoon mayonnaise

Instructions:
1. Preheat the Air fryer to 355 º F and grease an Air fryer basket.
2. Spread the mayonnaise and melted butter over one side of each bread slice.
3. Sprinkle the cheddar cheese over the buttered side of the 2 slices.
4. Cover with the remaining slices of bread and transfer into the Air fryer basket.
5. Cook for about 5 minutes and dish out to serve warm.

Nutrition Facts Per Serving:
Calories: 445, Fat: 8.1g, Carbohydrates: 85.5g, Sugar: 7.8g, Protein: 9.7g, Sodium: 191mg

Tortilla Chips

Prep time: 10 minutes, cook time: 6 minutes; Serves 6

5 Ingredients:
- 8 corn tortillas, cut into triangles

What you' ll need from the store cupboard:
- 1 tablespoon olive oil
- Salt, to taste

Instructions:
1. Preheat the Air fryer to 390 º F and grease an Air fryer basket.
2. Drizzle the tortilla chips with olive oil and season with salt.
3. Arrange half of the tortilla chips in the Air fryer basket and cook for about 3 minutes, flipping in between.
4. Repeat with the remaining tortilla chips and dish out to serve warm.

Nutrition Facts Per Serving:
Calories: 90, Fat: 3.2g, Carbohydrates: 14.3g, Sugar: 0.3g, Protein: 1.8g, Sodium: 42mg

Sweet Corn and Bell Pepper Sandwich with Barbecue Sauce

Prep time: 15 minutes, cook time: 23 minutes; Serves 2

5 Ingredients:

- 2 tablespoons butter, softened
- 1 cup sweet corn kernels
- 1 roasted green bell pepper, chopped
- 4 bread slices, trimmed and cut horizontally

What you'll need from the store cupboard:

- ¼ cup barbecue sauce

Instructions:

1. Preheat the Air fryer to 355 º F and grease an Air fryer basket.
2. Heat butter in a skillet on medium heat and add corn.
3. Sauté for about 2 minutes and dish out in a bowl.
4. Add bell pepper and barbecue sauce to the corn.
5. Spread corn mixture on one side of 2 bread slices and top with remaining slices.
6. Dish out and serve warm.

Nutrition Facts Per Serving:
Calories: 286, Fat: 15.3g, Carbohydrates: 36.1g, Sugar: 12.6g, Protein: 4.6g, Sodium: 377mg

Potato Bread Rolls

Prep time: 20 minutes, cook time: 13 minutes; Serves 8

5 Ingredients:

- 5 large potatoes, boiled and mashed
- 2 small onions, chopped finely
- 2 green chilies, seeded and chopped
- 2 curry leaves
- 8 bread slices, trimmed

What you'll need from the store cupboard:

- 2 tablespoons vegetable oil, divided
- ½ teaspoon ground turmeric
- Salt, to taste

Instructions:

1. Preheat the Air fryer to 390 º F and grease an Air fryer basket.
2. Heat 1 teaspoon of vegetable oil in a skillet on medium heat and add onions.
3. Sauté for about 5 minutes and add green chilies, curry leaves and turmeric.
4. Sauté for about 1 minute and add mashed potatoes and salt.
5. Stir well until combined and remove from heat.
6. Make 8 equal sized oval shaped patties from the mixture.
7. Wet the bread slices completely with water and press the bread slices to drain completely.
8. Put a patty in a bread slice and roll it in a spindle shape.
9. Seal the edges to secure the filling and coat with vegetable oil.
10. Repeat with the remaining bread slices, filling mixture and vegetable oil.
11. Place the potato rolls in the Air fryer basket and cook for about 13 minutes.
12. Remove from the Air fryer and serve warm.

Nutrition Facts Per Serving:
Calories: 221, Fats: 4g, Carbohydrates: 42.7g, Sugar: 3.9g, Proteins: 4.8g, Sodium: 95mg

Beet Chips

Prep time: 10 minutes, cook time: 15 minutes; Serves 6

5 Ingredients:

- 4 medium beetroots, peeled and thinly sliced
- ¼ teaspoon smoked paprika

What you'll need from the store cupboard:

- ½ teaspoon salt
- 2 tablespoons olive oil

Instructions:

1. Preheat the Air fryer to 325 º F and grease an Air fryer basket.
2. Mix together all the ingredients in a bowl until well combined.
3. Arrange the beet slices in the Air fryer basket and cook for about 15 minutes.
4. Dish out and serve warm.

Nutrition Facts Per Serving:
Calories: 60, Fat: 4.8g, Carbohydrates: 5.3g, Sugar: 3.7g, Protein: 0.9g, Sodium: 236mg

Avocado Fries

Prep time: 20 minutes, cook time: 7 minutes; Serves 2

5 Ingredients:

- ¼ cup all-purpose flour
- 1 egg
- 1 teaspoon water
- ½ cup panko breadcrumbs
- 1 avocado, peeled, pitted and sliced into 8 pieces

What you' ll need from the store cupboard:

- Salt and black pepper, to taste

Instructions:

1. Preheat the Air fryer to 400 º F and grease an Air fryer basket.
2. Place flour, salt and black pepper in a shallow dish and whisk the egg with water in a second dish.
3. Place the breadcrumbs in a third shallow dish.
4. Coat the avocado slices evenly in flour and dip in the egg mixture.
5. Roll into the breadcrumbs evenly and arrange the avocado slices in an Air fryer basket.
6. Cook for about 7 minutes, flipping once in between and dish out to serve warm.

Nutrition Facts Per Serving:

Calories: 363, Fat: 22.4g, Carbohydrates: 35.7g, Sugar: 1.2g, Protein: 8.3g, Sodium:

Dill Pickle Fries

Prep time: 15 minutes, cook time: 28 minutes; Serves 12

5 Ingredients:

- 1½ (16-ounces) jars spicy dill pickle spears, drained and pat dried
- 1 cup all-purpose flour
- 1 egg, beaten
- ¼ cup milk
- 1 cup panko breadcrumbs

What you' ll need from the store cupboard:

- ½ teaspoon paprika

Instructions:

1. Preheat the Air fryer to 440 º F and grease an Air fryer basket.
2. Place flour and paprika in a shallow dish and whisk the egg with milk in a second dish.
3. Place the breadcrumbs in a third shallow dish.
4. Coat the pickle spears evenly in flour and dip in the egg mixture.
5. Roll into the breadcrumbs evenly and arrange half of the pickle spears in an Air fryer basket.
6. Cook for about 14 minutes, flipping once in between.
7. Repeat with the remaining pickle spears and dish out to serve warm.

Nutrition Facts Per Serving:

Calories: 76, Fat: 0.8g, Carbohydrates: 14.8g, Sugar: 1.2g, Protein: 2.7g, Sodium: 550mg

Radish Sticks

Prep time: 10 minutes, cook time: 12 minutes; Serves 2

5 Ingredients:

- 1 large radish, peeled and cut into sticks
- 1 tablespoon fresh rosemary, finely chopped

What you' ll need from the store cupboard:

- 1 tablespoon olive oil
- 2 teaspoons sugar
- ¼ teaspoon cayenne pepper
- Salt and black pepper, as needed

Instructions:

1. Preheat the Air fryer to 390 º F and grease an Air fryer basket.
2. Mix radish with all other ingredients in a bowl until well combined.
3. Arrange the radish sticks in the Air fryer basket and cook for about 12 minutes.
4. Dish out and serve warm.

Nutrition Facts Per Serving:

Calories: 96, Fat: 7.3g, Carbohydrates: 8.7g, Sugar: 5.8g, Protein: 0.4g, Sodium: 26mg

Spicy Broccoli Poppers

Prep time: 15 minutes, cook time: 10 minutes; Serves 4

5 Ingredients:
- 2 tablespoons plain yogurt
- 1 pound broccoli, cut into small florets
- 2 tablespoons chickpea flour

What you'll need from the store cupboard:
- ½ teaspoon red chili powder
- ¼ teaspoon ground cumin
- ¼ teaspoon ground turmeric
- Salt, to taste

Instructions:
1. Preheat the Air fryer to 400 º F and grease an Air fryer basket.
2. Mix together the yogurt, red chili powder, cumin, turmeric and salt in a bowl until well combined.
3. Stir in the broccoli and generously coat with marinade.
4. Refrigerate for about 30 minutes and sprinkle the broccoli florets with chickpea flour.
5. Arrange the broccoli florets in the Air fryer basket and cook for about 10 minutes, flipping once in between.
6. Dish out and serve warm.

Nutrition Facts Per Serving:
Calories: 69, Fat: 0.9g, Carbohydrates: 12.2g, Sugar: 3.2g, Protein: 4.9g, Sodium: 87mg

Crispy Cauliflower Poppers

Prep time: 10 minutes, cook time: 20 minutes; Serves 4

5 Ingredients:
- 1 large egg white
- ¾ cup panko breadcrumbs
- 4 cups cauliflower florets

What you'll need from the store cupboard:
- 3 tablespoons ketchup
- 2 tablespoons hot sauce

Instructions:
1. Preheat the Air fryer to 320 º F and grease an Air fryer basket.
2. Mix together the egg white, ketchup, and hot sauce in a bowl until well combined.
3. Stir in the cauliflower florets and generously coat with marinade.
4. Place breadcrumbs in a shallow dish and dredge the cauliflower florets in it.
5. Arrange the cauliflower florets in the Air fryer basket and cook for about 20 minutes, flipping once in between.
6. Dish out and serve warm.

Nutrition Facts Per Serving:
Calories: 94, Fat: 0.5g, Carbohydrates: 19.6g, Sugar: 5.5g, Protein: 4.6g, Sodium: 457mg

Cheese Filled Bell Peppers

Prep time: 15 minutes, cook time: 12 minutes; Serves 3

5 Ingredients:
- 1 small green bell pepper
- 1 small red bell pepper
- 1 small yellow bell pepper
- ½ cup mozzarella cheese
- ½ cup cream cheese

What you'll need from the store cupboard:
- 3 teaspoons red chili flakes

Instructions:
1. Preheat the Air fryer to 320 º F and grease an Air fryer basket.
2. Chop the tops of the bell peppers and remove all the seeds.
3. Mix together mozzarella cheese, cream cheese and red chili flakes in a bowl.
4. Stuff this cheese mixture in the bell peppers and put back the tops.
5. Arrange in the Air Fryer basket and cook for about 12 minutes.
6. Remove from the Air fryer and serve hot.

Nutrition Facts Per Serving:
Calories: 185, Fats: 13.9g, Carbohydrates: 12.8g, Sugar: 7.7g, Proteins: 4.7g, Sodium: 120mg

Cod Nuggets

Prep time: 15 minutes, cook time: 10 minutes; Serves 4

5 Ingredients:
- 1 cup all-purpose flour
- 2 eggs
- ¾ cup breadcrumbs
- 1 pound cod, cut into 1x2½-inch strips

What you'll need from the store cupboard:
- A pinch of salt
- 2 tablespoons olive oil

Instructions:
1. Preheat the Air fryer to 390 º F and grease an Air fryer basket.
2. Place flour in a shallow dish and whisk the eggs in a second dish.
3. Place breadcrumbs, salt, and olive oil in a third shallow dish.
4. Coat the cod strips evenly in flour and dip in the eggs.
5. Roll into the breadcrumbs evenly and arrange the nuggets in an Air fryer basket.
6. Cook for about 10 minutes and dish out to serve warm.

Nutrition Facts Per Serving:
Calories: 404, Fat: 11.6g, Carbohydrates: 36.8g, Sugar: 1.5g, Protein: 34.6g, Sodium: 307mg

Mozzarella Sticks

Prep time: 15 minutes, cook time: 24 minutes; Serves 4

5 Ingredients:
- ¼ cup white flour
- 2 eggs
- 3 tablespoons nonfat milk
- 1 cup plain breadcrumbs
- 1 pound Mozzarella cheese block, cut into 3x½-inch stick

What you'll need from the store cupboard:
- Salt and black pepper, to taste

Instructions:
1. Preheat the Air fryer to 440 º F and grease an Air fryer basket.
2. Place flour in a shallow dish and whisk the eggs with milk, salt and black pepper in a second dish.
3. Place breadcrumbs in a third shallow dish.
4. Coat the Mozzarella sticks with flour, then dip into egg mixture and finally, dredge in the breadcrumbs.
5. Arrange the Mozzarella sticks on a baking sheet and freeze for about 4 hours.
6. Transfer into the Air fryer and cook for about 12 minutes.
7. Dish out in a platter and serve warm.

Nutrition Facts Per Serving:
Calories: 191, Fat: 5g, Carbohydrates: 26.4g, Sugar: 2.4g, Protein: 9.6g, Sodium: 177mg

Bow Tie Pasta Chips

Prep time: 10 minutes, cook time: 10 minutes; Serves 6

5 Ingredients:
- 2 cups white bow tie pasta

What you'll need from the store cupboard:
- 1 tablespoon olive oil
- 1 tablespoon nutritional yeast
- 1½ teaspoons Italian seasoning blend
- ½ teaspoon salt

Instructions:
1. Cook the pasta for 1/2 the time called for on the package. Toss the drained pasta
2. with the olive oil or aquafaba, nutritional yeast, Italian seasoning, and salt.
3. Place about half of the mixture in your air fryer basket if yours is small; larger ones may be able to do cook in one batch.
4. Cook on 390°F (200°C) for 5 minutes. Shake the basket and cook 3 to 5 minutes more or until crunchy.

Nutrition Facts Per Serving:
Calories: 408, Fat: 23.1g, Carbohydrates: 52.6g, Sugar: 0g, Protein: 14.6g, Sodium: 688mg

Stuffed Mushrooms with Sour Cream

Prep time: 15 minutes, cook time: 8 minutes; Serves 12

5 Ingredients:
- ¼ orange bell pepper, diced
- ¾ cup Cheddar cheese, shredded
- 12 mushrooms caps, stems diced
- ½ onion, diced
- ½ small carrot, diced

What you'll need from the store cupboard:
- ¼ cup sour cream

Instructions:
1. Preheat the Air fryer to 350 º F and grease a baking tray.
2. Place mushroom stems, onion, orange bell pepper and carrot over medium heat in a skillet.
3. Cook for about 5 minutes until softened and stir in ½ cup Cheddar cheese and sour cream.
4. Stuff this mixture in the mushroom caps and arrange them on the baking tray.
5. Top with rest of the cheese and place the baking tray in the Air fryer basket.
6. Cook for about 8 minutes until cheese is melted and serve warm.

Nutrition Facts Per Serving:
Calories: 43, Fat: 3.1g, Carbohydrates: 1.7g, Sugar: 1g, Protein: 2.4g, Sodium: 55mg

Crispy Shrimps

Prep time: 15 minutes, cook time: 8 minutes; Serves 2

5 Ingredients:
- 1 egg
- ¼ pound nacho chips, crushed
- 10 shrimps, peeled and deveined

What you'll need from the store cupboard:
- 1 tablespoon olive oil
- Salt and black pepper, to taste

Instructions:
1. Preheat the Air fryer to 365 º F and grease an Air fryer basket.
2. Crack egg in a shallow dish and beat well.
3. Place the nacho chips in another shallow dish.
4. Season the shrimps with salt and black pepper, coat into egg and then roll into nacho chips.
5. Place the coated shrimps into the Air fryer basket and cook for about 8 minutes.
6. Dish out and serve warm.

Nutrition Facts Per Serving:
Calories: 514, Fat: 25.8g, Carbohydrates: 36.9g, Sugar: 2.3g, Protein: 32.5g, Sodium: 648mg

Sunflower Seeds Bread

Prep time: 15 minutes, cook time: 18 minutes; Serves 4

5 Ingredients:
- 2/3 cup whole wheat flour
- 2/3 cup plain flour
- 1/3 cup sunflower seeds
- 1 cup lukewarm water

What you'll need from the store cupboard:
- ½ sachet instant yeast
- 1 teaspoon salt

Instructions:
1. Preheat the Air fryer to 390 º F and grease a cake pan.
2. Mix together flours, sunflower seeds, yeast and salt in a bowl.
3. Add water slowly and knead for about 5 minutes until a dough is formed.
4. Cover the dough with a plastic wrap and keep in warm place for about half an hour.
5. Arrange the dough into a cake pan and transfer into an Air fryer basket.
6. Cook for about 18 minutes and dish out to serve warm.

Nutrition Facts Per Serving:
Calories: 156, Fat: 2.4g, Carbohydrates: 28.5g, Sugar: 0.5g, Protein: 4.6g, Sodium: 582mg

Air Fried Chicken Tenders

Prep time: 15 minutes, cook time: 10 minutes; Serves 4

5 Ingredients:
- 12 oz chicken breasts, cut into tenders
- 1 egg white
- 1/8 cup flour
- ½ cup panko bread crumbs

What you'll need from the store cupboard:
- Salt and black pepper, to taste

Instructions:
1. Preheat the Air fryer to 350 º F and grease an Air fryer basket.
2. Season the chicken tenders with salt and black pepper.
3. Coat the chicken tenders with flour, then dip in egg whites and then dredge in the panko bread crumbs.
4. Arrange in the Air fryer basket and cook for about 10 minutes.
5. Dish out in a platter and serve warm.

Nutrition Facts Per Serving:
Calories: 220, Fat: 17.1g, Carbohydrates: 6g, Sugar: 3.5g, Protein: 12.8g, Sodium: 332mg

Air Fryer Plantains

Prep time: 10 minutes, cook time: 10 minutes; Serves 4

5 Ingredients:
- 2 ripe plantains

What you'll need from the store cupboard:
- 2 teaspoons avocado oil
- 1/8 teaspoon salt

Instructions:
1. Preheat the Air fryer to 400 º F and grease an Air fryer basket.
2. Mix the plantains with avocado oil and salt in a bowl.
3. Arrange the coated plantains in the Air fryer basket and cook for about 10 minutes.
4. Dish out in a bowl and serve immediately.

Nutrition Facts Per Serving:
Calories: 112, Fat: 0.6g, Carbohydrates: 28.7g, Sugar: 13.4g, Protein: 1.2g, Sodium: 77mg

Buttered Dinner Rolls

Prep time: 15 minutes, cook time: 30 minutes; Serves 12

5 Ingredients:
- 1 cup milk
- 3 cups plain flour
- 7½ tablespoons unsalted butter

What you'll need from the store cupboard:
- 1 tablespoon coconut oil
- 1 tablespoon olive oil
- 1 teaspoon yeast
- Salt and black pepper, to taste

Instructions:
1. Preheat the Air fryer to 360 º F and grease an Air fryer basket.
2. Put olive oil, milk and coconut oil in a pan and cook for about 3 minutes.
3. Remove from the heat and mix well.
4. Mix together plain flour, yeast, butter, salt and black pepper in a large bowl.
5. Knead well for about 5 minutes until a dough is formed.
6. Cover the dough with a damp cloth and keep aside for about 5 minutes in a warm place.
7. Knead the dough for about 5 minutes again with your hands.
8. Cover the dough with a damp cloth and keep aside for about 30 minutes in a warm place.
9. Divide the dough into 12 equal pieces and roll each into a ball.
10. Arrange 6 balls into the Air fryer basket in a single layer and cook for about 15 minutes.
11. Repeat with the remaining balls and serve warm.

Nutrition Facts Per Serving:
Calories: 208, Fat: 10.3g, Carbohydrates: 25g, Sugar: 1g, Protein: 4.1g, Sodium: 73mg

Cheesy Dinner Rolls

Prep time: 10 minutes, cook time: 5 minutes; Serves 2

5 Ingredients:

- 2 dinner rolls
- ½ cup Parmesan cheese, grated
- 2 tablespoons unsalted butter, melted

What you'll need from the store cupboard:

- ½ teaspoon garlic bread seasoning mix

Instructions:

1. Preheat the Air fryer to 355 º F and grease an Air fryer basket.
2. Cut the dinner rolls in slits and stuff cheese in the slits.
3. Top with butter and garlic bread seasoning mix.
4. Arrange the dinner rolls into the Air fryer basket and cook for about 5 minutes.
5. Dish out in a platter and serve hot.

Nutrition Facts Per Serving:
Calories: 608, Fat: 33.1g, Carbohydrates: 48.8g, Sugar: 4.8g, Protein: 33.5g, Sodium: 2000mg

Pita Bread Cheese Pizza

Prep time: 10 minutes, cook time: 6 minutes; Serves 4

5 Ingredients:

- 1 pita bread
- ¼ cup Mozzarella cheese
- 7 slices pepperoni
- ¼ cup sausage
- 1 tablespoon yellow onion, sliced thinly

What you'll need from the store cupboard:

- 1 tablespoon pizza sauce
- 1 drizzle extra-virgin olive oil
- ½ teaspoon fresh garlic, minced

Instructions:

1. Preheat the Air fryer to 350 º F and grease an Air fryer basket.
2. Spread pizza sauce on the pita bread and add sausages, pepperoni, onions, garlic and cheese.
3. Drizzle with olive oil and place it in the Air fryer basket.
4. Cook for about 6 minutes and dish out to serve warm.

Nutrition Facts Per Serving:
Calories: 56, Fat: 3.6g, Carbohydrates: 6.7g, Sugar: 3.6g, Protein: 0.3g, Sodium: 0mg

Healthy Veggie Lasagna

Prep time: 15 minutes, cook time: 1 hour; Serves 4

5 Ingredients:

- 1½ pounds pumpkin, peeled and chopped finely
- ¾ pound tomatoes, cubed
- 1 pound cooked beets, sliced thinly
- ½ pound fresh lasagna sheets
- ¼ cup Parmesan cheese, grated

What you'll need from the store cupboard:

- 2 tablespoons sunflower oil

Instructions:

1. Preheat the Air fryer to 300 º F and lightly grease a baking dish.
2. Put pumpkin and 1 tablespoon sunflower oil in a skillet and cook for about 10 minutes.
3. Put the pumpkin mixture and tomatoes in a blender and pulse until smooth.
4. Return to the skillet and cook on low heat for about 5 minutes.
5. Transfer the pumpkin puree into the baking dish and layer with lasagna sheets.
6. Top with the beet slices and cheese and place in the Air fryer.
7. Cook for about 45 minutes and dish out to serve warm.

Nutrition Facts Per Serving:
Calories: 368, Fats: 10.3g, Carbohydrates: 59.8g, Sugar: 16.9g, Proteins: 13.4g, Sodium: 165mg

Portabella Pizza Treat

Prep time: 10 minutes, cook time: 6 minutes; Serves 2

5 Ingredients:
- 2 Portabella caps, stemmed
- 2 tablespoons canned tomatoes with basil
- 2 tablespoons mozzarella cheese, shredded
- 4 pepperoni slices
- 2 tablespoons Parmesan cheese, grated freshly

What you'll need from the store cupboard:
- 2 tablespoon olive oil
- 1/8 teaspoon dried Italian seasonings
- Salt, to taste
- 1 teaspoon red pepper flakes, crushed

Instructions:
1. Preheat the Air fryer to 320 º F and grease an Air fryer basket.
2. Drizzle olive oil on both sides of portabella cap and season salt, red pepper flakes and Italian seasonings.
3. Top canned tomatoes on the mushrooms, followed by mozzarella cheese.
4. Place portabella caps in the Air fryer basket and cook for about 2 minutes.
5. Top with pepperoni slices and cook for about 4 minutes.
6. Sprinkle with Parmesan cheese and dish out to serve warm.

Nutrition Facts Per Serving:
Calories: 242, Fat: 21.8g, Carbohydrates: 5.8g, Sugar: 2g, Protein: 8.8g, Sodium: 350mg

Croissant Rolls

Prep time: 10 minutes, cook time: 6 minutes; Serves 8

5 Ingredients:
- 1 (8-ounces) can croissant rolls
- 4 tablespoons butter, melted

What you'll need from the store cupboard:
- 1 tablespoon olive oil

Instructions:
1. Preheat the Air fryer to 320 º F and grease an Air fryer basket with olive oil.
2. Coat the croissant rolls with butter and arrange into the Air fryer basket.
3. Cook for about 6 minutes, flipping once in between.
4. Dish out in a platter and serve hot.

Nutrition Facts Per Serving:
Calories: 167, Fat: 12.6g, Carbohydrates: 11.1g, Sugar: 3g, Protein: 2.1g, Sodium: 223mg

Heirloom Tomato Sandwiches with Pesto

Prep time: 20 minutes, cook time: 16 minutes; Serves 4

5 Ingredients:
- 3 tablespoons pine nuts
- ½ cup fresh basil, chopped
- ½ cup fresh parsley, chopped
- 2 heirloom tomatoes, cut into ½ inch thick slices
- 8-ounce feta cheese, cut into ½ inch thick slices

What you'll need from the store cupboard:
- ½ cup plus 2 tablespoons olive oil, divided
- Salt, to taste
- 1 garlic clove, chopped

Instructions:
1. Preheat the Air fryer to 390 º F and grease an Air fryer basket.
2. Mix together 1 tablespoon of olive oil, pine nuts and pinch of salt in a bowl.
3. Place pine nuts in the Air fryer and cook for about 2 minutes.
4. Put the pine nuts, remaining oil, fresh basil, fresh parsley, garlic and salt and pulse until combined.
5. Dish out the pesto in a bowl, cover and refrigerate.
6. Spread 1 tablespoon of pesto on each tomato slice and top with a feta slice and onion.
7. Drizzle with olive oil and arrange the prepared tomato slices in the Air fryer basket.
8. Cook for about 14 minutes and serve with remaining pesto.

Nutrition Facts Per Serving:
Calories: 559, Fat: 55.7g, Carbohydrates: 8g, Sugar: 2.6g, Protein: 11.8g, Sodium: 787mg

Cheese Stuffed Tomatoes

Prep time: 15 minutes, cook time: 15 minutes; Serves 2

5 Ingredients:

- 2 large tomatoes, sliced in half and pulp scooped out
- ½ cup broccoli, finely chopped
- ½ cup cheddar cheese, shredded
- 1 tablespoon unsalted butter, melted

What you' ll need from the store cupboard:

- ½ teaspoon dried thyme, crushed

Instructions:

1. Preheat the Air fryer to 355 º F and grease an Air fryer basket.
2. Mix together broccoli and cheese in a bowl.
3. Stuff the broccoli mixture in each tomato.
4. Arrange the stuffed tomatoes into the Air fryer basket and drizzle evenly with butter.
5. Cook for about 15 minutes and dish out in a serving platter.
6. Garnish with thyme and serve warm.

Nutrition Facts Per Serving:
Calories: 206, Fat: 15.6g, Carbohydrates: 9.1g, Sugar: 5.3g, Protein: 9.4g, Sodium: 233mg

Hummus Mushroom Pizza

Prep time: 20 minutes, cook time: 6 minutes; Serves 4

5 Ingredients:

- 4 Portobello mushroom caps, stemmed and gills removed
- 3 ounces zucchini, shredded
- 2 tablespoons sweet red pepper, seeded and chopped
- 4 Kalamata olives, sliced
- ½ cup hummus

What you' ll need from the store cupboard:

- 1 tablespoon balsamic vinegar
- Salt and black pepper, to taste
- 4 tablespoons pasta sauce
- 1 garlic clove, minced
- 1 teaspoon dried basil

Instructions:

1. Preheat the Air fryer to 330 º F and grease an Air fryer basket.
2. Coat both sides of all Portobello mushroom cap with vinegar.
3. Season the inside of each mushroom cap with salt and black pepper.
4. Divide pasta sauce and garlic inside each mushroom.
5. Arrange mushroom caps into the Air fryer basket and cook for about 3 minutes.
6. Remove from the Air fryer and top zucchini, red peppers and olives on each mushroom cap.
7. Season with basil, salt, and black pepper and transfer into the Air fryer basket.
8. Cook for about 3 more minutes and dish out in a serving platter.
9. Spread hummus on each mushroom pizza and serve.

Nutrition Facts Per Serving:
Calories: 115, Fat: 4.1g, Carbohydrates: 15.4g, Sugar: 4.8g, Protein: 6.7g, Sodium: 264mg

Zucchini Air Fried Gratin

Prep time: 10 minutes, cook time: 15 minutes; Serves 4

5 Ingredients:

- 2 zucchinis, cut into 8 equal sized pieces
- 1 tablespoon fresh parsley, chopped
- 2 tablespoons bread crumbs
- 4 tablespoons Parmesan cheese, grated

What you' ll need from the store cupboard:

- 1 tablespoon vegetable oil
- Salt and black pepper, to taste

Instructions:

1. Preheat the Air fryer to 360 º F and grease an Air fryer basket.
2. Arrange the zucchini pieces in the Air fryer basket with their skin side down.
3. Top with the remaining ingredients and cook for about 15 minutes.
4. Dish out and serve warm.

Nutrition Facts Per Serving:
Calories: 481, Fat: 11.1g, Carbohydrates: 9.1g, Sugar: 3g, Protein: 7g, Sodium: 203mg

Jacket Potatoes

Prep time: 15 minutes, cook time: 15 minutes; Serves 2

5 Ingredients:

- 2 potatoes
- 1 tablespoon parmesan cheese, shredded
- 1 tablespoon butter, softened
- 1 teaspoon parsley, minced
- ¼ cup tomatoes, chopped

What you' ll need from the store cupboard:

- 3 tablespoons sour cream
- Salt and black pepper, to taste

Instructions:

1. Preheat the Air fryer to 355 º F and grease an Air fryer basket.
2. Make holes in the potatoes and transfer into the Air fryer basket.
3. Cook for about 15 minutes and dish out in a bowl.
4. Mix together rest of the ingredients in a bowl and combine well.
5. Cut the potatoes from the center and stuff in the cheese mixture to serve.

Nutrition Facts Per Serving:

Calories: 277, Fats: 12.2g, Carbohydrates: 34.8g, Sugar: 2.5g, Proteins: 8.2g, Sodium: 226mg

Cheese Stuffed Mushrooms

Prep time: 15 minutes, cook time: 8 minutes; Serves 4

5 Ingredients:

- 4 fresh large mushrooms, stemmed and gills removed
- ¼ cup Parmesan cheese, shredded
- 2 tablespoons white cheddar cheese, shredded
- 2 tablespoons sharp cheddar cheese, shredded

What you' ll need from the store cupboard:

- Salt and black pepper, to taste
- 1/3 cup vegetable oil4 ounces cream cheese, softened
- 1 teaspoon Worcestershire sauce
- 2 garlic cloves, chopped
- Salt and ground black pepper, as required

Instructions:

1. Preheat the Air fryer to 375 º F and grease an Air fryer basket.
2. Mix together Parmesan cheese, cheddar cheese, Worcestershire sauce, cream cheese, garlic, salt and black pepper in a bowl,
3. Stuff the cheese mixture in each mushroom and arrange in the Air fryer basket.
4. Cook for about 8 minutes and dish out in a serving platter.

Nutrition Facts Per Serving:

Calories: 156, Fat: 13.6g, Carbohydrates: 2.6g, Sugar: 0.7g, Protein: 6.5g, Sodium: 267mg

Cheesy Mushroom Pizza

Prep time: 15 minutes, cook time: 6 minutes; Serves 2

5 Ingredients:

- 2 Portobello mushroom caps, stemmed
- 2 tablespoons canned tomatoes, chopped
- 2 tablespoons Monterey Jack cheese, shredded
- 2 jalapeno peppers, pitted and sliced
- 2 tablespoons onions, chopped

What you' ll need from the store cupboard:

- 2 tablespoons olive oil
- 1 teaspoon dried oregano
- Salt and white pepper, to taste

Instructions:

1. Preheat the Air fryer to 320 º F and grease an Air fryer basket.
2. Coat both sides of all Portobello mushroom cap with olive oil.
3. Season the inside of each mushroom cap with salt and white pepper.
4. Divide pasta sauce and garlic inside each mushroom.
5. Arrange mushroom caps into the Air fryer basket and top with canned tomatoes, jalapeno peppers, onions and cheese.
6. Sprinkle with dried oregano and cook for about 6 minutes.
7. Remove from the Air fryer and serve warm.

Nutrition Facts Per Serving:

Calories: 251, Fat: 21g, Carbohydrates: 5.7g, Sugar: 0.7g, Protein: 13.4g, Sodium: 330mg

Rice Flour Crusted Tofu

Prep time: 15 minutes, cook time: 28 minutes; Serves 3

5 Ingredients:

- 1 (14-ounces) block firm tofu, pressed and cubed into ½-inch size
- 2 tablespoons cornstarch
- ¼ cup rice flour

What you'll need from the store cupboard:

- Salt and ground black pepper, as required
- 2 tablespoons olive oil

Instructions:

1. Preheat the Air fryer to 360 º F and grease an Air fryer basket.
2. Mix together cornstarch, rice flour, salt, and black pepper in a bowl.
3. Coat the tofu with flour mixture evenly and drizzle with olive oil.
4. Arrange the tofu cubes into the Air fryer basket and cook for about 28 minutes.
5. Dish out the tofu in a serving platter and serve warm.

Nutrition Facts Per Serving:
Calories: 241, Fat: 15g, Carbohydrates: 17.7g, Sugar: 0.8g, Protein: 11.6g, Sodium: 67mg

Beans and Veggie Burgers

Prep time: 20 minutes, cook time: 23 minutes; Serves 4

5 Ingredients:

- 1 cup cooked black beans
- 2 cups boiled potatoes, peeled and mashed
- 1 cup fresh spinach, chopped
- 1 cup fresh mushrooms, chopped
- 6 cups fresh baby greens

What you'll need from the store cupboard:

- 2 teaspoons Chile lime seasoning
- Olive oil cooking spray

Instructions:

1. Preheat the Air fryer to 375 º F and grease an Air fryer basket.
2. Mix together potatoes, spinach, beans, mushrooms and Chile lime seasoning in a large bowl.
3. Make 4 equal-sized patties from this mixture and place the patties into the prepared Air fryer basket.
4. Spray with olive oil cooking spray and cook for about 20 minutes, flipping once in between.
5. Set the Air fryer to 90 º F and cook for about 3 more minutes.
6. Dish out in a platter and serve alongside the baby greens.

Nutrition Facts Per Serving:
Calories: 249, Fat: 1.1g, Carbohydrates: 48.8g, Sugar: 2.9g, Protein: 13.7g, Sodium: 47mg

Spiced Soy Curls

Prep time: 15 minutes, cook time: 10 minutes; Serves 2

5 Ingredients:

- 3 cups boiling water
- 4 ounces soy curls, soaked in boiling water for about 10 minutes and drained
- ¼ cup fine ground cornmeal

What you'll need from the store cupboard:

- ¼ cup nutritional yeast
- 2 teaspoons Cajun seasoning
- 1 teaspoon poultry seasoning
- Salt and ground white pepper, to taste

Instructions:

1. Preheat the Air fryer to 385 º F and grease an Air fryer basket.
2. Mix together cornmeal, nutritional yeast, Cajun seasoning, poultry seasoning, salt and white pepper in a bowl.
3. Coat the soy curls generously with this mixture and arrange in the Air fryer basket.
4. Cook for about 10 minutes, flipping in between and dis out in a serving platter.

Nutrition Facts Per Serving:
Calories: 317, Fat: 10.2g, Carbohydrates: 30.8g, Sugar: 2g, Protein: 29.4g, Sodium: 145mg

Tofu in Sweet and Spicy Sauce

Prep time: 15 minutes, cook time: 6 minutes; Serves 2

5 Ingredients:
- 1 (14-ounces) block firm tofu, pressed and cubed
- ½ cup arrowroot flour
- 2 scallions (green part), chopped

What you' ll need from the store cupboard:
- ½ teaspoon sesame oil
- 4 tablespoons low-sodium soy sauce
- 1½ tablespoons rice vinegar
- 1½ tablespoons chili sauce
- 1 tablespoon agave nectar
- 2 large garlic cloves, minced
- 1 teaspoon fresh ginger, peeled and grated

Instructions:
1. Preheat the Air fryer to 360 º F and grease an Air fryer basket.
2. Mix together tofu, arrowroot flour, and sesame oil in a bowl.
3. Arrange the tofu into the Air fryer basket and cook for about 20 minutes.
4. Meanwhile, mix together remaining ingredients except scallions in a bowl to make a sauce.
5. Place the tofu and sauce in a skillet and cook for about 3 minutes, stirring occasionally.
6. Garnish with green parts of scallions and serve hot.

Nutrition Facts Per Serving:
Calories: 153, Fat: 6.4g, Carbohydrates: 13.5g, Sugar: 13.4g, Protein: 13.4g, Sodium: 1300mg

Ranch Dipped Fillets

Prep time: 5 minutes, cook time: 13 minutes; Serves 2

5 Ingredients:
- ¼ cup panko breadcrumbs
- 1 egg beaten
- 2 tilapia fillets
- Garnish: Herbs and chilies

What you' ll need from the store cupboard:
- ½ packet ranch dressing mix powder
- 1¼ tablespoons vegetable oil

Instructions:
1. Preheat the Air fryer to 350 º F and grease an Air fryer basket.
2. Mix ranch dressing with panko breadcrumbs in a bowl.
3. Whisk eggs in a shallow bowl and dip the fish fillet in the eggs.
4. Dredge in the breadcrumbs and transfer into the Air fryer basket.
5. Cook for about 13 minutes and garnish with chilies and herbs to serve.

Nutrition Facts Per Serving:
Calories: 301, Fat: 12.2g, Carbohydrates: 1.5g, Sugar: 1.4g, Protein: 28.8g, Sodium: 276mg

Baked Egg Plant with Bacon

Prep time: 15 minutes, cook time: 35 minutes; Serves 2

5 Ingredients:
- 2 egg plants, cut in half lengthwise
- ½ cup cheddar cheese, shredded
- ½ can (7.5 oz.) chili without beans
- 2 tablespoons cooked bacon bits
- Fresh scallions, thinly sliced

What you' ll need from the store cupboard:
- 2 teaspoons kosher salt
- 2 tablespoons sour cream

Instructions:
1. Preheat the Air fryer to 390 º F and grease an Air fryer basket.
2. Place the egg plants with their skin side down in the Air fryer basket.
3. Cook for about 35 minutes and remove the egg plants from the Air fryer basket.
4. Top each half with salt, chili and cheddar cheese and transfer them back in the Air fryer basket.
5. Cook for 3 more minutes and dish out in a bowl.
6. Garnish with sour cream, bacon bits and scallions to serve.

Nutrition Facts Per Serving:
Calories: 548, Fat: 22.9g, Carbohydrates: 7.5g, Sugar: 10.9g, Protein: 40.1g, Sodium: 350mg

Bacon Filled Poppers

Prep time: 5 minutes, cook time: 15 minutes; Serves 4

5 Ingredients:

- 4 strips crispy cooked bacon
- 3 tablespoons butter
- ½ cup jalapeno peppers, diced
- 2/3 cup almond flour
- 2 oz. Cheddar cheese, white, shredded

What you' ll need from the store cupboard:

- 1 pinch cayenne pepper
- 1 tablespoon bacon fat
- 1 teaspoon kosher salt
- Black pepper, ground, to taste

Instructions:

1. Preheat the Air fryer to 390 º F and grease an Air fryer basket.
2. Mix together butter with salt and water on medium heat in a skillet.
3. Whisk in the flour and sauté for about 3 minutes.
4. Dish out in a bowl and mix with the remaining ingredients to form a dough.
5. Wrap plastic wrap around the dough and refrigerate for about half an hour.
6. Make small popper balls out of this dough and arrange in the Air fryer basket.
7. Cook for about 15 minutes and dish out to serve warm.

Nutrition Facts Per Serving:
Calories: 385, Fat: 32.8g, Carbohydrates: 5.2g, Sugar: 0.4g, Protein: 17g, Sodium: 1532mg

Chicken Stuffed Mushrooms

Prep time: 10 minutes, cook time: 15 minutes; Serves 12

5 Ingredients:

- 12 large fresh mushrooms, stems removed
- 1 cup chicken meat, cubed
- ½ lb. imitation crabmeat, flaked
- 2 cups butter

What you' ll need from the store cupboard:

- Garlic powder, to taste
- 2 cloves garlic, peeled and minced
- Salt and black pepper, to taste
- 1 (8 oz.) package cream cheese, softened
- Crushed red pepper, to taste

Instructions:

1. Preheat the Air fryer to 375 º F and grease an Air fryer basket.
2. Heat butter on medium heat in a nonstick skillet and add chicken.
3. Sauté for about 5 minutes and stir in the remaining ingredients except mushrooms.
4. Stuff this filling mixture in the mushroom caps and arrange in the Air fryer basket.
5. Cook for about 10 minutes and dish out to serve warm.

Nutrition Facts Per Serving:
Calories: 383, Fat: 36.3g, Carbohydrates: 4.3g, Sugar: 1.7g, Protein: 7.3g, Sodium: 444mg

Chapter 8 Desserts Recipes

Fiesta Pastries

Prep time: 15 minutes, cook time: 20 minutes; Serves 8

5 Ingredients:

- ½ of apple, peeled, cored and chopped
- 1 teaspoon fresh orange zest, grated finely
- 7.05-ounce prepared frozen puff pastry, cut into 16 squares

What you' ll need from the store cupboard:

- ½ tablespoon white sugar
- ½ teaspoon ground cinnamon

Instructions:

1. Preheat the Air fryer to 390 ° F and grease an Air fryer basket.
2. Mix all ingredients in a bowl except puff pastry.
3. Arrange about 1 teaspoon of this mixture in the center of each square.
4. Fold each square into a triangle and slightly press the edges with a fork.
5. Arrange the pastries in the Air fryer basket and cook for about 10 minutes.
6. Dish out and serve immediately.

Nutrition Facts Per Serving:
Calories: 147, Fat: 9.5g, Carbohydrates: 13.8g, Sugar: 2.1g, Protein: 1.9g, Sodium: 62mg

Classic Buttermilk Biscuits

Prep time: 15 minutes, cook time: 8 minutes; Serves 4

5 Ingredients:

- ½ cup cake flour
- 1¼ cups all-purpose flour
- ¾ teaspoon baking powder
- ¼ cup + 2 tablespoons butter, cut into cubes
- ¾ cup buttermilk

What you' ll need from the store cupboard:

- 1 teaspoon granulated sugar
- Salt, to taste

Instructions:

1. Preheat the Air fryer to 400 ° F and grease a pie pan lightly.
2. Sift together flours, baking soda, baking powder, sugar and salt in a large bowl.
3. Add cold butter and mix until a coarse crumb is formed.
4. Stir in the buttermilk slowly and mix until a dough is formed.
5. Press the dough into ½ inch thickness onto a floured surface and cut out circles with a 1¾-inch round cookie cutter.
6. Arrange the biscuits in a pie pan in a single layer and brush butter on them.
7. Transfer into the Air fryer and cook for about 8 minutes until golden brown.

Nutrition Facts Per Serving:
Calories: 374, Fat: 18.2g, Carbohydrates: 45.2g, Sugar: 3.4g, Protein: 7.3g, Sodium: 291mg

Crispy Fruit Tacos

Prep time: 5 minutes, cook time: 5 minutes; Serves 2

5 Ingredients:

- 2 soft shell tortillas
- 4 tablespoons strawberry jelly
- ¼ cup blueberries
- ¼ cup raspberries

What you' ll need from the store cupboard:

- 2 tablespoons powdered sugar

Instructions:

1. Preheat the Air fryer to 300 ° F and grease an Air fryer basket.
2. Put 2 tablespoons of strawberry jelly over each tortilla and top with blueberries and raspberries.
3. Sprinkle with powdered sugar and transfer into the Air fryer basket.
4. Cook for about 5 minutes until crispy and serve.

Nutrition Facts Per Serving:
Calories: 202, Fat: 0.8g, Carbohydrates: 49.2g, Sugar: 34.5g, Protein: 1.7g, Sodium: 11mg

Coconut-Coated White Chocolate Cookies

Prep time: 15 minutes, cook time: 12 minutes; Serves 8

5 Ingredients:

- 3½-ounce butter
- 1 small egg
- 5-ounce self-raising flour
- 1¼-ounce white chocolate, chopped
- 3 tablespoons desiccated coconut

What you'll need from the store cupboard:

- 2¼-ounce caster sugar
- 1 teaspoon vanilla extract

Instructions:

1. Preheat the Air fryer to 355 º F and grease a baking sheet lightly.
2. Mix sugar and butter in a large bowl and beat till fluffy.
3. Whisk in the egg, vanilla extract, flour and chocolate and mix until well combined.
4. Place coconut in a shallow dish and make small balls from the mixture.
5. Roll the balls into coconut evenly and arrange them onto baking sheet.
6. Press each ball into a cookie-like shape and transfer into the Air fryer.
7. Cook for about 8 minutes and set the Air fryer to 320 º F.
8. Cook for about 4 minutes and dish out to serve.

Nutrition Facts Per Serving:
Calories: 231, Fat: 13.7g, Carbohydrates: 24.8g, Sugar: 10.9g, Protein: 0.9g, Sodium: 83mg

Tasty Lemony Biscuits

Prep time: 15 minutes, cook time: 5 minutes; Serves 10

5 Ingredients:

- 8½ ounce self-rising flour
- 3½-ounce cold butter
- 1 small egg
- 1 teaspoon fresh lemon zest, grated finely

What you'll need from the store cupboard:

- 3½-ounce caster sugar
- 2 tablespoons fresh lemon juice
- 1 teaspoon vanilla extract

Instructions:

1. Preheat the Air fryer to 355 º F and grease a baking sheet lightly.
2. Mix flour and sugar in a large bowl.
3. Add cold butter and mix until a coarse crumb is formed.
4. Stir in the egg, lemon zest and lemon juice and mix until a dough is formed.
5. Press the dough into ½ inch thickness onto a floured surface and cut dough into medium-sized biscuits.
6. Arrange the biscuits on a baking sheet in a single layer and transfer into the Air fryer.
7. Cook for about 5 minutes until golden brown and serve with tea.

Nutrition Facts Per Serving:
Calories: 203, Fats: 8.7g, Carbohydrates: 28.5g, Sugar: 10.2g, Proteins: 3.1g, Sodium: 63mg

Basic Butter Cookies

Prep time: 10 minutes, cook time: 10 minutes; Serves 8

5 Ingredients:

- 4-ounce unsalted butter
- 1 cup all-purpose flour
- ¼ teaspoon baking powder

What you'll need from the store cupboard:

- 1¼-ounce icing sugar

Instructions:

1. Preheat the Air fryer to 340 º F and grease a baking sheet lightly.
2. Mix butter, icing sugar, flour and baking powder in a large bowl.
3. Mix well until a dough is formed and transfer into the piping bag fitted with a fluted nozzle.
4. Pipe the dough onto a baking sheet and arrange the baking sheet in the Air fryer.
5. Cook for about 10 minutes until golden brown and serve with tea.

Nutrition Facts Per Serving:
Calories: 176, Fat: 11.6g, Carbohydrates: 16.4g, Sugar: 4.4g, Protein: 1.7g, Sodium: 82mg

Perfect Apple Pie

Prep time: 15 minutes, cook time: 30 minutes; Serves 6

5 Ingredients:
- 1 frozen pie crust, thawed
- 1 large apple, peeled, cored and chopped
- 1 tablespoon butter, chopped
- 1 egg, beaten

What you' ll need from the store cupboard:
- 3 tablespoons sugar, divided
- 1 tablespoon ground cinnamon
- 2 teaspoons fresh lemon juice
- ½ teaspoon vanilla extract

Instructions:
1. Preheat the Air fryer to 320 º F and grease a pie pan lightly.
2. Cut 2 crusts, first about 1/8-inch larger than pie pan and second, a little smaller than first one.
3. Arrange the large crust in the bottom of pie pan.
4. Mix apple, 2 tablespoons of sugar, cinnamon, lemon juice and vanilla extract in a large bowl.
5. Put the apple mixture evenly over the bottom crust and top with butter.
6. Arrange the second crust on top and seal the edges.
7. Cut 4 slits in the top crust carefully and brush with egg.
8. Sprinkle with sugar and arrange the pie pan in the Air fryer basket.
9. Cook for about 30 minutes and dish out to serve.

Nutrition Facts Per Serving:
Calories: 182, Fat: 9.7g, Carbohydrates: 22.6g, Sugar: 10.9g, Protein: 2g, Sodium: 161mg

Healthy Fruit Muffins

Prep time: 10 minutes, cook time: 10 minutes; Serves 6

5 Ingredients:
- 1 cup milk
- 1 pack Oreo biscuits, crushed
- ¾ teaspoon baking powder
- 1 banana, peeled and chopped
- 1 apple, peeled, cored and chopped

What you' ll need from the store cupboard:
- 1 teaspoon cocoa powder
- 1 teaspoon honey
- 1 teaspoon fresh lemon juice
- Pinch of ground cinnamon

Instructions
1. Preheat the Air fryer to 320 º F and grease 6 muffin cups lightly.
2. Mix milk, biscuits, cocoa powder, baking soda and baking powder in a bowl until a smooth mixture is formed.
3. Divide this mixture into the prepared muffin cups and transfer into the Air fryer basket.
4. Cook for about 10 minutes and remove from Air fryer.
5. Mix banana, apple, honey, lemon juice and cinnamon in a bowl.
6. Scoop out some portion from center of muffins and fill with the fruit mixture.
7. Refrigerate for 2 hours and serve chilled.

Nutrition Facts Per Serving:
Calories: 152, Fat: 5.2g, Carbohydrates: 24.5g, Sugar: 9.3g, Protein: 3.3g, Sodium: 342mg

Chocolate Lover's Muffins

Prep time: 10 minutes, cook time: 10 minutes; Serves 8

5 Ingredients:
- 1½ cups all-purpose flour
- 2 teaspoons baking powder
- 1 egg
- 1 cup yogurt
- ½ cup mini chocolate chips

What you' ll need from the store cupboard:
- ¼ cup sugar
- Salt, to taste
- 1/3 cup vegetable oil
- 2 teaspoons vanilla extract

164

Instructions:

1. Preheat the Air fryer to 355 º F and grease 8 muffin cups lightly.
2. Mix flour, baking powder, sugar and salt in a bowl.
3. Whisk egg, oil, yogurt and vanilla extract in another bowl.
4. Combine the flour and egg mixtures and mix until a smooth mixture is formed.
5. Fold in the chocolate chips and divide this mixture into the prepared muffin cups.
6. Transfer into the Air fryer basket and cook for about 10 minutes.
7. Refrigerate for 2 hours and serve chilled.

Nutrition Facts Per Serving:
Calories: 279, Fat: 13.3g, Carbohydrates: 33.3g, Sugar: 14.1g, Protein: 5.6g, Sodium: 59mg

Delicate Pear Pouch

Prep time: 10 minutes, cook time: 15 minutes; Serves 4

5 Ingredients:

- 2 small pears, peeled, cored and halved
- 2 cups prepared vanilla custard
- 4 puff pastry sheets
- 1 egg, beaten lightly

What you' ll need from the store cupboard:

- 2 tablespoons sugar
- Pinch of ground cinnamon
- 2 tablespoons whipped cream

Instructions:

1. Preheat the Air fryer to 330 º F and grease an Air fryer basket.
2. Place a spoonful of vanilla custard and a pear half in the center of each pastry sheet.
3. Mix sugar and cinnamon in a bowl and sprinkle on the pear halves.
4. Pinch the corners of sheets together to shape into a pouch and transfer into the Air fryer basket.
5. Cook for about 15 minutes and top with whipped cream.
6. Dish out and serve with remaining custard.

Nutrition Facts Per Serving:
Calories: 622, Fat: 35.9g, Carbohydrates: 64.1g, Sugar: 27.7g, Protein: 12.1g, Sodium: 436mg

Spongy Cinnamon Donuts

Prep time: 10 minutes, cook time: 8 minutes; Serves 8

5 Ingredients:

For Donuts:

- 2¼ cups plain flour
- 1½ teaspoons baking powder
- 2 large egg yolks
- 2 tablespoons butter, melted

What you' ll need from the store cupboard:

For Donuts:

- Salt, to taste
- ½ cup sugar
- ½ cup sour cream

For Cinnamon Sugar:

- 1/3 cup caster sugar
- 1 teaspoon cinnamon

Instructions:

1. Preheat the Air fryer to 355 º F and grease an Air fryer basket lightly.
2. Sift together flour, baking powder and salt in a large bowl.
3. Add sugar and cold butter and mix until a coarse crumb is formed.
4. Stir in the egg yolks, ½ of the sour cream and 1/3 of the flour mixture and mix until a dough is formed.
5. Add remaining sour cream and 1/3 of the flour mixture and mix until well combined.
6. Stir in the remaining flour mixture and combine well.
7. Roll the dough into ½ inch thickness onto a floured surface and cut into donuts with a donut cutter.
8. Coat butter on both sides of the donuts and arrange in the Air fryer basket.
9. Cook for about 8 minutes until golden and sprinkle with cinnamon sugar to serve.

Nutrition Facts Per Serving:
Calories: 247, Fat: 6.5g, Carbohydrates: 43.7g, Sugar: 18.7g, Protein: 4.3g, Sodium: 288mg

Red Velvet Cupcakes

Prep time: 15 minutes, cook time: 12 minutes; Serves 12

5 Ingredients:

For Cupcakes:
- 2 cups refined flour
- ¾ cup peanut butter
- 3 eggs

For Frosting:
- 1 cup butter
- 1 cup cream cheese

What you' ll need from the store cupboard:

For Cupcakes:
- ¾ cup icing sugar
- 2 teaspoons beet powder
- 1 teaspoon cocoa powder

For Frosting:
- ¾ cup icing sugar
- ¼ cup strawberry sauce
- 1 teaspoon vanilla essence

Instructions:
1. Preheat the Air fryer to 340 º F and grease 12 silicon cups lightly.

For cupcakes:
2. Mix all the ingredients in a large bowl until well combined.
3. Transfer the mixture into silicon cups and place in the Air fryer basket.
4. Cook for about 12 minutes and dish out.

For Frosting:
5. Mix all the ingredients in a large bowl until well combined.
6. Top each cupcake evenly with frosting and serve.

Nutrition Facts Per Serving:
Calories: 455, Fats: 31.5g, Carbohydrates: 36.1g, Sugar: 17.8g, Proteins: 9.4g, Sodium: 260mg

Apple Dumplings

Prep time: 10 minutes, cook time: 25 minutes; Serves 2

5 Ingredients:
- 2 sheets puff pastry
- 2 small apples, peeled and cored
- 2 tablespoons raisins
- 2 tablespoons butter, melted

What you' ll need from the store cupboard:
- 1 tablespoon brown sugar

Instructions:
1. Preheat the Air fryer to 355 º F and grease an Air fryer basket.
2. Mix sugar and raisins in a bowl and fill each apple core with it.
3. Place the apple in the center of each pastry sheet and fold to completely cover the apple.
4. Seal the edges and transfer the dumplings into the Air fryer basket.
5. Cook for about 25 minutes and dish out in a platter.

Nutrition Facts Per Serving:
Calories: 500, Fat: 29.8g, Carbohydrates: 57.9g, Sugar: 29g, Protein: 4.3g, Sodium: 203mg

Sweet Wontons

Prep time: 15 minutes, cook time: 8 minutes; Serves 12

5 Ingredients:

For Wonton Wrappers:
- 18-ounce cream cheese, softened
- 1 Package of wonton wrappers

For Raspberry Syrup:
- 1 (12-ounce) package frozen raspberries

What you' ll need from the store cupboard:

For Wonton Wrappers:
- ½ cup powdered sugar
- 1 teaspoon vanilla extract

For Raspberry Syrup:
- ¼ cup water
- ¼ cup sugar
- 1 teaspoon vanilla extract

Instructions:
1. Preheat the Air fryer to 350 º F and grease an Air fryer basket.

For Wonton Wrappers:
2. Mix sugar, cream cheese and vanilla extract in a bowl and place a wonton wrapper on a work surface.

3. Place about 1 tablespoon of the cream cheese mixture in the center of each wonton wrapper.
4. Fold the wrappers around the filling and seal the edges.
5. Place the wontons in the Air fryer basket and cook for about 8 minutes.

For Raspberry Syrup:

6. Put water, sugar, raspberries and vanilla in a skillet on medium heat and cook for about 5 minutes, stirring continuously.

7. Transfer the mixture into the food processor and blend until smooth.
8. Drizzle the raspberry syrup over the wontons to serve.

Nutrition Facts Per Serving:
Calories: 297, Fat: 15.3g, Carbohydrates: 34.2g, Sugar: 15.4g, Protein: 6.2g, Sodium: 289mg

Heavenly Tasty Lava Cake

Prep time: 10 minutes, cook time: 3 minutes; Serves 6

5 Ingredients:

- 2/3 cup unsalted butter
- 2 eggs
- 2/3 cup all-purpose flour
- 1 cup chocolate chips, melted
- 1/3 cup fresh raspberries

What you'll need from the store cupboard:

- 5 tablespoons sugar
- Salt, to taste

Instructions:

1. Preheat the Air fryer to 355 º F and grease 6 ramekins lightly.

2. Mix sugar, butter, eggs, chocolate mixture, flour and salt in a bowl until well combined.
3. Fold in the melted chocolate chips and divide this mixture into the prepared ramekins.
4. Transfer into the Air fryer basket and cook for about 3 minutes.
5. Garnish with raspberries and serve immediately.

Nutrition Facts Per Serving:
Calories: 443, Fat: 30.4g, Carbohydrates: 38.2g, Sugar: 24.9g, Protein: 5.7g, Sodium: 215mg

Apple Cake

Prep time: 10 minutes, cook time: 45 minutes; Serves 6

5 Ingredients:

- 1 cup all-purpose flour
- ½ teaspoon baking soda
- 1 egg
- 2 cups apples, peeled, cored and chopped

What you'll need from the store cupboard:

- 1/3 cup brown sugar
- 1 teaspoon ground nutmeg
- 1 teaspoon ground cinnamon
- Salt, to taste
- 5 tablespoons plus 1 teaspoon vegetable oil
- ¾ teaspoon vanilla extract

Instructions:

1. Preheat the Air fryer to 355 º F and grease a baking pan lightly.

2. Mix flour, sugar, spices, baking soda and salt in a bowl until well combined.
3. Whisk egg with oil and vanilla extract in another bowl.
4. Stir in the flour mixture slowly and fold in the apples.
5. Pour this mixture into the baking pan and cover with the foil paper.
6. Transfer the baking pan into the Air fryer and cook for about 40 minutes.
7. Remove the foil and cook for 5 more minutes.
8. Allow to cool completely and cut into slices to serve.

Nutrition Facts Per Serving:
Calories: 244, Fat: 13.2g, Carbohydrates: 29.4g, Sugar: 11.9g, Protein: 3.2g, Sodium: 145mg

Nutella and Banana Pastries

Prep time: 10 minutes, cook time: 12 minutes; Serves 4

5 Ingredients:
- 1 puff pastry sheet, cut into 4 equal squares
- ½ cup Nutella
- 2 bananas, sliced

What you' ll need from the store cupboard:
- 2 tablespoons icing sugar

Instructions:
1. Preheat the Air fryer to 375 º F and grease an Air fryer basket.
2. Spread Nutella on each pastry square and top with banana slices and icing sugar.
3. Fold each square into a triangle and slightly press the edges with a fork.
4. Arrange the pastries in the Air fryer basket and cook for about 12 minutes.
5. Dish out and serve immediately.

Nutrition Facts Per Serving:
Calories: 158, Fat: 6.1g, Carbohydrates: 25.6g, Sugar: 13.7g, Protein: 1.8g, Sodium: 32mg

Sweet Potato Pie

Prep time: 15 minutes, cook time: 1 hour; Serves 4

5 Ingredients:
- 6-ounce sweet potato
- 1 (9-inch) prepared frozen pie dough, thawed
- 2 large eggs
- 1 tablespoon butter, melted

What you' ll need from the store cupboard:
- 1 teaspoon olive oil
- ¼ cup heavy cream
- 2 tablespoons maple syrup
- 1 tablespoon light brown sugar
- ½ teaspoon ground cinnamon
- 1/8 teaspoon ground nutmeg
- Salt, to taste
- ¾ teaspoon vanilla extract

Instructions:
1. Preheat the Air fryer to 400 º F and grease a pie pan.
2. Rub the sweet potato with oil and arrange in the Air fryer basket.
3. Cook for about 30 minutes and dish out in a bowl.
4. Allow to cool and mash it completely.
5. Add rest of the ingredients and mix until well combined.
6. Arrange the shell into a pie pan and place the mixture over the pie shell.
7. Transfer the pie pan in the Air fryer basket and cook for about 30 minutes.
8. Dish out and serve warm.

Nutrition Facts Per Serving:
Calories: 469, Fat: 24.3g, Carbohydrates: 57.4g, Sugar: 34.1g, Protein: 6.7g, Sodium: 455mg

Citric Chocolate Pudding

Prep time: 10 minutes, cook time: 14 minutes; Serves 4

5 Ingredients:
- ½ cup butter
- 2/3 cup dark chocolate, chopped
- 2 medium eggs
- 2 teaspoons fresh orange rind, grated finely
- 2 tablespoon self-rising flour

What you' ll need from the store cupboard:
- ¼ cup caster sugar
- ¼ cup fresh orange juice

Instructions:
1. Preheat the Air fryer to 355 º F and grease 4 ramekins lightly.
2. Microwave butter and chocolate in a bowl on high for about 2 minutes.
3. Add sugar, eggs, orange rind and juice and mix until well combined.
4. Stir in the flour and mix well.
5. Divide this mixture into the ramekins and cook for about 12 minutes.
6. Dish out and serve chilled.

Nutrition Facts Per Serving:
Calories: 454, Fat: 33.6g, Carbohydrates: 34.2g, Sugar: 28.4g, Protein: 5.7g, Sodium: 217mg

Vanilla Soufflé

Prep time: 15 minutes, cook time: 40 minutes; Serves 6

5 Ingredients:

- ¼ cup butter, softened
- ¼ cup all-purpose flour
- 1 cup milk
- 4 egg yolks
- 5 egg whites

What you' ll need from the store cupboard:

- ½ cup sugar
- 3 teaspoons vanilla extract, divided
- 1 teaspoon cream of tartar
- 1-ounce sugar

Instructions:

1. Preheat the Air fryer to 330 ° F and grease 6 ramekins lightly.
2. Mix butter and flour in a bowl until a smooth paste is formed.
3. Put milk and ½ cup of sugar in a bowl on medium-low heat and cook for about 3 minutes.
4. Bring to a boil and stir in the flour mixture.
5. Let it simmer for about 4 minutes and remove from heat.
6. Whisk egg yolks and vanilla extract in a bowl until well combined.
7. Combine the egg yolk mixture with milk mixture until mixed.
8. Mix egg whites, cream of tartar, remaining sugar and vanilla extract in another bowl.
9. Combine the egg white mixture into milk mixture and divide this mixture into the ramekins.
10. Transfer 3 ramekins into the Air fryer basket and cook for about 16 minutes.
11. Repeat with the remaining ramekins and dish out to serve.

Nutrition Facts Per Serving:
Calories: 245, Fat: 11.6g, Carbohydrates: 28.6g, Sugar: 23.8g, Protein: 6.8g, Sodium: 107mg

Apple Pie Crumble

Prep time: 10 minutes, cook time: 25 minutes; Serves 4

5 Ingredients:

- 1 (14-ounce) can apple pie
- ¼ cup butter, softened
- 9 tablespoons self-rising flour

What you' ll need from the store cupboard:

- 7 tablespoons caster sugar
- Pinch of salt

Instructions:

1. Preheat the Air fryer to 320 ° F and grease a baking dish.
2. Mix all the ingredients in a bowl until a crumbly mixture is formed.
3. Arrange the apple pie in the baking dish and top with the mixture.
4. Transfer the baking dish into the Air fryer basket and cook for about 25 minutes.
5. Dish out in a platter and serve.

Nutrition Facts Per Serving:
Calories: 296, Fats: 11.9g, Carbohydrates: 48.1g, Sugar: 31.4g, Proteins: 2.2g, Sodium: 122mg

Simple Donuts

Prep time: 10 minutes, cook time: 25 minutes; Serves 12

5 Ingredients:

- 2 cups all-purpose flour
- 2 teaspoons baking powder
- 1 egg
- 1 tablespoon butter, softened
- ½ cup milk

What you' ll need from the store cupboard:

- Salt, to taste
- ¾ cup sugar
- 2 teaspoons vanilla extract
- 2 tablespoons icing sugar

Instructions:

1. Preheat the Air fryer to 390 ° F and grease an Air fryer basket lightly.
2. Sift together flour, baking powder and salt in a large bowl.
3. Add sugar and egg and mix well.

4. Stir in the butter, milk and vanilla extract and mix until a dough is formed.
5. Refrigerate the dough for at least 1 hour and roll the dough into ½ inch thickness onto a floured surface.
6. Cut into donuts with a donut cutter and arrange the donuts in the Air fryer basket in 3 batches.

7. Cook for about 8 minutes until golden and serve.

Nutrition Facts Per Serving:
Calories: 150, Fat: 1.7g, Carbohydrates: 30.7g, Sugar: 14.4g, Protein: 3g, Sodium: 30mg

Walnut Banana Cake

Prep time: 5 minutes, cook time: 40 minutes; Serves 6

5 Ingredients:
- 1½ cups cake flour
- 1 teaspoon baking soda
- 2 eggs
- 3 medium bananas, peeled and mashed
- ½ cup walnuts, chopped

What you'll need from the store cupboard:
- ½ teaspoon ground cinnamon
- Salt, to taste
- ½ cup vegetable oil
- ½ cup sugar
- ½ teaspoon vanilla extract

Instructions:
1. Preheat the Air fryer to 300 º F and grease a 6-inch round baking pan lightly.
2. Mix flour, baking soda, cinnamon and salt in a bowl until well combined.

3. Whisk egg with oil, vanilla extract, sugar and bananas in another bowl.
4. Stir in the flour mixture slowly and fold in the apples.
5. Pour this mixture into the baking pan and top with walnuts and raisins.
6. Cover with the foil paper and transfer the baking pan into the Air fryer.
7. Cook for about 30 minutes and remove the foil.
8. Cook for 10 more minutes and cut into slices to serve.

Nutrition Facts Per Serving:
Calories: 462, Fat: 23.2g, Carbohydrates: 59.6g, Sugar: 27.8g, Protein: 7.2g, Sodium: 260mg

Super Moist Chocolate Cake

Prep time: 5 minutes, cook time: 40 minutes; Serves 9

5 Ingredients:
- 1/3 cup plain flour
- ¼ teaspoon baking powder
- 1½ tablespoons unsweetened cocoa powder
- 2 eggs, yolks and whites separated
- 3¾ tablespoons milk

What you'll need from the store cupboard:
- 1½-ounce castor sugar, divided
- 2 tablespoon vegetable oil
- 1 teaspoon vanilla extract
- 1/8 teaspoon cream of tartar

Instructions:
1. Preheat the Air fryer to 330 º F and grease a chiffon pan lightly.
2. Mix flour, baking powder and cocoa powder in a bowl.

3. Combine the remaining ingredients in another bowl until well combined.
4. Stir in the flour mixture slowly and pour this mixture into the chiffon pan.
5. Cover with the foil paper and poke some holes in the foil paper.
6. Transfer the baking pan into the Air fryer basket and cook for about 30 minutes.
7. Remove the foil and set the Air fryer to 285 º F.
8. Cook for 10 more minutes and cut into slices to serve.

Nutrition Facts Per Serving:
Calories: 94, Fat: 4.9g, Carbohydrates: 10.6g, Sugar: 5.8g, Protein: 2.5g, Sodium: 14mg

Strawberry Cupcakes

Prep time: 10 minutes, cook time: 8 minutes; Serves 10

5 Ingredients:
For Cupcakes:
- 7 tablespoons butter
- 2 eggs
- 7/8 cup self-rising flour

For Icing:
- 3½ tablespoons butter
- ¼ cup fresh strawberries, blended

What you'll need from the store cupboard:
For Cupcakes:
- ½ cup caster sugar
- ½ teaspoon vanilla essence

For Icing:
- 1 cup icing sugar
- 1 tablespoon whipped cream
- ½ teaspoon pink food color

Instructions:

1. Preheat the Air fryer to 340 º F and grease 8 muffin tins lightly.

For Cupcakes:
2. Mix all the ingredients in a large bowl until well combined.
3. Transfer the mixture into muffin tins and place in the Air fryer basket.
4. Cook for about 8 minutes and dish out.

For Icing:
5. Mix all the ingredients in a large bowl until well combined.
6. Fill the pastry bag with icing and top each cupcake evenly with frosting to serve.

Nutrition Facts Per Serving:
Calories: 250, Fat: 13.5g, Carbohydrates: 30.7g, Sugar: 22.1g, Protein: 2.4g, Sodium: 99mg

Bread Pudding

Prep time: 10 minutes, cook time: 12 minutes; Serves 2

5 Ingredients:
- 1 cup milk
- 1 egg
- 2 tablespoons raisins, soaked in hot water for about 15 minutes
- 2 bread slices, cut into small cubes
- 1 tablespoon chocolate chips

What you'll need from the store cupboard:
- 1 tablespoon brown sugar
- ½ teaspoon ground cinnamon
- ¼ teaspoon vanilla extract
- 1 tablespoon sugar

Instructions:
1. Preheat the Air fryer to 375 º F and grease a baking dish lightly.
2. Mix milk, egg, brown sugar, cinnamon and vanilla extract until well combined.
3. Stir in the raisins and mix well.
4. Arrange the bread cubes evenly in the baking dish and top with the milk mixture.
5. Refrigerate for about 20 minutes and sprinkle with chocolate chips and sugar.
6. Transfer the baking pan into the Air fryer and cook for about 12 minutes.
7. Dish out and serve immediately.

Nutrition Facts Per Serving:
Calories: 214, Fat: 6.6g, Carbohydrates: 32g, Sugar: 24.6g, Protein: 8.2g, Sodium: 156mg

Fruity Meringue

Prep time: 20 minutes, cook time: 2 hours 20 minutes; Serves 4

5 Ingredients:
- 5 egg whites
- 1 papaya, peeled and chopped
- 1 mango, peeled, pitted and chopped
- 1 pineapple, peeled and chopped
- 4 passion fruit, chopped

What you'll need from the store cupboard:
- 2 teaspoons cornstarch, sieved
- 3½-ounce super-fine sugar, divided
- 1 teaspoon fresh lemon juice
- 1 cup whipped cream

Instructions:
1. Preheat the Air fryer to 210 º F and grease an

Air fryer grill pan.

2. Whisk egg whites in a bowl and add the cornstarch and 2¾-ounce of sugar slowly.
3. Cut 2 sheets from a parchment paper and divide the egg white mixture evenly onto both sheets.
4. Put 1 sheet in the Air fryer grill pan and cook for about 1 hour.
5. Repeat with the other sheet and remove the egg white mixture from sheets.
6. Place about ¼ cup of each fruit in a bowl and reserve them.
7. Put the remaining fruit and lemon juice in a food processor and pulse till a puree forms.
8. Mix whipped cream and remaining sugar in a bowl and beat till stiff.
9. Transfer the whipped cream in a piping bag with a star nozzle and place the reserve chopped fruit over meringue.
10. Top with fruit puree and decorate with whipped cream to serve.

Nutrition Facts Per Serving:
Calories: 407, Fat: 10.1g, Carbohydrates: 78.5g, Sugar: 63.3g, Protein: 7.4g, Sodium: 67mg

Apple Tart

Prep time: 15 minutes, cook time: 25 minutes; Serves 2

5 Ingredients:

- 2½-ounce butter, chopped and divided
- 3 ½-ounce flour
- 1 egg yolk
- 1 large apple, peeled, cored and cut into 12 wedges

What you' ll need from the store cupboard:

- 1-ounce sugar

Instructions:

1. Preheat the Air fryer to 390 º F and grease a baking pan lightly.
2. Mix half of the butter and flour in a bowl until a soft dough is formed.
3. Roll the dough into 6-inch round on a floured surface.
4. Place the remaining butter and sugar in a baking pan and arrange the apple wedges in a circular pattern.
5. Top with rolled dough and press gently along the edges of the pan.
6. Transfer the baking pan in the Air fryer basket and cook for about 25 minutes.
7. Dish out and serve hot.

Nutrition Facts Per Serving:
Calories: 573, Fat: 21.7g, Carbohydrates: 67.8g, Sugar: 26g, Protein: 7.1g, Sodium: 210mg

Pecan Pie

Prep time: 10 minutes, cook time: 35 minutes; Serves 6

5 Ingredients:

- 1/3 cup butter, melted
- 2 large eggs
- 1¾ tablespoons flour
- 1 cup pecan halves
- 1 frozen pie crust, thawed

What you' ll need from the store cupboard:

- ¾ cup brown sugar
- ¼ cup caster sugar
- 1 teaspoon vanilla extract

Instructions:

1. Preheat the Air fryer to 300 º F and grease a pie pan lightly.
2. Mix both sugars, eggs and butter in a bowl until smooth.
3. Stir in the flour, milk and vanilla extract and beat until well combined.
4. Fold in the pecan halves and arrange the crust in the bottom of pie pan.
5. Put the pecan mixture in pie crust evenly and transfer in the Air fryer basket.
6. Cook for about 20 minutes and set the Air fryer to 285 º F.
7. Cook for about 15 more minutes more and dish out to serve hot.

Nutrition Facts Per Serving:
Calories: 479, Fat: 33.8g, Carbohydrates: 41.6g, Sugar: 27.9g, Protein: 5.7g, Sodium: 239mg

Peach Parcel

Prep time: 10 minutes, cook time: 15 minutes; Serves 2

5 Ingredients:

- 1 peach, peeled, cored and halved
- 1 cup prepared vanilla custard
- 2 puff pastry sheets
- 1 egg, beaten lightly

What you' ll need from the store cupboard:

- 1 tablespoon sugar
- Pinch of ground cinnamon
- 1 tablespoon whipped cream

Instructions:

1. Preheat the Air fryer to 340 º F and grease an Air fryer basket.
2. Place a spoonful of vanilla custard and a peach half in the center of each pastry sheet.
3. Mix sugar and cinnamon in a bowl and sprinkle on the peach halves.
4. Pinch the corners of sheets together to shape into a parcel and transfer into the Air fryer basket.
5. Cook for about 15 minutes and top with whipped cream.
6. Dish out and serve with remaining custard.

Nutrition Facts Per Serving:
Calories: 622, Fat: 35.9g, Carbohydrates: 64.1g, Sugar: 27.7g, Protein: 12.1g, Sodium: 436mg

Walnut Brownies

Prep time: 10 minutes, cook time: 22 minutes; Serves 8

5 Ingredients:

- ½ cup chocolate, chopped roughly
- 1/3 cup butter
- 1 large egg, beaten
- 5 tablespoons self-rising flour
- ¼ cup walnuts, chopped

What you' ll need from the store cupboard:

- 5 tablespoons sugar
- 1 teaspoon vanilla extract
- Pinch of salt

Instructions:

1. Preheat the Air fryer to 355 º F and line a baking pan with greased parchment paper.
2. Microwave chocolate and butter on high for about 2 minutes.
3. Mix sugar, egg, vanilla extract, salt and chocolate mixture in a bowl until well combined.
4. Stir in the flour mixture slowly and fold in the walnuts.
5. Pour this mixture into the baking pan and smooth the top surface of mixture with the back of spatula.
6. Transfer the baking pan into the Air fryer basket and cook for about 20 minutes.
7. Dish out and cut into 8 equal sized squares to serve.

Nutrition Facts Per Serving:
Calories: 205, Fat: 13.8g, Carbohydrates: 18g, Sugar: 13.1g, Protein: 3.1g, Sodium: 91mg

Shortbread Fingers

Prep time: 10 minutes, cook time: 12 minutes; Serves 10

5 Ingredients:

- 1 2/3 cups plain flour
- ¾ cup butter

What you' ll need from the store cupboard:

- 1/3 cup caster sugar

Instructions:

1. Preheat the Air fryer to 355 º F and grease a baking sheet lightly.
2. Mix sugar, flour and butter in a bowl to form a dough.
3. Cut the dough into 10 equal sized fingers and prick the fingers lightly with a fork.
4. Transfer the fingers into the Air fryer basket and cook for about 12 minutes.
5. Dish out and serve warm.

Nutrition Facts Per Serving:
Calories: 223, Fats: 14g, Carbohydrates: 22.6g, Sugar: 6.7g, Proteins: 2.3g, Sodium: 99mg

Decadent Cheesecake

Prep time: 15 minutes, cook time: 33 minutes; Serves 6

5 Ingredients:
- 3 eggs, separated
- 1 cup white chocolate, chopped
- ½ cup cream cheese, softened
- 2 tablespoons cocoa powder
- ¼ cup apricot jam

What you' ll need from the store cupboard:
- 2 tablespoons powdered sugar

Instructions:
1. Preheat the Air fryer to 285 º F and grease a cake pan lightly.
2. Refrigerate egg whites in a bowl to chill before using.
3. Microwave chocolate and cream cheese on high for about 3 minutes.
4. Remove from microwave and whisk in the egg yolks.
5. Whisk together egg whites until firm peaks form and combine with the chocolate mixture.
6. Transfer the mixture into a cake pan and arrange in the Air fryer basket.
7. Cook for about 30 minutes and dish out.
8. 1Dust with powdered sugar and spread jam on top to serve.

Nutrition Facts Per Serving:
Calories: 298, Fat: 18.3g, Carbohydrates: 29.7g, Sugar: 25.4g, Protein: 6.3g, Sodium: 119mg

Nutty Fudge Muffins

Prep time: 5 minutes, cook time: 10 minutes; Serves 10

5 Ingredients:
- 1 package fudge brownie mix
- 1 egg
- 2 teaspoons water
- ¼ cup walnuts, chopped

What you' ll need from the store cupboard:
- 1/3 cup vegetable oil

Instructions:
1. Preheat the Air fryer to 300 º F and grease 10 muffin tins lightly.
2. Mix brownie mix, egg, oil and water in a bowl.
3. Fold in the walnuts and pour the mixture in the muffin cups.
4. Transfer the muffin tins in the Air fryer basket and cook for about 10 minutes.
5. Dish out and serve immediately.

Nutrition Facts Per Serving:
Calories: 355, Fat: 18.6g, Carbohydrates: 47.1g, Sugar: 0g, Protein: 3.7g, Sodium: 191mg

Semolina Cake

Prep time: 15 minutes, cook time: 15 minutes; Serves 8

5 Ingredients:
- 2½ cups semolina
- 1 cup milk
- 1 cup Greek yogurt
- 2 teaspoons baking powder
- ½ cup walnuts, chopped

What you' ll need from the store cupboard:
- ½ cup vegetable oil
- 1 cup sugar
- Pinch of salt

Instructions:
1. Preheat the Air fryer to 360 º F and grease a baking pan lightly.
2. Mix semolina, oil, milk, yogurt and sugar in a bowl until well combined.
3. Cover the bowl and keep aside for about 15 minutes.
4. Stir in the baking soda, baking powder and salt and fold in the walnuts.
5. Transfer the mixture into the baking pan and place in the Air fryer.
6. Cook for about 15 minutes and dish out to serve.

Nutrition Facts Per Serving:
Calories: 482, Fat: 17.8g, Carbohydrates: 70.3g, Sugar: 30.5g, Protein: 12.2g, Sodium: 127mg

Luscious Cheesecake

Prep time: 10 minutes, cook time: 25 minutes; Serves 8

5 Ingredients:
- 17.6-ounce ricotta cheese
- 3 eggs
- 3 tablespoons corn starch

What you'll need from the store cupboard:
- ¾ cup sugar
- 1 tablespoon fresh lemon juice
- 2 teaspoons vanilla extract
- 1 teaspoon fresh lemon zest, grated finely

Instructions:

1. Preheat the Air fryer to 320 ° F and grease a baking dish lightly.
2. Mix all the ingredients in a bowl and transfer the mixture into the baking dish.
3. Place the baking dish in the Air fryer basket and cook for 25 about minutes.
4. Dish out and serve immediately.

Nutrition Facts Per Serving:
Calories: 197, Fat: 6.6g, Carbohydrates: 25.7g, Sugar: 19.2g, Protein: 9.2g, Sodium: 102mg

Flavor-Packed Clafoutis

Prep time: 10 minutes, cook time: 25 minutes; Serves 4

5 Ingredients:
- 1½ cups fresh cherries, pitted
- ¼ cup flour
- 1 egg
- 1 tablespoon butter

What you'll need from the store cupboard:
- 3 tablespoons vodka
- 2 tablespoons sugar
- Pinch of salt
- ½ cup sour cream
- ¼ cup powdered sugar

Instructions:

1. Preheat the Air fryer to 355 ° F and grease a baking pan lightly.
2. Mix cherries and vodka in a bowl.
3. Sift together flour, sugar and salt in another bowl.
4. Stir in the sour cream and egg until a smooth dough is formed.
5. Transfer the dough evenly into the baking pan and top with the cherry mixture and butter.
6. Place the baking pan in the Air fryer basket and cook for about 25 minutes.
7. Dust with powdered sugar and serve warm.

Nutrition Facts Per Serving:
Calories: 264, Fat: 10.1g, Carbohydrates: 34.7g, Sugar: 13.5g, Protein: 3.3g, Sodium: 99mg

Stuffed Apples

Prep time: 10 minutes, cook time: 13 minutes; Serves 4

5 Ingredients:
- 4 small firm apples, cored
- ½ cup golden raisins
- ½ cup blanched almonds

What you'll need from the store cupboard:
- 4 tablespoons sugar, divided
- ½ cup whipped cream
- ½ teaspoon vanilla extract

Instructions:

1. Preheat the Air fryer to 355 ° F and grease a baking dish lightly.
2. Put raisins, almond and half of sugar in a food processor and pulse until chopped.
3. Stuff the raisin mixture inside each apple and arrange the apples in the prepared baking dish.
4. Transfer the baking dish in the Air fryer basket and cook for about 10 minutes.
5. Put cream, remaining sugar and vanilla extract on medium heat in a pan and cook for about 3 minutes, continuously stirring.
6. Remove from the heat and serve apple with vanilla sauce.

Nutrition Facts Per Serving:
Calories: 308, Fat: 11g, Carbohydrates: 54.6g, Sugar: 42.3g, Protein: 3.9g, Sodium: 9mg

Fruity Crumble

Prep time: 15 minutes, cook time: 20 minutes; Serves 4

5 Ingredients:

- ½ pound fresh apricots, pitted and cubed
- 1 cup fresh blackberries
- 7/8 cup flour
- 1 tablespoon cold water
- ¼ cup chilled butter, cubed

What you' ll need from the store cupboard:

- 1/3 cup sugar, divided
- 1 tablespoon fresh lemon juice
- Pinch of salt

Instructions:

1. Preheat the Air fryer to 390 º F and grease a baking pan lightly.
2. Mix apricots, blackberries, 2 tablespoons of sugar and lemon juice in a bowl.
3. Combine the remaining ingredients in a bowl and mix until a crumbly mixture is formed.
4. Pour the apricot mixture in the baking pan and top with the crumbly mixture.
5. Transfer the baking pan in the Air fryer basket and cook for about 20 minutes.
6. Dish out in a bowl and serve warm.

Nutrition Facts Per Serving:
Calories: 307, Fat: 12.4g, Carbohydrates: 47.3g, Sugar: 23.7g, Protein: 4.2g, Sodium: 243mg

Cream Cheese Cupcakes

Prep time: 10 minutes, cook time: 20 minutes; Serves 10

5 Ingredients:

- 4½-ounce self-rising flour
- ½-ounce cream cheese, softened
- 4¾-ounce butter, softened
- 2 eggs
- ½ cup fresh raspberries

What you' ll need from the store cupboard:

- Pinch of salt
- 4¼-ounce caster sugar
- 2 teaspoons fresh lemon juice

Instructions:

1. Preheat the Air fryer to 365 º F and grease 10 silicon cups.
2. Mix flour, baking powder and salt in a bowl.
3. Combine cream cheese, sugar, eggs and butter in another bowl.
4. Mix the flour mixture with the cream cheese mixture and squeeze in the lemon juice.
5. Transfer the mixture into 10 silicon cups and top each cup with 2 raspberries.
6. Place the silicon cups in the Air fryer basket and cook for about 20 minutes.
7. Dish out and serve to enjoy.

Nutrition Facts Per Serving:
Calories: 209, Fat: 12.5g, Carbohydrates: 22.8g, Sugar: 12.4g, Protein: 2.7g, Sodium: 110mg

Brownies Muffins

Prep time: 10 minutes, cook time: 10 minutes; Serves 12

5 Ingredients:

- 1 package Betty Crocker fudge brownie mix
- ¼ cup walnuts, chopped
- 1 egg
- 2 teaspoons water

What you' ll need from the store cupboard:

- 1/3 cup vegetable oil

Instructions:

1. Preheat the Air fryer to 300 º F and grease 12 muffin molds lightly.
2. Mix all the ingredients in a bowl and divide evenly into the muffin molds.
3. Arrange the molds in the Air Fryer basket and cook for about 10 minutes.
4. Dish out and invert the muffins onto wire rack to completely cool before serving.

Nutrition Facts Per Serving:
Calories: 241, Fat: 9.6g, Carbohydrates: 36.9g, Sugar: 25g, Protein: 2.8g, Sodium: 155mg

Chocolate Balls

Prep time: 15 minutes, cook time: 13 minutes; Serves 8

5 Ingredients:

- 2 cups plain flour
- 2 tablespoons cocoa powder
- ¾ cup chilled butter
- ¼ cup chocolate, chopped into 8 chunks

What you' ll need from the store cupboard:

- ½ cup icing sugar
- Pinch of ground cinnamon
- 1 teaspoon vanilla extract

Instructions:

1. Preheat the Air fryer to 355 º F and grease a baking dish lightly.
2. Mix flour, icing sugar, cocoa powder, cinnamon and vanilla extract in a bowl.
3. Add cold butter and buttermilk and mix until a smooth dough is formed.
4. Divide the dough into 8 equal balls and press 1 chocolate chunk in the center of each ball.
5. Cover completely with the dough and arrange the balls in a baking dish.
6. Transfer into the Air fryer and cook for about 8 minutes.
7. Set the Air fryer to 320 º F and cook for 5 more minutes.
8. Dish out in a platter and serve to enjoy.

Nutrition Facts Per Serving:
Calories: 328, Fats: 19.3g, Carbohydrates: 35.3g, Sugar: 10.2g, Proteins: 4g, Sodium: 128mg

Banana Split

Prep time: 10 minutes, cook time: 10 minutes; Serves 8

5 Ingredients:

- 1 cup panko bread crumbs
- 4 bananas, peeled and halved lengthwise
- ½ cup corn flour
- 2 eggs
- 2 tablespoons walnuts, chopped

What you' ll need from the store cupboard:

- 3 tablespoons coconut oil
- 3 tablespoons sugar
- ¼ teaspoon ground cinnamon

Instructions:

1. Preheat the Air fryer to 280 º F and grease an Air fryer basket lightly.
2. Heat coconut oil in a skillet on medium heat and add bread crumbs.
3. Cook for 4 minutes until golden brown and transfer into a bowl.
4. Place the flour in a shallow dish and whisk the eggs in another shallow dish.
5. Coat banana slices evenly with flour and dip in eggs and dredge again in the bread crumbs.
6. Mix the sugar and cinnamon in a small bowl and sprinkle over the banana slices.
7. Arrange the banana slices in the Air fryer basket and cook for about 10 minutes.
8. Top with walnuts and serve.

Nutrition Facts Per Serving:
Calories: 221, Fat: 18.5g, Carbohydrates: 33.7g, Sugar: 12.7g, Protein: 4.8g, Sodium: 115mg

Rich Layered Cake

Prep time: 15 minutes, cook time: 25 minutes; Serves 8

5 Ingredients:

For Cake:

- 3½-ounce plain flour
- 3½-ounce butter, softened
- 2 medium eggs

For Filling:

- 1¾-ounce butter, softened
- 2 tablespoons strawberry jam

What you' ll need from the store cupboard:

For Cake:

- 1 teaspoon ground cinnamon
- Pinch of salt
- 7 tablespoons sugar

For Filling:

- 1 tablespoon whipped cream
- 2/3 cup icing sugar

Instructions:

1. Preheat the Air fryer to 355 º F and grease a cake pan lightly.

For Cake:
2. Mix flour, cinnamon and salt in a large bowl.
3. Beat together sugar, eggs and butter in another bowl until creamy.
4. Stir in the flour mixture slowly and beat until well combined
5. Transfer the mixture into the cake pan and cook for about 15 minutes.
6. Set the Air fryer to 335 degrees F and cook for about 10 minutes.
7. Remove the cake from the Air fryer and cut the cake in 2 portions.

For Filling:
8. Mix butter, cream and icing sugar in a bowl and beat until creamy.
9. Place 1 cake portion in a plate, cut side up and spread jam evenly over cake.
10. Top with the butter mixture and place another cake, cut side down over filling to serve.

Nutrition Facts Per Serving:
Calories: 298, Fat: 16.9g, Carbohydrates: 30.5g, Sugar: 20.4g, Protein: 2.9g, Sodium: 143mg

Chocolate Yogurt Pecans Muffins

Prep time: 15 minutes, cook time: 10 minutes; Serves 9

5 Ingredients:
- 1½ cups all-purpose flour
- 2 teaspoons baking powder
- 1 cup yogurt
- ¼ cup mini chocolate chips
- ¼ cup pecans, chopped

What you'll need from the store cupboard:
- ¼ cup sugar
- ½ teaspoon salt
- 1/3 cup vegetable oil
- 2 teaspoons vanilla extract

Instructions:
1. Preheat the Air fryer to 355 ° F and grease 9 muffin molds lightly.
2. Mix flour, sugar, baking powder, and salt in a bowl.
3. Mix the yogurt, oil, and vanilla extract in another bowl.
4. Fold in the chocolate chips and pecans and divide the mixture evenly into the muffin molds.
5. Arrange the muffin molds into the Air fryer basket and cook for about 10 minutes.
6. Remove the muffin molds from Air fryer and invert the muffins onto wire rack to cool completely before serving.

Nutrition Facts Per Serving:
Calories: 246, Fat: 12.9g, Carbohydrates: 27.3g, Sugar: 10.2g, Protein: 5g, Sodium: 159mg

Double Chocolate Muffins

Prep time: 20 minutes, cook time: 30 minutes; Serves 12

5 Ingredients:
- 1 1/3 cups self-rising flour
- 2½ tablespoons cocoa powder
- 3½ ounces butter
- 5 tablespoons milk
- 2½ ounces milk chocolate, finely chopped

What you'll need from the store cupboard:
- 2/3 cup plus 3 tablespoons caster sugar
- ½ teaspoon vanilla extract

Instructions:
1. Preheat the Air fryer to 355 ° F and grease 12 muffin molds lightly.
2. Mix flour, sugar, and cocoa powder in a bowl.
3. Stir in the butter, milk, vanilla extract and the chopped chocolate and mix until well combined.
4. Transfer the mixture evenly into the muffin molds and arrange in the Air fryer basket in 2 batches.
5. Cook for about 9 minutes and set the Air fryer to 320 ° F.
6. Cook for about 6 minutes and remove from the Air fryer to serve.

Nutrition Facts Per Serving:
Calories: 207, Fat: 9.6g, Carbohydrates: 28.1g, Sugar: 16.5g, Protein: 3.3g, Sodium: 66mg

Raspberry Cupcakes

Prep time: 15 minutes, cook time: 15 minutes; Serves 10

5 Ingredients:

- 4½ ounces self-rising flour
- ½ teaspoon baking powder
- ½ ounce cream cheese, softened
- 4¾ ounces butter, softened
- ½ cup fresh raspberries

What you' ll need from the store cupboard:

- A pinch of salt
- 4¼ ounces caster sugar
- 2 teaspoons fresh lemon juice

Instructions:

1. Preheat the Air fryer to 320 º F and grease 10 silicon cups lightly.
2. Mix flour, baking powder, and salt in a large bowl until well combined.
3. Combine well the cream cheese, sugar, eggs, butter, lemon juice and flour mixture in another bowl.
4. Transfer the mixture into silicon cups and place in the Air fryer basket.
5. Cook for about 15 minutes and invert the cupcakes onto wire rack to completely cool.

Nutrition Facts Per Serving:
Calories: 209, Fat: 12.5g, Carbohydrates: 22.8g, Sugar: 12.5g, Protein: 2.7g, Sodium: 110mg

Fruity Oreo Muffins

Prep time: 15 minutes, cook time: 10 minutes; Serves 6

5 Ingredients:

- 1 cup milk
- 1 pack Oreo biscuits, crushed
- ¾ teaspoon baking powder
- 1 banana, peeled and chopped
- 1 apple, peeled, cored and chopped

What you' ll need from the store cupboard:

- 1 teaspoon cocoa powder
- 1 teaspoon honey
- 1 teaspoon fresh lemon juice
- A pinch of ground cinnamon

Instructions:

1. Preheat the Air fryer to 320 º F and grease 6 muffin cups lightly.
2. Mix milk, biscuits, cocoa powder, baking soda, and baking powder in a bowl until well combined.
3. Transfer the mixture into the muffin cups and cook for about 10 minutes.
4. Remove from the Air fryer and invert the muffin cups onto a wire rack to cool.
5. Meanwhile, mix the banana, apple, honey, lemon juice, and cinnamon in another bowl.
6. Scoop some portion of muffins from the center and fill with fruit mixture to serve.

Nutrition Facts Per Serving:
Calories: 182, Fat: 3.1g, Carbohydrates: 31.4g, Sugar: 19.5g, Protein: 3.1g, Sodium: 196mg

Chocolate Mug Cake

Prep time: 15 minutes, cook time: 13 minutes; Serves 1

5 Ingredients:

- ¼ cup self-rising flour
- 1 tablespoon cocoa powder
- 3 tablespoons whole milk

What you' ll need from the store cupboard:

- 5 tablespoons caster sugar
- 3 tablespoons coconut oil

Instructions:

1. Preheat the Air fryer to 390 º F and grease a large mug lightly.
2. Mix all the ingredients in a shallow mug until well combined.
3. Arrange the mug into the Air fryer basket and cook for about 13 minutes.
4. Dish out and serve warm.

Nutrition Facts Per Serving:
Calories: 729, Fat: 43.3g, Carbohydrates: 88.8g, Sugar: 62.2g, Protein: 5.7g, Sodium: 20mg

Dark Chocolate Cheesecake

Prep time: 20 minutes, cook time: 34 minutes; Serves 6

5 Ingredients:
- 3 eggs, whites and yolks separated
- 1 cup dark chocolate, chopped
- ½ cup cream cheese, softened
- 2 tablespoons cocoa powder
- ¼ cup dates jam

What you' ll need from the store cupboard:
- 2 tablespoons powdered sugar

Instructions:
1. Preheat the Air fryer to 285 º F and grease a cake pan lightly.
2. Refrigerate egg whites in a bowl to chill before using.
3. Microwave chocolate and cream cheese on high for about 3 minutes.
4. Remove from microwave and whisk in the egg yolks.
5. Whisk together egg whites until firm peaks form and combine with the chocolate mixture.
6. Transfer the mixture into a cake pan and arrange in the Air fryer basket.
7. Cook for about 30 minutes and dish out.
8. Dust with powdered sugar and spread dates jam on top to serve.

Nutrition Facts Per Serving:
Calories: 298, Fat: 18.3g, Carbohydrates: 29.7g, Sugar: 24.5g, Protein: 6.3g, Sodium: 119mg

Cream Doughnuts

Prep time: 15 minutes, cook time: 16 minutes; Serves 8

5 Ingredients:
- 4 tablespoons butter, softened and divided
- 2 egg yolks
- 2¼ cups plain flour
- 1½ teaspoons baking powder

What you' ll need from the store cupboard:
- ½ cup sugar
- 1 teaspoon salt
- ½ cup sour cream
- ½ cup heavy cream

Instructions:
1. Preheat the Air fryer to 355 º F and grease an Air fryer basket lightly.
2. Sift together flour, baking powder and salt in a large bowl.
3. Add sugar and cold butter and mix until a coarse crumb is formed.
4. Stir in the egg yolks, ½ of the sour cream and 1/3 of the flour mixture and mix until a dough is formed.
5. Add remaining sour cream and 1/3 of the flour mixture and mix until well combined.
6. Stir in the remaining flour mixture and combine well.
7. Roll the dough into ½ inch thickness onto a floured surface and cut into donuts with a donut cutter.
8. Coat butter on both sides of the donuts and arrange in the Air fryer basket.
9. Cook for about 8 minutes until golden and top with heavy cream to serve.

Nutrition Facts Per Serving:
Calories: 297, Fats: 13g, Carbohydrates: 40.7g, Sugar: 12.6g, Proteins: 5g, Sodium: 346mg

Apple Doughnuts

Prep time: 20 minutes, cook time: 5 minutes; Serves 6

5 Ingredients:
- 2½ cups plus 2 tablespoons all-purpose flour
- 1½ teaspoons baking powder
- 2 tablespoons unsalted butter, softened
- 1 egg
- ½ pink lady apple, peeled, cored and grated

What you' ll need from the store cupboard:
- 1 cup apple cider
- ½ teaspoon ground cinnamon
- ½ teaspoon salt
- ½ cup brown sugar

Instructions:
1. Preheat the Air fryer to 360 º F and grease an Air fryer basket lightly.

2. Boil apple cider in a medium pan over medium-high heat and reduce the heat.
3. Let it simmer for about 15 minutes and dish out in a bowl.
4. Sift together flour, baking powder, baking soda, cinnamon, and salt in a large bowl.
5. Mix the brown sugar, egg, cooled apple cider and butter in another bowl.
6. Stir in the flour mixture and grated apple and mix to form a dough.
7. Wrap the dough with a plastic wrap and refrigerate for about 30 minutes.
8. Roll the dough into 1-inch thickness and cut the doughnuts with a doughnut cutter.
9. Arrange the doughnuts into the Air fryer basket and cook for about 5 minutes, flipping once in between.
10. Dish out and serve warm.

Nutrition Facts Per Serving:
Calories: 433, Fat: 11g, Carbohydrates: 78.3g, Sugar: 35g, Protein: 6.8g, Sodium: 383mg

Doughnuts Pudding

Prep time: 15 minutes, cook time: 1 hour; Serves 4

5 Ingredients:
- 6 glazed doughnuts, cut into small pieces
- ¾ cup frozen sweet cherries
- ½ cup raisins
- ½ cup semi-sweet chocolate baking chips
- 4 egg yolks

What you' ll need from the store cupboard:
- ¼ cup sugar
- 1 teaspoon ground cinnamon
- 1½ cups whipping cream

Instructions:
1. Preheat the Air fryer to 310 º F and grease a baking dish lightly.
2. Mix doughnut pieces, cherries, raisins, chocolate chips, sugar, and cinnamon in a large bowl.
3. Whisk the egg yolks with whipping cream in another bowl until well combined.
4. Combine the egg yolk mixture into the doughnut mixture and mix well.
5. Arrange the doughnuts mixture evenly into the baking dish and transfer into the Air fryer basket.
6. Cook for about 60 minutes and dish out to serve warm.

Nutrition Facts Per Serving:
Calories: 786, Fat: 43.2g, Carbohydrates: 9.3g, Sugar: 60.7g, Protein: 11g, Sodium: 419mg

Chocolate Soufflé

Prep time: 15 minutes, cook time: 16 minutes; Serves 2

5 Ingredients:
- 3 ounces semi-sweet chocolate, chopped
- ¼ cup butter
- 2 eggs, egg yolks and whites separated
- 2 tablespoons all-purpose flour

What you' ll need from the store cupboard:
- 3 tablespoons sugar
- ½ teaspoon pure vanilla extract
- 1 teaspoon powdered sugar plus extra for dusting

Instructions:
1. Preheat the Air fryer to 330 º F and grease 2 ramekins lightly.
2. Microwave butter and chocolate on high heat for about 2 minutes until smooth.
3. Whisk the egg yolks, sugar, and vanilla extract in a bowl.
4. Add the chocolate mixture and flour and mix until well combined.
5. Whisk the egg whites in another bowl until soft peaks form and fold into the chocolate mixture.
6. Sprinkle each with a pinch of sugar and transfer the mixture into the ramekins.
7. Arrange the ramekins into the Air fryer basket and cook for about 14 minutes.
8. Dish out and serve sprinkled with the powdered sugar to serve.

Nutrition Facts Per Serving:
Calories: 569, Fat: 38.8g, Carbohydrates: 54.1g, Sugar: 42.2g, Protein: 6.9g, Sodium: 225mg

Fried Banana Slices

Prep time: 15 minutes, cook time: 15 minutes; Serves 8

5 Ingredients:
- 4 medium ripe bananas, peeled and cut in 4 pieces lengthwise
- 1/3 cup rice flour, divided
- 4 tablespoons corn flour
- 2 tablespoons desiccated coconut
- ½ teaspoon baking powder

What you'll need from the store cupboard:
- ½ teaspoon ground cardamom
- A pinch of salt

Instructions:
1. Preheat the Air fryer to 390 ° F and grease an Air fryer basket.
2. Mix coconut, 2 tablespoons of rice flour, corn flour, baking powder, cardamom, and salt in a shallow bowl.
3. Stir in the water gradually and mix until a smooth mixture is formed.
4. Place the remaining rice flour in a second bowl and dip in the coconut mixture.
5. Dredge in the rice flour and arrange the banana slices into the Air fryer basket in a single layer.
6. Cook for about 15 minutes, flipping once in between and dish out onto plates to serve.

Nutrition Facts Per Serving:
Calories: 260, Fat: 6g, Carbohydrates: 51.2g, Sugar: 17.6g, Protein: 4.6g, Sodium: 49mg

Chocolaty Squares

Prep time: 15 minutes, cook time: 20 minutes; Serves 4

5 Ingredients:
- 2-ounce cold butter
- 3-ounce self-rising flour
- ½ tablespoon milk
- 2-ounce chocolate, chopped

What you'll need from the store cupboard:
- 1¼-ounce brown sugar
- 1/8 cup honey

Instructions:
1. Preheat the Air fryer to 320 ° F and grease a tin lightly.
2. Mix butter, brown sugar, flour and honey and beat till smooth.
3. Stir in the chocolate and milk and pour the mixture into a tin.
4. Transfer into the Air fryer basket and cook for about 20 minutes.
5. Dish out and cut into desired squares to serve.

Nutrition Facts Per Serving:
Calories: 322, Fat: 15.9g, Carbohydrates: 42.2g, Sugar: 24.8g, Protein: 3.5g, Sodium: 97mg

Cherry Pie

Prep time: 20 minutes, cook time: 15 minutes; Serves 4

5 Ingredients:
- ½ (21-ounce) can cherry pie filling
- 1 refrigerated pre-made pie crust
- ½ tablespoon milk
- 1 egg yolk

What you'll need from the store cupboard:
- 1 tablespoon vegetable oil

Instructions:
1. Preheat the Air fryer to 320 ° F and press pie crust into a pie pan.
2. Poke the holes with a fork all over dough and transfer the pie pan into the Air fryer basket.
3. Cook for about 5 minutes and remove from the Air fryer.
4. Pour the cherry pie filling into pie crust.
5. Cut the remaining pie crust into ¾-inch strips and place the strips in a crisscross manner.
6. Whisk egg and milk in a small bowl and brush the egg wash on the top of pie.
7. Transfer the pie pan into the Air fryer basket and cook for about 15 minutes to serve.

Nutrition Facts Per Serving:
Calories: 307, Fat: 1.4g, Carbohydrates: 70g, Sugar: 57.9g, Protein: 1g, Sodium: 130mg

Marshmallow Pastries

Prep time: 20 minutes, cook time: 5 minutes; Serves 8

5 Ingredients:
- 4-ounce butter, melted
- 8 phyllo pastry sheets, thawed
- ½ cup chunky peanut butter
- 8 teaspoons marshmallow fluff

What you'll need from the store cupboard:
- Pinch of salt

Instructions:
1. Preheat the Air fryer to 360 ° F and grease an Air fryer basket.
2. Brush butter over 1 filo pastry sheet and top with a second filo sheet.
3. Brush butter over second filo pastry sheet and repeat with all the remaining sheets.
4. Cut the phyllo layers in 8 strips and put 1 tablespoon of peanut butter and 1 teaspoon of marshmallow fluff on the underside of a filo strip.
5. Fold the tip of the sheet over the filling to form a triangle and fold repeatedly in a zigzag manner.
6. Arrange the pastries into the Air fryer basket and cook for about 5 minutes.
7. Season with a pinch of salt and serve warm.

Nutrition Facts Per Serving:
Calories: 283, Fat: 20.6g, Carbohydrates: 20.2g, Sugar: 3.4g, Protein: 6g, Sodium: 320mg

Avocado Walnut Bread

Prep time: 5 minutes, cook time: 35 minutes; Serves 6

5 Ingredients:
- ¾ cup (3 oz.) almond flour, white
- ¼ teaspoon baking soda
- 2 ripe avocados, cored, peeled and mashed
- 2 large eggs, beaten
- 2 tablespoons (3/4 oz.) Toasted walnuts, chopped roughly

What you'll need from the store cupboard:
- 1 teaspoon cinnamon ground
- ½ teaspoon kosher salt
- 2 tablespoons vegetable oil
- ½ cup granulated swerve
- 1 teaspoon vanilla extract

Instructions:
1. Preheat the Air fryer to 310 ° F and line a 6-inch baking pan with parchment paper.
2. Mix almond flour, salt, baking soda, and cinnamon in a bowl.
3. Whisk eggs with avocado mash, yogurt, swerve, oil, and vanilla in a bowl.
4. Stir in the almond flour mixture and mix until well combined.
5. Pour the batter evenly into the pan and top with the walnuts.
6. Place the baking pan into the Air fryer basket and cook for about 35 minutes.
7. Dish out in a platter and cut into slices to serve.

Nutrition Facts Per Serving:
Calories: 248, Fat: 15.7g, Carbohydrates: 8.4g, Sugar: 1.1g, Protein: 14.1g, Sodium: 94mg

Air Fryer Chocolate Cake

Prep time: 10 minutes, cook time: 25 minutes; Serves 6

5 Ingredients:
- 3 eggs
- 1 cup almond flour
- 1 stick butter, room temperature
- 1/3 cup cocoa powder
- 1½ teaspoons baking powder

What you'll need from the store cupboard:
- ½ cup sour cream
- 2/3 cup swerve
- 2 teaspoons vanilla

Instructions:
1. Preheat the Air fryer to 360 ° F and grease a cake pan lightly.
2. Mix all the ingredients in a bowl and beat well.
3. Pour the batter in the cake pan and transfer into the Air fryer basket.
4. Cook for about 25 minutes and cut into slices to serve.

Nutrition Facts Per Serving:
Calories: 313, Fats: 134g, Carbohydrates: 5.3g, Sugar: 19g, Proteins: 4.6g, Sodium: 62mg

Pumpkin Bars

Prep time: 10 minutes, cook time: 25 minutes; Serves 6

5 Ingredients:

- ¼ cup almond butter
- 1 tablespoon unsweetened almond milk
- ½ cup coconut flour
- ¾ teaspoon baking soda
- ½ cup dark sugar free chocolate chips, divided

What you' ll need from the store cupboard:

- 1 cup canned sugar free pumpkin puree
- ¼ cup swerve
- 1 teaspoon cinnamon
- 1 teaspoon vanilla extract
- ¼ teaspoon nutmeg
- ½ teaspoon ginger
- 1/8 teaspoon salt
- 1/8 teaspoon ground cloves

Instructions:

1. Preheat the Air fryer to 360 º F and layer a baking pan with wax paper.
2. Mix pumpkin puree, swerve, vanilla extract, milk, and butter in a bowl.
3. Combine coconut flour, spices, salt, and baking soda in another bowl.
4. Combine the two mixtures and mix well until smooth.
5. Add about 1/3 cup of the sugar free chocolate chips and transfer this mixture into the baking pan.
6. Transfer into the Air fryer basket and cook for about 25 minutes.
7. Microwave sugar free chocolate bits on low heat and dish out the baked cake from the pan.
8. Top with melted chocolate and slice to serve.

Nutrition Facts Per Serving:
Calories: 249, Fat: 11.9g, Carbohydrates: 1.8g, Sugar: 0.3g, Protein: 5g, Sodium: 79mg

Double Layer Lemon Bars

Prep time: 10 minutes, cook time: 25 minutes; Serves 6

5 Ingredients:

For the crust:

- 1 cup coconut flour, sifted
- 1 tablespoon butter, melted

For the lemon topping:

- 3 eggs
- 2 teaspoons coconut flour, sifted

What you' ll need from the store cupboard:

For the crust:

- ½ cup coconut oil, melted
- A pinch of salt
- Swerve, to taste

For the lemon topping:

- Swerve, to taste
- 2 teaspoons lemon zest
- ½ cup fresh lemon juice

Instructions:

1. Preheat the Air fryer to 350 º F and grease a 6-inch baking pan lightly.
2. Mix butter, swerve, salt, and oil in a bowl until foamy.
3. Stir in the coconut flour and mix until a smooth dough is formed.
4. Place the dough into the baking pan and press it thoroughly.
5. Transfer into the Air fryer and cook for about 8 minutes.
6. Meanwhile, whisk eggs with swerve, lemon zest, coconut flour and lemon juice in a bowl and mix well until smooth.
7. Pour this filling into the air fried crust and place into the Air fryer.
8. Set the Air fryer to 370 º F and cook for about 23 minutes.
9. Cut into slices and serve.

Nutrition Facts Per Serving:
Calories: 301, Fat: 12.2g, Carbohydrates: 2.5g, Sugar: 1.4g, Protein: 8.8g, Sodium: 276mg

Cinnamon Doughnuts

Prep time: 10 minutes, cook time: 12 minutes; Serves 6

5 Ingredients:

- 1 cup white almond flour
- 1 teaspoon baking powder
- 2 tablespoons water
- ¼ cup almond milk

What you'll need from the store cupboard:

- ¼ cup swerve
- ½ teaspoon salt
- 1 tablespoon coconut oil, melted
- 2 teaspoons cinnamon

Instructions:

1. Preheat the Air fryer to 360 º F and grease an Air fryer basket.
2. Mix flour, swerve, salt, cinnamon and baking powder in a bowl.
3. Stir in the coconut oil, water, and soy milk until a smooth dough is formed.
4. Cover this dough and refrigerate for about 1 hour.
5. Mix ground cinnamon with 2 tablespoons swerve in another bowl and keep aside.
6. Divide the dough into 12 equal balls and roll each ball in the cinnamon swerve mixture.
7. Transfer 6 balls in the Air fryer basket and cook for about 6 minutes.
8. Repeat with the remaining balls and dish out to serve.

Nutrition Facts Per Serving:
Calories: 166, Fat: 4.9g, Carbohydrates: 9.3g, Sugar: 2.7g, Protein: 2.4g, Sodium: 3mg

Dark Chocolate Cake

Prep time: 10 minutes, cook time: 10 minutes; Serves 4

5 Ingredients:

- 1½ tablespoons almond flour
- 3½ oz. unsalted butter
- 3½ oz. sugar free dark chocolate, chopped
- 2 eggs

What you'll need from the store cupboard:

- 3½ tablespoons swerve

Instructions:

1. Preheat the Air fryer to 375 º F and grease 4 regular sized ramekins.
2. Microwave all chocolate bits with butter in a bowl for about 3 minutes.
3. Remove from the microwave and whisk in the eggs and swerve.
4. Stir in the flour and mix well until smooth.
5. Transfer the mixture into the ramekins and arrange in the Air fryer basket.
6. Cook for about 10 minutes and dish out to serve.

Nutrition Facts Per Serving:
Calories: 379, Fat: 29.7g, Carbohydrates: 3.7g, Sugar: 1.3g, Protein: 5.2g, Sodium: 193mg

Blueberry Cake

Prep time: 10 minutes, cook time: 25 minutes; Serves 6

5 Ingredients:

- 3 eggs
- 1 cup almond flour
- 1 stick butter, room temperature
- 1/3 cup blueberries
- 1½ teaspoons baking powder

What you'll need from the store cupboard:

- ½ cup sour cream
- 2/3 cup swerve
- 2 teaspoons vanilla

Instructions:

1. Preheat the Air fryer to 370 º F and grease a baking pan lightly.
2. Mix all the ingredients in a bowl except blueberries.
3. Pour the batter in the baking pan and fold in the blueberries.
4. Mix well and transfer the pan in the Air fryer basket.
5. Cook for about 25 minutes and cut into slices to serve.

Nutrition Facts Per Serving:
Calories: 323, Fat: 14g, Carbohydrates: 5.3g, Sugar: 1.4g, Protein: 4.6g, Sodium: 92mg

Prep time: 10 minutes, cook time: 1 hour; Serves 6

5 Ingredients:

Pop-tarts:
- 1 cup coconut flour
- 1 cup almond flour
- ½ cup of ice-cold water

What you' ll need from the store cupboard:

Pop-tarts:
- ¼ teaspoon salt
- 2 tablespoons swerve
- 2/3 cup very cold coconut oil
- ½ teaspoon vanilla extract

Lemon Glaze:
- 1¼ cups powdered swerve
- 2 tablespoons lemon juice
- zest of 1 lemon
- 1 teaspoon coconut oil, melted
- ¼ teaspoon vanilla extract

Instructions:

Pop-tarts:
1. Preheat the Air fryer to 375 º F and grease an Air fryer basket.
2. Mix all the flours, swerve, and salt in a bowl and stir in the coconut oil.
3. Mix well with a fork until an almond meal mixture is formed.
4. Stir in vanilla and 1 tablespoon of cold water and mix until a firm dough is formed.
5. Cut the dough into two equal pieces and spread in a thin sheet.
6. Cut each sheet into 12 equal sized rectangles and transfer 4 rectangles in the Air fryer basket.
7. Cook for about 10 minutes and repeat with the remaining rectangles.

Lemon Glaze:
8. Meanwhile, mix all the ingredients for the lemon glaze and pour over the cooked tarts.
9. Top with sprinkles and serve.

Nutrition Facts Per Serving:
Calories: 368, Fat: 6g, Carbohydrates: 2.8g, Sugar: 2.9g, Protein: 7.2g, Sodium: 103mg

Prep time: 10 minutes, cook time: 13 minutes; Serves 8

5 Ingredients:
- 10 egg yolks

What you' ll need from the store cupboard:
- 4 cups heavy cream
- 2 tablespoons sugar
- 2 tablespoons vanilla extract

Instructions:
1. Preheat the Air fryer to 370 º F and grease 8 (6-ounce) ramekins lightly.
2. Mix all the ingredients in a bowl except stevia until well combined.
3. Divide the mixture evenly in the ramekins and transfer into the Air fryer.
4. Cook for about 13 minutes and remove from the Air fryer.
5. Let it cool slightly and refrigerate for about 3 hours to serve.

Nutrition Facts Per Serving:
Calories: 295, Fat: 27.8g, Carbohydrates: 5.8g, Sugar: 3.6g, Protein: 4.6g, Sodium: 33mg

Tea Cookies

Prep time: 15 minutes, cook time: 25 minutes; Serves 15

5 Ingredients:

- ½ cup salted butter, softened
- 2 cups almond meal
- 1 organic egg

What you'll need from the store cupboard:

- 1 teaspoon ground cinnamon
- 2 teaspoons sugar
- 1 teaspoon organic vanilla extract

Instructions:

1. Preheat the Air fryer to 370 ° F and grease an Air fryer basket.
2. Mix all the ingredients in a bowl until well combined.
3. Make equal sized balls from the mixture and transfer in the Air fryer basket.
4. Cook for about 5 minutes and press down each ball with fork.
5. Cook for about 20 minutes and allow the cookies cool to serve with tea.

Nutrition Facts Per Serving:
Calories: 291, Fat: 14g, Carbohydrates: 30.3g, Sugar: 2.3g, Protein: 11.9g, Sodium: 266mg

Zucchini Brownies

Prep time: 5 minutes, cook time: 35 minutes; Serves 12

5 Ingredients:

- 1 cup butter
- 1 cup dark chocolate chips
- 1½ cups zucchini, shredded
- ¼ teaspoon baking soda
- 1 egg

What you'll need from the store cupboard:

- 1 teaspoon vanilla extract
- 1/3 cup applesauce, unsweetened
- 1 teaspoon ground cinnamon
- ½ teaspoon ground nutmeg

Instructions:

1. Preheat the Air fryer to 345 ° F and grease 3 large ramekins.
2. Mix all the ingredients in a large bowl until well combined.
3. Pour evenly into the prepared ramekins and smooth the top surface with the back of spatula.
4. Transfer the ramekin in the Air fryer basket and cook for about 35 minutes.
5. Dish out and cut into slices to serve.

Nutrition Facts Per Serving:
Calories: 195, Fat: 18.4g, Carbohydrates: 8.2g, Sugar: 6.4g, Protein: 1.5g, Sodium: 143mg

Lemon Mousse

Prep time: 15 minutes, cook time: 10 minutes; Serves 6

5 Ingredients:

- 12-ounces cream cheese, softened

What you'll need from the store cupboard:

- ¼ teaspoon salt
- 1 teaspoon lemon liquid stevia
- 1/3 cup fresh lemon juice
- 1½ cups heavy cream

Instructions:

1. Preheat the Air fryer to 345 degrees F and grease a large ramekin lightly.
2. Mix all the ingredients in a large bowl until well combined.
3. Pour into the ramekin and transfer into the Air fryer.
4. Cook for about 10 minutes and pour into the serving glasses.
5. Refrigerate to cool for about 3 hours and serve chilled.

Nutrition Facts Per Serving:
Calories: 305, Fat: 31g, Carbohydrates: 2.6g, Sugar: 0.4g, Protein: 5g, Sodium: 279mg

Appendix:Recipes Index

Printed in Great Britain
by Amazon